Early Civilizations
of Southeast Asia

ARCHAEOLOGY OF SOUTHEAST ASIA (ASEA)

Series Editor:
Charles Higham
University of Otago, New Zealand

Archaeological research in Southeast Asia has produced many major discoveries, but few works of synthesis have been published to bring these discoveries to a broader audience. This series is designed to encompass the great span of time from earliest mankind to recent historical eras, especially by drawing on the work of archaeologists in the field. ASEA will put the early cultures of Southeast Asia on a world stage for the first time.

SERIES EDITOR:

Charles Higham, Research Professor, Department of Anthropology, University of Otago, Dunedin, New Zealand and Visiting Scholar, St. Catharine's College, Cambridge.

BOOKS IN THE SERIES

Early Civilizations of Southeast Asia, by Dougald O'Reilly (2007), is the first book in this series.

SUBMISSION GUIDELINES

Prospective authors of single- or co-authored books and editors of anthologies should submit a manuscript or proposal (including a brief abstract of the entire work, a table of contents, and at least one complete chapter) along with a curriculum vitae. Please send your book manuscript or proposal packet to:

Archaeology of Southeast Asia Series, AltaMira Press, 4501 Forbes Blvd, Suite 200, Lanham, Maryland 20706 U.S.A. / www.altamirapress.com

Early Civilizations
of Southeast Asia

Dougald JW O'Reilly

ALTAMIRA
PRESS

A Division of

ROWMAN & LITTLEFIELD PUBLISHERS, INC.
Lanham • New York • Toronto • Plymouth, UK

AltaMira Press
A Division of Rowman & Littlefield Publishers, Inc.
A wholly owned subsidiary of The Rowman & Littlefield Publishing Group, Inc.
4501 Forbes Boulevard, Suite 200
Lanham, MD 20706
www.altamirapress.com

Estover Road, Plymouth PL6 7PY, United Kingdom

British Library Cataloguing in Publication Information Available

Library of Congress Cataloging-in-Publication Data
O'Reilly, Dougald J. W., 1965-
  Early civilizations of Southeast Asia / Dougald J.W. O'Reilly.
    p. cm. — (Archaeology of Southeast Asia)
  Includes bibliographical references and index.
  ISBN-13: 978-0-7591-0278-1 (cloth : alk. paper)
  ISBN-10: 0-7591-0278-3 (cloth : alk. paper)
  ISBN-13: 978-0-7591-0279-8 (pbk. : alk. paper)
  ISBN-10: 0-7591-0279-1 (pbk. : alk. paper)
  1. Southeast Asia—Civilization. 2. Southeast Asia—Antiquities. I. Title.

  DS523.2.O73 2007
  959'.01—dc22

                                                        2006021776

Printed in the United States of America

♾™ The paper used in this publication meets the minimum requirements of American National Standard for Information Sciences—Permanence of Paper for Printed Library Materials, ANSI/NISO Z39.48-1992.

Contents

v

Figures and Maps

FIGURES

MAPS

Foreword

Charles Higham

When I was invited by AltaMira Press to develop a series of books on early Southeast Asia, my first thought was to encourage younger authors to place their ideas before the reader. Dougald O'Reilly is one such scholar. He came to New Zealand from Canada to study Southeast Asian prehistory at the University of Otago, and impressed me as one both committed to the discipline and imbued with the resolve to make a major contribution. He participated in my fieldwork in northeast Thailand, with the difficult brief of excavating a large and important Iron Age site called Non Muang Kao, the Mound of the Ancient City. This provided the basis for his doctoral dissertation. He then took a post at the Royal University of Fine Arts in Cambodia and continued his fieldwork at a second Iron Age settlement, Phum Snay. Cambodia is undergoing a nightmare of looting of archaeological sites, and Dougald has founded Heritage Watch as a medium to educate and, hopefully, stem this cultural suicide. Few have visited more sites, and cared more for the cultural heritage of Cambodia than he.

He has now put together, for this volume, his views on the origins of the early Southeast Asian civilizations. He is well familiar with the Thai data, is virtually unrivaled in terms of Cambodia and has traveled widely in Vietnam. It is time for a fresh look at the origins of the civilizations that are the foundations of modern states of Southeast Asia. Much new data are at hand, and old ideas are in need of invigoration by the next generation of scholars. This is the first book in a new and imaginative series, one that is destined to make a major contribution to our appreciation of one of the most fascinating parts of the ancient world.

Acknowledgments

I thank the many individuals who assisted and supported me while I researched this book. The support and encouragement of my wife, Ashley, and my parents, Ann and Joe O'Reilly, were especially valuable, as were those of my many friends in Cambodia and Canada. Thanks also to my colleagues who provided photographs, information, and valuable insights into their research, including Professor Charles Higham, Professor Michael Vickery, Professor Peter Bellwood, Professor Miriam Stark, Professor Ian Glover, Associate Professor John Miksic, Dr. Pamela Gutman, Dr. Phuong Tran Ky, Dr. William Southworth, and Dr. Bob Hudson. I am also grateful for the assistance provided by the editorial staff at AltaMira Press. This book would not be possible without the warm hospitality and kindness of all the people of Southeast Asia who welcomed me and offered advice and assistance and whose magnificent cultural heritage should be an inspiration to all.

I would like to take this opportunity to alert all those who care about the past, present, and future of Southeast Asia to the scale of heritage destruction taking place in many ASEAN countries. If left unchecked, this frenzy of looting that feeds the international antiquities market will take from us any chance of knowing a poorly understood but incredibly rich prehistoric and historic past. The pages that follow illustrate the need for further research in Southeast Asia to flesh out our skeletal understanding of past developments.

1

Introduction

> It is just as if a man, travelling along a wilderness track, were to see an ancient path, an ancient road, travelled by people of former times. He would follow it. Following it, he would see an ancient city, an ancient capital, complete with parks, groves, and pools, walled, delightful.
>
> —Buddhist text, Samyutta Nikaya XII.65

> The monuments and roads are made of marble, and are intact. The sculptures are also intact, as if they were modern. There is a strong wall. The moat, stone lined, can admit boats. The bridges are supported by stone giants. Where the canals end, one sees the vestiges of gardens. . . . And in all this city, when the natives discovered it, there were no people, no animals, nothing living.
>
> —Bartolomé L. de Argensola writing of Angkor in 1609.

The archaeology of Southeast Asia, for many, conjures images of the enigmatic faces of long forgotten god-kings peering down from the jungle canopy. The remains of the great empires of the remote past are still scattered throughout Southeast Asia, and it is surprising that the area is often overlooked in terms of archaeological research. This is especially true of the late prehistoric/early historic period. The early centuries of the first millennium saw the florescence of a number of cultures. Complex societies on the cusp of statehood arose from modern Myanmar to the shores of Vietnam. A considerable amount of research has been undertaken on the earlier prehistoric societies of Southeast Asia, particularly in Thailand and Vietnam, but there is a lacuna in our understanding of the period that preceded the rise of the complex state in the region. It is hoped that this book will go

1

some way to enlighten the reader of the research that has been undertaken to date and perhaps to inspire further research into this most important formative period.

Mainland Southeast Asia is difficult to define but it is usually considered to incorporate Myanmar, Laos, Thailand, Malaysia, Cambodia, and Vietnam. Within this geographic area there is great diversity. The region may be divided into a number of geographic subregions including central Thailand, the river valleys and deltas of northern Vietnam, the lower Mekong River, the Tonlé Sap plains, and the upland areas that separate these subregions. All of these areas are affected by the seasonal monsoon to different degrees. From October through April the winds blow from the northeast, but in May this pattern is reversed and they blow from the southwest. Rainfall is heavy along the southwest coast of Cambodia and Thailand as the cloudbanks are forced upward by the Cardamom and Petchabun mountain ranges. Similarly the Truong Son cordillera, which runs like a spine up the center of Vietnam, receives heavy rainfall. Central and northeast Thailand, the Tonlé Sap plains, and the coastal areas of Vietnam get considerably less rainfall during this period.

The dry period, which occurs from October through February, heralds a temperature drop and a sharp decrease in precipitation in the areas that lie to the west of the Truong Son cordillera. In the north of Vietnam this time period brings heavy cloud cover and constant rain. Each of these geographic regions are comprised of distinct biospheres including the marine interfaces of the coastal regions through to the expansive river deltas to the inland plains, plateaus, and mountains. Prior to significant alteration as a result of human settlement, much of lowland Southeast Asia was covered by subtropical moist forest made up of deciduous species which are able to survive long periods without rainfall. Dipterocarp trees share the land with smaller shrubs and grasses below, a result of their annual leaf fall that allows moisture and light to the forest floor. Such an environment is conducive to a wide range of animal species including grazing animals and arboreal creatures. At the higher elevations the increased rainfall changes the character of the forest, creating a canopy where little sunlight penetrates to ground level. Here the arboreal animals dominate the faunal spectrum. The most mountainous areas are covered with subtropical wet forests with an abundance of evergreen trees species. Coastal Southeast Asia at one time boasted healthy mangrove forests, one of the richest and most diverse environments known. Mangrove thrive in brackish water on mud flats. These areas are breeding grounds for incredible numbers of shell fish and other aquatic species as well as a few mammals. The delta areas of Southeast Asia are largely grass covered as they are too wet to support forest cover, but they make attractive feeding grounds for grazing mammals.

The language map of Southeast Asia over the past two millennium is kaleidoscopic, as the fortunes of various culture groups rose and fell, and it continues to change. The main language groups of Southeast Asia are Thai, Austroasiatic, and Austronesian. The Thai group originated in southern China or what is now northern Vietnam and has expanded southward over the last millennium into what is today Thailand. Previously, these areas were probably occupied by speakers of the Austroasiatic language group, specifically Mon and Khmer. Austronesian languages are found throughout Malaysia as well as in Vietnam. The Cham language belongs to this group and is spoken by the inhabitants of central, coastal Vietnam, as well as some populations in Cambodia.

The human colonization of Southeast Asia has resulted in a huge range of ethnic and linguistic groups occupying different parts of the region. Gradually the smaller groups are being subsumed into the more dominant cultures but at least a dozen major language families still exist. Perhaps the most predominant language family is Thai, which spreads over a vast area of Southeast Asia, although the Thai group has only inhabited the country known as Thailand for about a thousand years. Cambodia is dominated by Khmer speakers who have inhabited the area for at least two thousand years. Languages related to Khmer are also widely spoken in the Truong Son uplands. This language was at one time spoken far into the Mekong Delta, an area now predominantly Vietnamese as is all of the coastal area of eastern Southeast Asia. Cham was once widely spoken in central Vietnam. Languages belonging to the Burmese, Karen, and Mon families are spoken in Myanmar and western Thailand. Chinese is spoken all over the region by ethnic Chinese migrants.

Although there is much work to be done before we have a good understanding of the events that shaped early Mainland Southeast Asia, it is possible to paint a general picture thanks to the advances of archaeological science in the region.

The earliest human inhabitants of Southeast Asia were hunter/gatherers who adapted to life in different ecological niches including the interior, uplands, and coastal areas. The interior inhabitants were likely more mobile than the others, who enjoyed such bounty that extended habitation in one locale appears to have been possible. The earliest peoples are classified as belonging to the "Hoabinhian culture," named for one of the first hunter/gatherer sites found in Hoa Binh province, Vietnam. A broadly similar tool kit of roughly chipped stone implements has led to the application of the term to other parts of Southeast Asia.

The period following the Hoabinhian in Southeast Asia is known as the Neolithic period. It appears that rice agriculture began to be practiced in Mainland Southeast Asia from around 3000 B.C.E. The technology appears to have been transmitted up and down the rivers of the region although it is unclear whether the arrival of agriculture represents an intrusive population or the adoption of new technology by indigenous inhabitants or both. Linguistics seem to indicate that the origin of rice agriculture lies in the Yangtze Valley of southern China. From there it appears as if groups speaking languages belonging to the Austroasiatic group spread. It is difficult to overstate the importance of the introduction of agricultural technology as it ushered in sweeping changes including changes in tool technology and the introduction of domesticated animals including cattle, pigs, dogs, and fowl.

The ability to forge iron was introduced into the region about one thousand years after the introduction of bronze. It is unclear from where the technology was introduced. A Chinese source is a strong possibility but we must not rule out local innovation or Indian influence, although the latter's production methodology differed.

The Bronze Age of Southeast Asia is poorly understood, especially the nature of the social structure and the appearance of indigenously produced copper alloys (Kennedy 1977; Bayard 1980; Bayard 1984; Higham 1984; Higham 1989a; Glover 1991; Hutterer 1991; Solheim 1968; Vallibhotama 1991; Pautreau, Matringhem, et al. 1997a). In some areas, this period appears to have been characterized by conflict while, in others, evidence is fugitive. Indications of warfare, in the form of weaponry, increase as the Bronze Age progresses, especially in Vietnam and Southern China (Higham 1996, 96, 100), while White (1982, 45–49) has proposed that the Bronze Age in Thailand was a relatively peaceful period. White argues that inter-community conflict was reduced because access to resources was not circumscribed. She believes that unrestricted access to raw materials, such as salt and copper ore, made it difficult for any particular community to establish and maintain a dominant position in Bronze Age society. This is not to say that hierarchy did not exist during the Bronze Age, but this form of social organization does not appear to have had lasting significance in that evidence for it is largely absent in Bronze Age cemeteries.

Although many sites in Thailand share a similar inventory of imported artifacts, it is possible to identify localized pottery traditions (Wilen 1982–1983). White (1995, 105) believes that Bronze Age Thailand was populated by individual, culturally localized, autonomous communities. It is apparent, based upon the finds of burnishing stones and anvils, that villages produced their own ceramics resulting in regional variation. White and Pigott (1996, 157), referring to copper mining and bronze production, state that "several lines of archaeological evidence support the view that production organization was characterized by independent specialists." This evidence includes small-scale production, absence of permanent villages exploiting raw materials, seasonal production, and a "differentiated production and distribution system" (White and Pigott 1996, 158).

The data from Bronze Age sites in Thailand does not accord well with many traditional theoretical models of sociopolitical organization including the templates of tribe, band, or chiefdom. Higham (1989a,187–88) has proposed that Bronze Age settlements were most likely autonomous units comprising no more than 500 individuals. Within these villages he notes that "the attainment of status was flexible rather than fixed [and that] the relative position of each autonomous settlement was given to fluctuation and, therefore, instability." White (1995) has presented a similar picture of Bronze Age social organization in Thailand. She has taken the argument a step further, interpreting the evidence from a heterarchical perspective, a paradigm that differs from the often inflexible models of social organization normally applied to archaeological societies. In Bronze Age cemeteries there appears to be social differentiation based upon age, sex, and social and economic roles but no "elite class" (White and Pigott 1996, 157).

Broadly contemporaneous sites in Thailand, such as Ban Lum Khao, Ban Kao, Non Nok Tha, Ban Na Di and Khok Phanom Di, share a widely related mortuary tradition. In all of these, the quantity and range of associated grave goods cut across age and sex boundaries. There appears to be a continuum in the burials from poor to wealthy. Often it is difficult to distinguish any definitive social divisions demarcated by wealth or symbols. Similarly, there is scant evidence of elite control of resources or craft production and, consequently, no evidence of control over distribution. In short, the evidence from these sites conforms to the models of social organization proposed by Higham (1989a) and White and Pigott (1996).

The next major event in Southeast Asian prehistory was the advent of bronze technology, which was also likely introduced from China. From around 2000 or 1500 B.C.E. bronze begins to appear frequently in the archaeological record. The technology used to cast bronze is broadly similar from northern Vietnam through Myanmar. Local groups mining copper and tin entered into an extensive trade network to supply the smiths in areas devoid of metal deposits.

There are a number of indications that social stress increased during the Iron Age. The number of excavated cemeteries dating to this period is limited, but it is apparent that the inclusion of weaponry in burials is more common than it was during the preceding Bronze Age. Sørensen's (1973, 155–59) excavations at Tham Ongbah in Thailand revealed individuals buried with lances, spearheads, halberds, and projectile points. More recently, excavations at Ban Wang Hi in northern Thailand have exposed graves containing decorated swords and large spears, interpreted by the excavators to have been used in warfare (Pautreau and Mornais 1998, 12). While it would be imprudent to suggest that the appearance of sites ringed with moats is indicative of fortification, it is possible that a large, fenced ditch near the center of Non Yang, in the Mun River valley, is related to defense

(Nitta 1991, 6). Similar evidence of apparent militarization is found at Phum Snay, a late Iron Age site in northwest Cambodia (O'Reilly and Peng 2001).

There is evidence that population aggregation started to develop in northeast Thailand during the Iron Age. In the Mun and Chi River basins, some sites grew very large and Higham (1989a, 219) estimates that settlements such as Non Chai and Ban Chiang Hian would have accommodated 1000 and 2000 people, respectively. There is some indication that there was a movement onto agriculturally marginal land in the Mun River valley (Moore 1986; McNeill and Welch 1991). Site density was also high during the Iron Age in the Huay Sai Khao basin (Wilen 1987, 107–10). Increasing population has been posited as a causative factor in the development of hierarchies (Johnson 1982), and analysis of settlement pattern has led Welch (1984) to suggest that social organization was probably at the level of complex chiefdom in the Phimai region.

Iron Age sites on the Khorat Plateau are notable for their encircling moats. Although we are unsure what the purpose of the moats was, it is clear that a great deal of effort was expended in their construction. The moats and reservoir at Ban Chiang Hian are estimated to have taken 500 adults one year to dig (Chataratiyakarn 1984). It could be argued that such a large mobilization of people would require a centralized societal structure (Wittfogel 1957), evidence of which is hinted at in Iron Age cemeteries.

The structure and content of cemeteries seem to have altered during the Iron Age. Sites such as Non Pa Kluay tend to contain a greater number and wider variety of items. Exotic items, including glass and carnelian beads, are common, as well as metal items of value (Wilen 1992, 106). The accumulated weight of this evidence seems to indicate that there was a shift from unranked social organizations circa 500 B.C.E. to those which may have been more stratified and enduring.

The first centuries of the first millennium witnessed the development of even more complex societies in Southeast Asia. In the Mekong Delta, what appears to have been a protostate began to develop. Later, similar early politically complex structures arose further up the Mekong River and in the Chao Phraya River valley in Thailand, as well as along the coast of the Malaysian peninsula and later in Vietnam. These early polities were led by indigenous leaders who sought to expand the territory under their control through domination and alliance. It appears that they adopted aspects of the Indic culture, perhaps in an effort to enhance their political and religious positions. It is on this period which this book focuses. Bringing together the threads of evidence from archaeology, linguistics, epigraphy, and history, I examine the earliest polities of modern Myanmar, Malaysia, Thailand, Cambodia, and Vietnam.

2

The Tircul (Pyu) and Arakan of Myanmar

Pagan, with its hundreds of crumbling brick stupas scattered over the landscape, is among the most famous of cultural sites in Southeast Asia. Less well known are the great cities of the Pyu, or Tircul, as they likely called themselves. The Tircul established a number of significant urban centers throughout central Myanmar in the early centuries of the first millennium. They spoke a Tibeto-Burmese language and appear to have been among the earliest immigrants into Myanmar (formerly Burma) (Aung Thaw 1978; Wheatley 1983). There are few inscriptions and, with just over one hundred words identified, the language is poorly understood (Tun Aung Chain 2003). The existing lexicon is the result of the discovery of an equivalent of the Rosetta Stone at Pagan: a four-faced pillar inscribed with Mon, Pali, Burmese, and Tircul, which led to the partial deciphering of the language (Blagden 1911). The oldest script dates from the 7th century C.E. and seems to be derived from a South Indian Kadamba alphabet of Vanavasi and the Pallava script of Andhra (Aung Thaw 1978). Tircul Sanskrit inscriptions can be dated to the end of the 7th century (Wheatley 1983).

The earliest written evidence of the Tircul is found in Chinese texts citing early reports from the Tsin dynasty (265–420 C.E.) that mention a people, known to the Chinese as the *P'iao*, who lived beyond the fierce Burmese border tribes. These people were reportedly civilized, in that "prince and minister, father and son, elder and younger, have each their order of precedence." They are also reported to have recognized Confucian doctrine (*Hau-Han Shu*, chuan 116 f. 18 verso). The *P'iao* are mentioned again by Ch'ang Ch'u, who lived during the middle of the 4th century C.E.

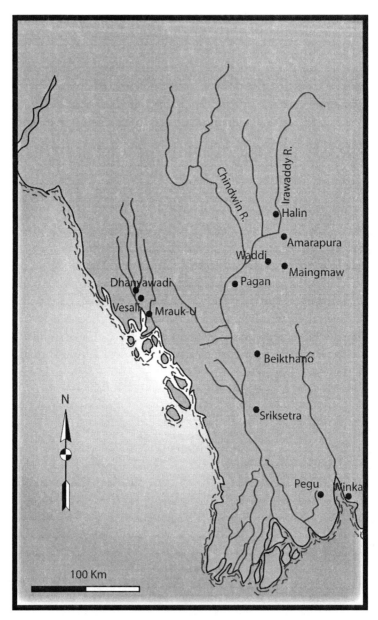

Map 2.1.   Sites located in Myanmar mentioned in the text.

Although the Chinese referred to these peoples as the *P'iao* or Pyu, we learn from the Chinese sources that these people called themselves *t'u-lo-chu*, they were known to the Javanese as *t'u-lich'u*, and to the Arab author, Ya'qubi (880 C.E.), they were known as the T.sūl. This latter name has been transliterated into English as Tircul and is probably the most accurate name for these people, as it is what they called themselves (Luce 1985).

The Tircul dominated central Myanmar from the 2nd to the 9th century C.E., leaving behind traces of enormous fortified urban sites, hydraulic works, and religious foundations from the modern cities of Pyay in the south to Schwebo in the north. According to the chronicles of the T'ang dynasty, Tircul power stretched for 3,000 *li* (~ 1,080 kilometers) from Dvaravati to the east to India to the west, and for up to 5,000 *li* (~ 1,800 kilometers) from Nanchao in the north to the sea in the south. Within this territory the T'ang chronicles claim there existed at least eight fortified cities (Hla 1979).

The origins of the Tircul people are unclear but Luce (1985, 52) contends that the Tircul were not indigenous to Myanmar but migrated from the northeast, moving slowly southward and establishing contacts with India and the Mon polities both in southern Myanmar and Thailand.

RELIGION

The Tircul were predominantly Buddhist but Hinduism appears to have been tolerated and practiced as well. Megaliths may hint at an earlier pre-Buddhist religion (Luce 1985). Most are large stone slabs, but some circular and squared "thrones" have been found. Beikthano and Halin may both harbor evidence of pre-Buddhist Tircul traditions, in the layout and supposed solar orientation of the buildings, in the group cremation burials, and in the shape of the urns (Stargardt 1990). Stargardt (1990) asserts that the transition to Buddhism was gradual and ended in an assimilation of the original Tircul beliefs and the teachings of the Buddha. She cites the continued use of urn cemeteries as evidence of this assimilation, a process that she says began at Beikthano in the early 4th century C.E.

At Sri Ksetra several sculptures have been recovered which portray Vishnu. One depicts Vishnu and his consort Lakshmi, another has the god riding his mount, Garuda, with Lakshmi on a giant lotus flower holding a trident. In another sculpture, Vishnu sleeps on Ananata in a depiction of the Hindu creation myth. From his navel spring three lotuses, each with a seated figure, Brahma, Vishnu, and Siva. The inscriptions on religious art indicate that both the Pali canon and another canon, written in Sanskrit, was known (Aung Thaw 1978).

The majority of religious sculpture, however, is Buddhist. Images of the Buddha are abundant at Sri Ksetra and are usually carved on large slabs in relief. Votive tablets are a common find, except at Halin. These are usually fashioned from clay and bear an image of the Buddha and a short inscription. Of particular interest was the chance recovery of a golden manuscript which dates to the 5th century C.E., in which twenty sheets of inscribed gold were bound between two thicker gold covers (Aung 1970; Aung Thaw 1978).

POLITICAL ORGANIZATION

During the 7th century, Chinese monks Hsuan Tsang and I Ching recorded a kingdom called Sri Ksetra. During this time a Sanskrit inscription records two Tircul dynasties, one whose members names ended in *–vikrama*, the other with *–varman*. The dynasties ruled over two unknown cities that appear to have been of unequal status. In the inscription, a Jayacandravarman calls Harivikrama, the ruler of the other city, his "younger brother" (Wheatley 1983, 175). As we shall see below, the *-vikrama* dynasty ruled Sri Ksetra. We must rely on the historical accounts of the Tircul that have survived to understand the political organization of this group, and without further archaeological investigation we are at a loss as to how to classify this civilization. Wheatley (1983, 306), based on present evidence, prefers to characterize the Tircul as having "a tiered political hierarchy that is most readily construed as a chiefdom."

The ancient Chinese text the *Chiu T'ang Shu* reports that the Tircul boasted eighteen "dependencies" and that thirty-two "tribes" recognized the Tircul as their overlords. Wheatley (1983) contends that one of the dependencies, Mi-ch'ên, was located in southern Myanmar, Mon territory. The *Chiu T'ang Shu* further describes 290 tribes "eating [the Tircul] territories" (Luce 1985). The dependencies listed by the Chinese are quite surprising in some cases as they include Fo-tai, which has been interpreted as relating to Sri Vijaya, possibly the island of Bali in modern Indonesia, Champa, and Java (Luce 1985).

SOCIAL ORGANIZATION

Wheatley's assessment of the Tircul is probably correct, and this assessment applies equally well to the social organization. The paucity of archaeological data makes it very difficult to judge the workings of Tircul society. It certainly appears that the Tircul were successful people, judging from the substantial urban remains and rich material culture they have left behind. Stargardt (1986, 32) attributes this success to the hydraulic engineering which they employed to great effect, enabling them to produce a significant surplus.

A recurring theme regarding the Tircul seems to be their love of music, mentioned by Chinese officials who were visited by a delegation on their way to the Chinese capital. This report seems to be confirmed by the discovery of a number of small bronze figures, most 11.5 centimeters in height, portraying a dancer, a singer, a drummer, and a dwarf dressed as a clown (Aung Thaw 1978).

SETTLEMENT PATTERN

We know very little of Tircul settlement patterns. No intensive archaeological survey has been conducted to identify smaller sites that may have been contemporaneous with the large Tircul urban enclaves. Almost certainly the landscape around these cities was populated, but we have little data on this aside from limited survey (Donovan, Fukui, and Itoh 1998) and excavations and for this reason cannot even begin to propose the nature of the large sites with surrounding settlements. There is some evidence for other large sites, aside from those that are known. The *Hsin T'ang Shu* reports the existence of nine "garrison towns," three of which Wheatley (1983, 180) identifies as His-lioi, T'u-min, and Mi-no-tao-li. Pagan may also be counted among the Tircul settlements although it is not cited in any of the Chinese histories regarding the Tircul (Wheatley 1983, 181). The Tircul remains near Pagan are today known as Tagaung. The site backs onto the Irrawaddy River and traces of the old wall are apparent. According to Moore and Myint (1991, 91), "[t]hese form two parts, with the northern walled area being irregularly rounded, and the larger southern part being more quadrangular, with angular corners."

Wheatley (1983) chooses to interpret the Chinese information regarding Tircul settlement patterns as a hierarchy of sites. The "capital" city was probably the home of the royal court and it oversaw a specifically delimited territory. This territory was kept secure by the garrison towns. Wheatley believes that the dependencies were probably subordinate chieftainships "ruled in the manner of patrimonial benefices, perhaps by heads of junior lineages." As for the tribes mentioned by the Chinese, he believes that this may be an indication that the Tircul were attempting to create administrative centers for groups of villages—a three-tiered system with the capital at the top, a number of regional settlements overseen by a governor, and then the village level, which comprised nearly 300 settlements according to the Chinese accounts. These accounts give a good impression of the breadth of the Tircul territory circa the 9th century C.E., saying that the boundaries of the "empire" stretched from the "Chenla kingdom" in the east to eastern India in the west, reaching the ocean to the south and Nanchao to the north (Luce 1985).

Recent research seems to indicate that the Tircul settlements of Burma were politically independent (Hudson 2004). It is argued that the larger Tircul sites were, in effect, city-states that fall within the definition of a "highly centralised micro-state consisting of one town (often walled) . . . settled with a stratified population [that is] ethnically affiliated with the population of neighbouring city-states . . . [with a] political identity focused on the city-state itself . . . [and a] large fraction of the population is settled in the town, [and] the others are settled in the hinterland, either dispersed in farmsteads or nucleated in villages, or both." The maximum extent of the hinterland, he suggests, is around 30 kilometers, "a day's march from the urban centre" (Hansen 2000). These arguments are based on present evidence that the Tircul urban foundations were broadly contemporaneous and, although they shared a similar culture, were probably politically autonomous (Hudson 2004).

Although intensive archaeological fieldwork has not been undertaken to identify the location of all the major Tircul sites, we can get a general idea of their distribution based on the discovery of the distinctive finger-marked bricks often associated with these sites. Such bricks have been found at the town of Maingmaw, about eighty kilometers south of Mandalay. This site is encircled by two rounded walls. From the outer wall the site measures 3 kilometers by 2.5 kilometers, and from the inner wall it is about 800 meters across. A canal runs through the center of the site. Preliminary work at Maingmaw indicates it may be the oldest Tircul site, predating even Beikthano (Moore and Myint 1991). The site comprises three walls—an outer circular wall enclosing 625 hectares, a rectangular wall enclosing one hundred hectares, and a circular wall enclosing forty-four hectares (Hudson 2004). Inside the walls may be found the remains of a few structures, and a cemetery was discovered in the early 20th century, which led to the recovery of many black onyx beads with white line designs, among others. Looters disinterred Tircul burials, which comprised pots filled with ash and sometimes silver coins, gold beads, and earplugs, as well as carnelian and agate beads (Moore and Myint 1993).

Close to Maingmaw is Pinle, another apparent Tircul site at which finger-marked bricks were found. This site does not have the same rounded shape as Maingmaw, one wall being straight and smaller, as well. Hudson (2004) believes this site may postdate the Tircul period based on the construction methods. Waddi is another poorly known Tircul site located in the eastern Irriwaddy valley. The site is round, surrounded by a brick wall, in which finger-marked bricks have been found. The diameter is approximately 1,500 meters.

Close to Beikthano, one of the older Tircul foundations, lies Taungdwingyi. Still inhabited today, the ancient walls of this city were quadrangular with rounded corners. Outside the walls lies a single moat, a feature which would lead one to think the city was founded after the establishment of Pagan. The presence of Tircul-style bricks may force us to reevaluate this assumption.

Another Tircul city lies close to the extensive urban enclave of Sri Ksetra. Thegon is surrounded by a rounded wall, elongated on the east-west axis so the site measures 2,500 meters by 1,000 meters. The western side of the site appears to have further fortifications, perhaps even three walls (Moore and Myint 1991).

TIRCUL URBAN FOUNDATIONS

Beikthano

One of the earliest known Tircul settlements, Beikthano, is located near the modern city of Taungdwingyi near the Yin River. The name of the city may be translated as Vishnu city (Wheatley 1983). Beikthano is, perhaps, the earliest urban expression in Southeast Asia with a suggested foundation during the 1st or 2nd century B.C.E. (Stargardt 1990, 46), although the smaller site of Waddi may be earlier (Moore and Myint 1991). The four available radiocarbon dates from Beikthano indicate that the part of the buildings from which they came date between 180 B.C.E. and 610 C.E. (Hudson 2004). Further evidence is available in the form of thermoluminescence dates, which indicate that earthenware from the site was manufactured between the 4th and 8th centuries C.E. The presence of stamp-decorated pottery supports these dates as this form of pottery is widely thought to have been introduced to Southeast Asia from India during the 4th to 8th centuries C.E. (Indrawooth 2004).

The walls of this impressive city encircle approximately nine square kilometers and were about 2.5 meters thick and three to four meters in height. It is, however, unclear when the walls of the city were erected (Bellwood 1992). The walls were constructed by building two facings and filling the interior with rubble (Hla 1979, 96). There is no indication that the city was further defended by moats, a feature that appears in later Tircul settlements. The site is roughly square and walled on three sides. The western side appears to have been defended by a large body of water, originally almost two kilometers long and 720 meters wide, on which the other walls abutted. Beikthano is bisected by a small, irregular wall that runs from the north to south of the city. The city was entered through twelve gates each about six meters across. At every gate the walls curved inward for twenty-six meters and were further protected by a guardhouse built into the projecting wall. The entrances were protected by a wooden gate, the remains of which have been found, with the nails and iron hinges on which they swung (Aung Thaw 1978).

Figure 2.1.   A section through the outer wall at Beikthano.

Excavations at Beikthano have revealed a number of masonry structures
built using the characteristically large Tircul bricks, as well as silver coins
with a variety of symbols on them, straight-sided burial urns, clay and stone
beads, pipes, and domestic pottery (Aung Thaw 1968). There is a notable
lack of Buddhist iconography at Beikthano, however, which may indicate
that the site was founded during a time when there was a proscription
against portraying the Buddha in human form. Some of the burial urns
were associated with skeletal remains, which may be indicative of a secondary burial practice at the site (Aung Thaw 1968).

To date, nearly one hundred structural remains have been located within
and around the enceinte of Beikthano. These structures appear to have
served various purposes—the foundations of *stupas*, living quarters of Buddhist monks, and bead workshops have been found. Similarities between
these religious structures and those found at Nagarjunakonda in southern
India have been noted (Aung Thaw 1978). The foundations of the stupa
and the residential quarters are in close proximity. The latter was a rectangular structure with eight small cells situated along a hallway. Excavation resulted in the recovery of a clay seal inscribed with Brahmi script datable to
the 2nd century C.E., a date supported by radiocarbon determinations indicating occupations from the 1st or 2nd century and the 3rd or early 4th
century C.E. (Wheatley 1983).

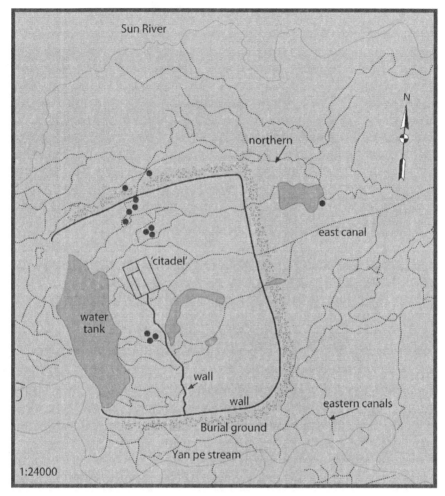

Map 2.2.   Map of Beikthano (after Stargardt 1990).

The remains of another type of structure at Beikthano have been interpreted as serving a religious purpose. Originally these structures, of which
there are three, comprised a square base on which it is thought a low hemi-
spherical dome was built. These structures are thought to derive from stupas found at Nagarjunakonda (Aung Thaw 1978). Burial urns were found
associated with these buildings and an inhumation burial and secondary
burial were discovered in another. The excavators suggest that the burial
urns were deposited en masse at certain locations and around structures
rather than buried singly (Aung Thaw 1978). The burial urns indicate a

Figure 2.2.   Partially reconstructed living quarters for monks at Beikthano.

cultural relationship between Beikthano and other Tircul sites discussed later.

Near the center of the site lies what has been interpreted as the remains of a "palace" or citadel that measures 480 meters by 410 meters. The structure interrupts the wall that divides the site in two and appears to be divided by a wall itself. On the east side, the brick enclosure had a gate similar to those entering the city, with guardhouses incorporated in them. A large statue once stood near the entrance to the citadel, of which the feet remain.

Stargardt (1990, 72) has noted that Beikthano has provided only limited evidence of exchange activities in comparison to other early Southeast Asian settlements. The longevity and wealth of the city are attributable perhaps instead to the development of an effective agrarian and hydraulic regimen. The Tircul appear to have been skilled hydraulic engineers in that they diverted water from the nearby river and channeled it through the urban complex and a network of distributary canals and then back to the source. Channels were not the only hydraulic works at Beikthano. Numerous tanks dot the landscape but none as large as that found on the western margin of the site which may have served as the defensive perimeter mentioned above.

This enormous tank may have been as deep as five meters and capable of holding 4,500,000 cubic meters of water. All of the tanks at Beikthano both inside and outside the walls are estimated to have been capable of storing

Figure 2.3.   Partially reconstructed brick wall that runs through the center of Beikthano.

6,992,400 cubic meters, the majority of which was held inside the urban area (Stargardt 1990). Stargardt (1990, 71) estimates that, at its peak, the irrigation system was capable of supplying water to an area in excess of 200 square kilometers. Such a system of irrigation was critical if Beikthano was to sustain a sizeable population. The region in which the city is situated is known for its aridity and without intensive irrigation could not support large communities of permanent residents. Another interesting point is the amount of space that appears to have been dedicated to agricultural land within the enceinte. In times of strife the population may have withdrawn behind the defenses and would have been assured a reliable source of food, at least for a limited time. It appears that the inhabitants of Beikthano were not unfamiliar with civil strife, as the necessity for walls will attest. There is also evidence that the city was razed sometime during the 4th or 5th century C.E. After this time another Tircul settlement appears to have been in ascendance, Sri Ksetra. It is likely, however, that a small population remained at Beikthano up until the end of the Tircul period (the beginning of the 9th century C.E.).

Sri Ksetra

Sri Ksetra, which means "honored field," is located on the left bank of the Irrawaddy River, a few kilometers from the modern town of Pyay (known in colonial times as Prome). The ruins incorporate a number of villages, the largest of which is Hmwaza. Based on archaeological discoveries and epigraphic evidence from Sri Ksetra, the city was at its height between the fifth and ninth centuries during which time it became the preeminent Tircul center (Aung Thaw 1978). It has been suggested that many of the important statues and inscriptions from Beikthano were relocated to Sri Ksetra (Stargardt 1990, 72). The rainfall in this area was considerably higher (1250 millimeters per annum) than in the northern region where Beikthano and another Tircul site, Halin, were located.

Sri Ksetra is oval shaped and covers an area of almost nineteen square kilometers (Stargardt 1990, 48). The site is surrounded by formidable brick walls. There is evidence that there was an outer, middle, and inner wall on the southeast, southwest, and western sides of the site. Each of these walls was separated by wide moats (fifteen to twenty meters across) for a total of three (Stargardt 1990, 86). There is, however, an anomaly in the defenses surrounding Sri Ksetra. The eastern side of the site is protected by only one wall much less robust than any of the others. Stargardt (1990, 86) has suggested that the eastern side of the site did not need to be fortified by brick walls due to the existence of a large reservoir similar to that found at Beikthano. The reservoir no longer exists, but there is evidence that it once existed in the form of a large swampy depression. Stargardt believes that during the occupation of the city the tank began to shrink necessitating the construction of the defensive wall on the eastern side of the urban area. The city was entered through gates that curved inwards, similar in construction to those of Beikthano. Topographically, the city slopes, and in the north the land is low lying and was probably used in rice cultivation while the southern section is comparatively high (Aung Thaw 1978, 19; Luce 1985, 52).

It is in this elevated area in which most of the ruins are located, and these are even found beyond the limits of the city wall. The most impressive struc-

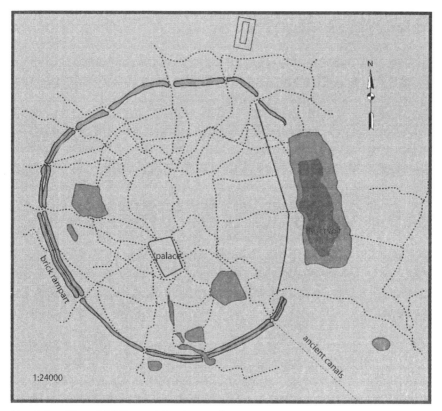

Map 2.3.   Map of Sri Ksetra (after Stargardt 1990).

tures are religious in nature, including many stupas and vaulted chambers. On many of the structures, vaults of the Indian type are employed with the bricks laid parallel to the arch-face. This technique differs from the vaulting used by Chinese architects of the Han period in Vietnam where the bricks are laid at right angles to the vault. Of note, however, is the fact that these vaults may predate those of eastern India (Luce 1985).

The Bawbawgyi is a solid brick stupa, coated with lime plaster, located to the south of Sri Ksetra and rises an impressive 153 meters. This undecorated cylindrical stupa is constructed atop five circular terraces, two of which are no longer visible. The upper portion of the stupa is conical and may represent an intermediate stage in the development of Tircul stupa but the inspiration is clearly derived from the Sanchi and Amaravati types of south India (Aung Thaw 1978). The votive tablets and epigraphy indicate that the stupa probably dates to circa 6th to 7th century C.E.

Other significant structures found at Sri Ksetra include the Bebe, which is a hollow stupa. The Bebe comprises a square structure with an eastward

Figure 2.4.   The Bawbawgyi stupa at Sri Ksetra.

facing porch. The sides of the structure are lined by pilasters and arched doors atop which are three terraces each smaller than the one below. A cylinder with a rounded top caps the structure.

The East Zegu temple is square in plan and measures 8.2 meters by 7.3 meters. The main entrance faces the east, but there are large projections on each side of the structure and the sides are all decorated with pilasters between arched doors. The East Zegu was probably built to house a huge bas relief, measuring 6.8 meters, of the Buddha's first sermon. It is unclear what the upper portion of the structure looked like as it has been destroyed.

The Yahanda-gu is a rather unimpressive monument and has been heavily restored. This long, narrow construction with its vaulted roof is usually described as resembling a cave. It is entered through low doorways on either end and a third in the middle. Set along the western wall are two stone slabs bearing a row of eight, seated Buddhas.

The center of the urban enclave is occupied by a rectangular citadel, 650 by 350 meters, which may also have been surrounded by a moat. These citadels had surrounding walls, more like fences, and were always oriented on a north-south axis.

Significant burial grounds have been found in close association with Sri Ksetra. The Tircul practiced cremation, storing the ashes of the deceased in urns. The urns were often placed outside the urban areas in brick terraces. The urn was sometimes placed on a bed of white pebbles, and burial offerings, usually inside the urn, consisted of gold rings and star-shaped artifacts,

Figure 2.5.   The Bebe stupa at Sri Ksetra.

inscribed gold and silver leaf, coins, and jadeite. Most common, however, were iron objects, including knives, nails, hooks, and pins. Another common grave good is a barbed rod, flattened or pierced at one end, the function of which is unknown (Luce 1985). These cemeteries contain large numbers of funerary urns of various sizes and shapes. Most are earthenware vessels that contain cremated human remains but some are made of copper and stone, these presumably used by the elite (Aung Thaw 1978, 32). The cemeteries, located to the south of the urban area, are dotted with tanks which date to the occupation of the city. The burial terraces had canals passing through them which eventually fed into the main city moats (Stargardt 1990). The most impressive urns, made of stone, were found near the Payagyi pagoda. One has a Tircul inscription which informs us that in 673 C.E. a presumed relative of an individual named Suriyavikrama died.

Figure 2.6.   A stone funerary urn *in situ* at Sri Ksetra.

Suriyavikrama was presumably a ruler of Sri Ksetra of the Vikrama dynasty. Another urn states that in 688 C.E. Suriyavikrama himself died. He was succeeded by Harivikrama who died in 695 C.E., and his presumed successor, Sihavikrama, died in 718 C.E. (Luce 1985).

There is some disagreement over the date of the inscriptions left at Sri Ksetra due to our inability to determine the dating system in use by the inscriber. It is possible that the urns date to the late 4th century C.E. if the Gupta calendar is used, the mid–first century C.E. if the Indian *Saka* calendar is used (Aung 1970), or even the 7th to 8th centuries if the Cula Era calendar is used. Most scholars seem to support the Cula Era date as the most accurate. This data has been supplemented by the partial translation of a recently discovered inscription on a burial urn from Sri Ksetra, which lists a number of kings of the Vikrama dynasty. The most recent opinion dates this inscription to the late seventh to early eighth century C.E. (San Win 2003).

The names on the urns have a clear Indian association, which could be interpreted as evidence of colonization by Indian rulers or, alternatively, the adoption of Indian regal names by Tircul royals (Aung Thaw 1978). There are other huge urns associated with Sri Ksetra, including those found in the Vishnu Queen's cemetery. These are laid on a bed of brick and are constructed of interlocking sandstone, a flat bottom, body, and stone collars measuring about 1.6 meters in height. Other urns are over 1.2 meters in outside diameter (Luce 1985).

Figure 2.7. The Payagyi pagoda at Sri Ksetra.

A great deal of the artifacts recovered from Sri Ksetra are religious in nature, mostly Mahayanist, illustrating Avalokitesvara, Maitreya, or Tara (Luce 1985, 55). A damaged gold-plated representation of the Avalokitesvara with six arms was recovered from the bank of the Yindaikkwin River. There are also many Vishnu images from the site. Excavations by Duroiselle (1926–1927) resulted in the recovery of many terra-cotta votive tablets, religious images in gold and silver, and decorative items including glass and stone beads. An impressive manuscript in gold leaf was also found, lettered in the local script, recording the *Tripitaka* (Luce 1985, 62).

Silver coins are another common find at Sri Ksetra. These coins are inscribed with sacred symbols, including the Svastika, Naga, conch, Vardhamana, and

Figure 2.8. A funerary urn
at Sri Ksetra.

rising sun symbol. These are very similar to the coinage used at Halin, the
last great urban enclave of the Tircul, but less similar to coins of the Candra
dynasty found on the west coast kingdom of Arakan (Luce 1985, 62).

Stargardt, studying aerial photographs of Sri Ksetra, has noted a significant integrated hydraulic system around, and including, the urban area. The
system was fed by a series of tanks and canals located along the higher
ridges outside the urban enclave. Inside the walls many water tanks are
readily apparent. A network of small and large canals that often form the
boundaries of religious monuments link the tanks. Stargardt (1990)
demonstrates that the water flowed in a circular direction entering the city
from the southwest and south, flowing around and through the site. The
water exited the city through at least seven different points to join with a
network of canals to the north and east.

As we have seen, there are some imposing architectural remains at Sri
Ksetra including three stupas, the Bawbawgyi, Payagyi, and Payama. The
cylindrical Bawbawgyi is located south of Sri Ksetra, while the other two are
found to the northwest and northeast. To date no dates for these structures

have been produced aside from attempts based on the chronicles and stylistic comparisons. It is probably safe to assume that they predate the 11th century. The site was probably occupied through the Bagan period when new religious structures were constructed (Zaini 2002). It is not clear whether the occupation of Sri Ksetra was continuous from the Tircul period.

It is unclear why the fortunes of Sri Ksetra declined but this occurred near the beginning of the 9th century C.E. Chinese histories record the sacking of a Tircul capital, either Sri Ksetra or the other large center, Halin, in 832 C.E. There is also a record of the last king of Sri Ksetra embarking on an expedition against a certain Kam:yan kingdom (possibly in Arakan Mahamuni). During this expedition the Tircul retreat was cut off leading to a military disaster (Luce 1985, 51).

HALINGYI

Halin, or Halingyi, is located near the modern city of Shwebo, in the Mu River catchment, upper Myanmar. According to Burmese tradition Halingyi was established by an Indian ruler who through certain misdeeds caused the eventual destruction of the city (Aung Thaw 1978). Stargardt (1990) has suggested that Halin's origins can be traced to the 3rd century C.E. She believes the walls date to circa first century C.E. but it was not until the 7th century that the city became powerful—probably being recognized as suzerain once the power of Sri Ksetra waned (Luce 1937, 316–17; Luce 1976). The radiocarbon evidence from Halin suggests the walls were constructed sometime between 50 C.E. and 450 C.E. (Hudson 2004). The sizeable remains of the site are consonant with what is described in Chinese histories including the *Hsin T'ang Shu* (*chuan* 222c f. 10 verso) and the *Man Shu* (*chuan* 10 p. 45), which describe the Tircul capital being situated in a barren environment; Halin receives only 750 millimeters of rain annually (Stargardt 1990).

The Chinese recorded information about the Tircul capital when Pyu envoys visited China in 802 and 807 C.E. According to these documents the city was surrounded by a moat and walls of glazed brick, circa 58,000 meters in circumference, or "one day's march" (Hla 1979). The presence of glazed bricks or tiles has yet to be confirmed archaeologically, however (Luce 1985, 72). According to the *Chiu T'ang Shu*, the city was inhabited by approximately 60,000 people, a figure Wheatley (1983, 177) suggests is rather inflated based on our knowledge of contemporary Southeast Asian capitals. The great walls of Halin were penetrated by a dozen gates, which were probably made of carved, gilded wood (Hla 1979, 98). At each corner of the city there was a pagoda, and other Buddhist foundations are reported to have existed by the T'ang chronicles, including "monasteries with courts and rooms, bedecked with gold and silver." The buildings, constructed of lychee, were roofed with tin or leaden tiles. The king inhabited a palace, which was decorated in a similar manner to the monasteries. Reportedly the palace housed one silver and one gold bell, which were used in times of strife, particularly before battle, to determine the outcome of the coming engagement. We are given another brief glimpse of Tircul beliefs by the T'ang chronicles, which record the presence of a huge white image near the gates of the palace which was used to determine civil law cases. Suppliants knelt before it and asked themselves whether their case was just or not, and at times the king supplicated himself before this image as well (Hla 1979).

The remains of the walls described in Chinese annals are still extant, although very degraded. The city wall is generally rectangular, with rounded corners, approximately 1.5 kilometers by 3 kilometers and is oriented on a north-south axis. It appears that the city grew in size at some point during its occupation. There are two eastern walls, and the construction of the second increased the area enclosed from approximately 4.4 to 5 square kilometers (Stargardt 1990).

Of the twelve gates described by the Chinese, three have been located archaeologically. The walls of the settlement curve inward at these points, so that two parallel walls extend inward creating a long passageway. Aung Thaw (1978) maintains that the remains of a moat may be discerned on all sides except the south. Stargardt (1990) disputes this, noting that no moats are evident on aerial photographs.

There are few structural remains at Halin, although the foundations of what is called a palace have been located just to the south of the center of the settlement. This citadel or palace is also aligned on a north-south axis. All of the buildings thus far exposed during excavation are rectangular, many with a quadrangular projection on one side (Aung Thaw 1978).

Both primary and cremation burials are found at Halin, one of which has been radiocarbon dated. It is likely that one burial area containing about fifty skeletons dates between 420 and 870 C.E. (Hudson 2004). Earthenware funerary urns have been found in association with these structures, and there is a possibility that these buildings were constructed expressly for mortuary purposes. At another location within the urban enclave, supine interments have been found in association with urns containing cremated remains. Local villagers have recovered burials from within a six-meter area, delimited by stones. Four skeletons were found buried with bronze tools. One of the graves contained the remains of a young woman who had had small pin-sized holes drilled in her teeth. These holes were then filled with strands of gold which were hammered flat producing small rosettes on the surface of her teeth (Anon 2001).

Halin has surrendered a range of artifacts, but religious artifacts are notably absent, whereas votive tablets and Buddha statues are commonly

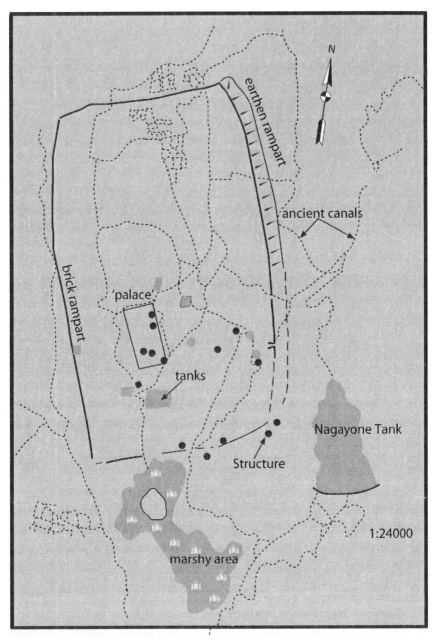

Map 2.4.　Map of Halin (after Stargardt 1990).

Figure 2.9. The remains of one of the gates at Halin.

found at the other Tircul sites. This may be indicative that Halin was under the influence of a different Buddhist sect, one that did not encourage image worship. A common find are coins. The majority of these bear the rising sun symbol. Coins bearing the Srivatsa symbol are not as common (Aung Thaw 1978). There are also coins bearing the *dharmacakra* symbol, resembling a wheel. Hudson (2004) feels that the range in coin styles found at Tircul sites in Myanmar may indicate a number of independent production centers. It is still not clear what the function of the Tircul coinage was, but its use as a currency cannot be ruled out (Wicks 1992).

There are a number of symbols commonly found on Tircul coins and some symbols are more predominant in certain geographic regions. The rising sun symbol is found from Shwebo down to Taungdwingyi. Coins bearing the image of a throne are found around Sri Ksetra. Another distinct group of coins appears to consist of copies of coins with auspicious symbols found in eastern central Myanmar (Mahlo 1998). This group of coins has been cited as evidence that, after the decline of the major Tircul centers, peripheral sites continued to manufacture coinage but with little familiarity of the purpose or meaning of the auspicious symbols (Hudson 2004). The fact that the coins are found at smaller Tircul sites and farther afield, including finds at sites in Thailand and Vietnam, indicates Tircul involvement in intra- and inter-regional networks.

Figure 2.10.   Tircul coins.

Some artifacts related to warfare have been found including caltrops, iron jacks with sharp spikes, used to impede attacking infantry and cavalry. The Archaeological Survey of Burma has recovered spears and arrowheads, and these items are commonly collected by the local inhabitants (Luce 1985). Other serendipitous finds include carnelian and agate beads, gold signet rings, seals, and miniature gold ornaments. The sophistication of craft production and the arts at the Tircul capital is also mentioned in the T'ang chronicles (Hla 1979, 97).

Many of the beads found are black and white, made either by painting, incising, or using an alkali resist (Moore and Myint 1993). Other beads are found at Tircul sites, including those made of carnelian, crystal, onyx, amber, jasper, jade, opalized wood, and amethyst. Generally speaking they are either spherical, cylindrical, or square in shape (Civico 1991).

The walls of Halin, Beikthano, and Sri Ksetra are all constructed of millions of bricks. Many of these have been found to bear markings, most commonly made by human fingers. While bricks from a wide range of sites are similar, each site seems to have some of its own distinct designs. Some bricks are stamped, one kind bearing the image of a horse and rider.

Several interesting stone slabs have been recovered from the site that record the death of an individual named Ruba; another mentions a probable female ruler, Sri Jatrajiku. Other slabs exist but are too damaged to read. One of these is particularly impressive, showing an unidentifiable sculpted figure in the seated position, below whom sit over fifty apparent worshippers (Aung Thaw 1978, 12). Another stone-slab inscription, datable to the 8th or 9th century, records several individuals, Siddham, Sri Trivikrama, and Va:ma. Other than these honorifics, the inscription remains untranslated (Aung Thaw 1978, 13). It is notable that a –*vikrama* name appears in a Halin inscription as this is the same suffix found on burial urns at Sri Ksetra. Other less monumental inscriptions are known from the site, including a piece of agate originally set in a signet ring. The stone is inscribed with South Indian characters identifying an individual named "Daya-danam" and has been dated to the 5th century (Aung Thaw 1978:14). The same name has also been found on a similar artifact from Oc Éo.

Figure 2.11. Assorted artifacts recovered by locals at Halin.

 Analysis of the hydraulic features in and around the urban enclave at Halin has led researchers to conclude that the city was situated to take advantage of tributaries to the east of the site. A number of irrigation-related features are apparent, including tanks and canals. The largest canal runs parallel to a ridge just under seven kilometers to the west of the site. The canal is unusual in that it only has one bank, on the down-slope side, to retain the water (Stargardt 1990, 76). From this canal ran a number of distributary canals that took the water farther to the west. Water entered the walls of Halin at the northeast corner, at which point it split into distributary channels the largest of which ran parallel to the eastern walls. Some of the incoming water was collected in a tank located in the southeast corner, and the rest exited the urban area and rejoined canals on the surrounding plains (Stargardt 1990, 83).

There are also a number of tanks associated with the ancient city, although caution should be exercised in relating these to the Tircul enclave as they have not been excavated or dated in any way. Although no large tanks are discernable within the walls of Halin, there are three large tanks outside the urban enclave and one smaller one, enough water to irrigate approximately 300 square kilometers. Although extensive, these are less substantial than those at either Beikthano or Sri Ksetra. According to Stargardt (1990), these tanks were created using preexisting depressions around which bunds were erected where necessary. Although there may have been substantial reserves of water, it is unclear just how productive the rice fields around Halin were. It has been noted above that the area is arid and the soils may not have retained water as well as the areas around other Tircul centers. Stargardt (1990, 84) suggests that perhaps the site was not as reliant on agriculture, due to its participation in various other activities including salt mining, gold panning, jade and ruby mining, and trade between China and India.

It is unlikely that Halin existed in a vacuum, and archaeological sites that are contemporary with the Tircul occupation probably exist nearby. The limited amount of research undertaken makes this proposition difficult to confirm. Stargardt (1990, 79) claims that there is, to date, no evidence of large-scale, pre-Pagan development on the eastern upstream bank of the Mu River, and the situation on the west bank is unknown but the Burmese chronicles claim that cities once existed in this area. A 400 square kilometer area around Halin appears devoid of archaeological sites contemporary with that urban center.

It appears that Halin suffered a catastrophic destruction at some point during the 2nd or 3rd century but the city was undoubtedly reoccupied as some of the structures there date to the 6th century C.E. (Aung Thaw 1978, 15) and artifacts datable to the Pagan period attest to its continued importance in later centuries.

ARAKAN—NORTHWEST MYANMAR

The area of northwestern Burma, stretching along the eastern shore of the Bay of Bengal, was the location of Arakan, a territory that covered no more than 40,000 square kilometers during its history. The earliest inhabitants of the area may have been people belonging to the Chin, Mro, and Sak ethnicities. Phayre (1967) notes that the language spoken in the area is similar to Burmese with a few dialectical differences. The area takes its name from the dominant ethnicity in the region today. The Rakhaing probably began to settle the region during the 9th century. The area is now called the Rakhine state after this dominant ethnic group. Arakanese chronicles indicate that the Mro were the inhabitants when the Arakanese entered it (Gutman 1976, 10). There is evidence of politically complex societies in the area from the 4th century C.E. with advanced art and architecture. It is possible to trace the political history through inscriptions left from these early times but the record is intermittent at best.

One of the earliest architectural remains in northwestern Burma is Dhanyawadi, a settlement dated to the late 4th to early 6th centuries C.E. The settlement was well located to exploit the sea and inland areas as well as being agriculturally productive. As was the case with other polities, especially those on the Indian Ocean, the fortunes of Dhanyawadi grew with the interruption of the overland trading routes through central Asia in the early first millennium. As with rulers on the Malaysian peninsula, the chiefs of Arakan possibly adopted the trappings of the Indian court to enhance their prestige and secure their positions. It is also likely that Arakan may have been among the first areas to adopt aspects of Indian culture based on its proximity to the subcontinent both by land and by sea.

The earliest ruler of Dhanyawadi that we know of was a man called Dvan Candra (r. approximately 370–425 C.E.) who reigned from a city surrounded by walls and a moat. The city's walls encircled an area of over four kilometers, and extraneous fortifications provided further protection for the city (Gutman 2001, 9). As is the case with some of the Tircul urban centers, the palace compound of Dhanyawadi, covering about 200 square meters, was also encircled by a stone wall. There are other similarities between Dhanyawadi and the Tircul foundations in that both seem to have developed complex irrigation systems.

The most important religious monument at Dhanyawadi is the Mahamuni shrine located on high ground northeast of the palace. The temple is said to have housed the only true known likeness of the Buddha. The temple retains Mahayana Buddhist sculptural elements that may be dated, stylistically, to the 5th and 6th centuries C.E. (Gutman 2001, 9). Although inspired by the Gupta, a dynasty that ruled north India from approximately 320–550 C.E., the art found at Dhanyawadi is unique and no prototypes are known on the subcontinent (Gutman 2001, 29).

Chronologically, the next city of importance in Arakan is Vesali, founded during the 6th century C.E. It eventually became the capital of Arakan but the date of this event is disputed (Hall 1950; Phayre 1967; Gutman 2001). Located only nine kilometers from Dhanyawadi, Vesali seems to have succeeded the former city as the seat of power in Arakan. The city is surrounded by an oval wall and moat enclosing about seven square kilometers. Again there is a "palace" located near the center of the settlement. Nine kings, bearing the name Candra, are thought to have reigned in succession for 169 years (788–957 C.E.) (Phayre 1967). It is possible that they were not native to Arakan and may have come from eastern India.

The material culture from Vesali indicates that it had wide-ranging contacts at various times during its history. Artifacts from the Tircul period are found, as are some from pre-Angkorian Cambodia (Gutman 2001, 11). Archaeological research at Vesali has revealed the existence of a large monastic foundation and an apparent royal shrine containing a stone bull, the royal symbol of the Candra dynasty who ruled both at Dhanyawadi and Vesali (Gutman 2001, 11). Although the Candra clan claimed descent from Siva, they were adherents of the Buddha's teachings.

Limited evidence is available of the early establishment of a ruling dynasty in Arakan. The Shit-Thuang pillar, which dates to the 8th century, was commissioned by king Anandacandra. The inscription traces twenty-two rulers back to the 4th century C.E. (Gutman 2001, 11).

The 8th century saw a number of changes in the political geography of ancient Myanmar. This is the period when the Mranmā peoples, speaking a Tibeto-Burman language, began to filter into Myanmar. Recent research on the genetics of the region seems to indicate that Tibeto-Burman populations of Myanmar derive from two groups, northern immigrants and native southerners. It is interesting to note that the admixture is biased toward males, indicating an influx of male immigrants southward some time in the past 2,600 years (Wen et al. 2004).

As is the case with many of the early polities of Southeast Asia, we see a mix of Buddhist and Hindu elements at Arakan. The former seems to have predominated, Therevada being dominant during the early centuries of the first millennium but Mahayana gradually taking hold. Gutman (2001, 26) believes that the artisans of Arakan were producing religious iconography in local workshops by the fifth century C.E., initially copying the Indian styles. For images that were not transportable and therefore unable to be faithfully copied, the Arakan artisans developed their own style of representation.

Hinduism is evident in the ancient cities of Arakan, and it appears as if the worship of Vishnu was prominent, particularly in the form practiced by the Gupta emperors (Gutman 2001, 27). Paleographic evidence indicates that the rulers built shrines for the Brahmans and donated land, servants, and musicians and maintained a royal cult in the Hindu tradition even though the rulers of the 7th century claimed to practice Mahayana Buddhism (Gutman 2001, 42). It is apparent that the Buddhist ideal of kingship, in the form of Dharmaraja, evidenced in the Mon sites of southern Myanmar and the Dvaravati sites of Thailand, was present at Arakan. The Mahayana sect probably infiltrated Arakan during the 6th and 7th centuries from northeast India and had an impact on the Pyu and Mon polities further to the south and east.

Excavations from the Vesali period have revealed lintels formerly above temple doors that are strikingly similar to 7th century lintels of the same date from present-day Thailand and Cambodia. Gutman (2001, 46) points out that there is no precedent for this form of lintel decoration in India but that the tradition almost certainly arose to the east of Arakan, probably in pre-Angkorian Cambodia.

Arakan was invaded during the 10th century first by the Shan, who may have ruled the area for a mere eighteen years (Murari 1985, 44), and later by Tibeto-Burman speaking peoples. The latter became the dominant force in the region until the present day. This was the same ethnic group that eventually came to dominate all of Myanmar and establish a capital at Pagan in the central part of the country.

The kingdom of Arakan seems to have used a system of coinage from which it has been possible to cross-check the names of various rulers of the Candra lineage with paleographic evidence (Murari 1985, 44). These coins have been estimated to date from the early 6th century C.E. (Majumdar 1963, 228). Gutman (1976, 131) presents the argument that there existed in Arakan an urbanized civilization that depended upon Indian trade for its economic survival and Indian traditions for its mandate to rule. To this she adds that the Arakanese polity had a currency at least as early as the fifth century C.E. and in use nearly continuously for six hundred years. The coins of Arakan are similar to those found at sites attributed to the Tircul, Mon, Dvaravati Mon, and Funan sites.

Arakan seems to follow a similar trajectory to the other polities discussed in later chapters in that its genesis resulted, at least in part, from maritime trade between polities in India and China. From the early third century C.E., chiefdoms seem to have developed along the coast of Arakan. Geographical circumscription prevented the foundation of agrarian urban centers for one hundred years until the foundation of Dhanyawadi (Gutman 1976, 317). The Arakanese prospered and, it seems, lived peacefully until political events in neighboring territories and possibly an invasion from the east forced the removal of their capital to Vesali (Gutman 1976, 318). By the beginning of the seventh century, it appears that the rulers of Arakan had been deposed and the territories may have reverted to rule by chiefs subordinate to a kingdom called Harikela (Gutman 1976, 319). Although briefly restored to its former glory during the early eighth century, Arakan seems to have been buffeted by political upheavals and sporadic attacks from its neighbors for the next several centuries. The Chin kingdoms attacked, as did the Tircul on occasion, and there is some evidence that even the Mon occupied part of Arakan in the tenth century C.E. (Gutman 1976, 319). The advent of the Mranmā or Burmans and the ascendancy of the Pagan polity had a profound effect on Arakan, with Mranmā kings ruling the northern part of Arakan. It seems that Arakan was more or less dominated by what is now Burma from the mid-ninth to at least the thirteenth century C.E. (Gutman 1976, 321).

CONCLUSION

The Tircul spoke a language that belonged to the Tibeto-Burman language family and seemed to meet with astounding success. These people probably relied heavily on the trade that was just beginning with India and China. Their hydraulic and cultivation skills probably allowed the production of a sizeable agricultural surplus, even in unfavorable areas. The success of the Pyu or Tircul is, perhaps, best represented by the size of the urban foundations they left behind, the most important discovered to date being Sri Ksetra, Halin, and Beikthano. Although the urban foundations of the Tircul were impressive and large, it is likely that the political apparatus of the civilization was not any more elaborate than that of a complex chiefdom that borrowed some of the trappings of a state-level society. The political power of the Tircul probably did not extend much farther than the impressive walled settlements which may have functioned as broadly contemporaneous city-"states." Each may have exercised power over a hinterland populated by smaller settlements and towns with which it engaged in exchange. Although we have only a limited knowledge of their material culture, it is apparent that they were heavily influenced by Indian religious ideals and seem to have been engaged in a vigorous trade with these people. Future archaeological research in Myanmar is desperately needed to expose more of this fascinating and poorly understood culture.

The Tircul, based upon the very scant evidence we have, appear to have been more culturally cohesive than the Mon of the Chao Phraya River valley and Khorat Plateau. One indication of this is the similarity in the patterns found on bricks used in the construction of the city walls. These were apparently marked by the makers, probably denoting that the village was fulfilling its requirements to the local power (Moore and Myint 1991). There are also wide similarities in the nature of the disposal of the dead and in the material culture found at disparate sites.

3

Peninsular Southeast Asia

Evidence of life in the pre- and protohistoric periods of Peninsular Southeast Asia is slowly emerging through the expansion of archaeological research. Nevertheless, we still have only a vague understanding of the developments during the crucial period when the peoples of this region began to adopt aspects of Indian culture. There can be little doubt that the first centuries of the first millennium C.E. were a dynamic period in Malaysia that saw sweeping changes in the social, political, and economic landscape.

Although the majority of cultural traits adopted in the Peninsula had their genesis in India, there was likely equal interaction with the other great economic power of the time, China. It is ironic that the Chinese provide us with the most insight on the events through their careful chronicling, while Indian culture, which had considerable influence in the area, left hardly any written records from this period.

Peninsular Southeast Asia was known to travelers as early as the 3rd century B.C.E. The Indian term "Malayadvipa" probably corresponds to the Malay Peninsula, and is used in tales dating to this period (Miksic 1999d). By the 1st century C.E. knowledge of Southeast Asia had reached the Mediterranean with mention being made by Greek authors of the *Aurea Cheronesus* or Golden Peninsula (Wheatley 1961).

LANGUAGE

Currently, Peninsular Southeast Asia is dominated by speakers of Austronesian languages, but in the past other language groups were also well represented. The Austronesian speakers, as is the case in the Indonesian archipelago, were clustered mainly on the coastal plains. These peoples are largely of the Southern Mongoloid phenotype and probably began to infiltrate the Malaysian archipelago and Peninsular Southeast Asia prior to 1000 B.C.E. (Bellwood 1985; 1997).

The interior of Malaysia was the domain of Austro-Melanesian peoples, and prior to the domination of Austronesian languages there was a diversity of languages spoken on the Peninsula, most notably Mon-Khmer Aslian languages (Vickery pers. comm.). The indigenous populations of Malaysia today are known as the Orang Asli. Two groups of these peoples speak languages related to Mon (Jacq-Hergoualc'h 2002, 25). The original inhabitants of Malaysia were skilled at exploiting the forest resources and lived by means of hunting and gathering. These skills probably saw them drawn into commercial relationships with the dominant ethnic group, the Malay, by the mid–first millennium C.E.

INSCRIPTIONS

The oldest surviving evidence for the Malay language is found in an inscription from Palembang, Sumatra, dating back to 682 C.E., written in the Pallava script. Although the Malay inscribers used Pallava script, it is clear that they adapted it to their own language, inserting Malay grammatical marks where necessary and omitting the proper Sanskrit endings. It is not clear whether the common people of 7th century Malaysia used Indic terms in their everyday language, but Sanskrit was certainly adopted by the ruling class to issue edicts on stone (Collins 1999, 102).

One of the most interesting inscriptions informing us of interactions between Malaysia and India comes from Seberang. It appears that the Malay played an important role in international trade. The inscription is succinct: "the great sea captain Buddhagupta, a resident of Raktamrttika." The locale is unknown in India, and a derivation of Raktamrttika is commonly found on maps of Malaysia today (Miksic 1999d, 64).

A number of other inscriptions have been found in Malaysia that date from the 5th or 6th century C.E. These are indicative of the level of cultural interchange during this period and hint at the longevity of the relationship as the texts have been written with local variations in ideology and text style (Miksic 1999d, 64).

INTERNATIONAL TRADE

It is apparent that the Malay Peninsula was involved in a regional network of exchange, probably as early as 500 B.C.E. Evidence of this exchange net-

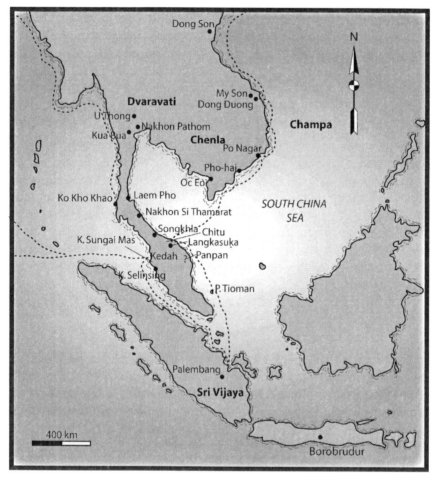

Map 3.1. Map showing probable ancient trade routes and locations mentioned in the text.

work is scant, but the discovery of bronze Dong Son drums is indicative that goods travelled great distances. The appearance of these decorative drums in many diverse parts of mainland and island Southeast Asia provides evidence of a sophisticated exchange network and advanced maritime technology at an early time.

The Dong Son culture existed in the Red River Valley of northern Vietnam. Although most of our knowledge of Dong Son comes from interment sites, there is one settlement site attributed to the culture, Co Loa (Higham 2002). Co Loa is a moated site with two, round external moats and an inner, rectangular rampart. The Dong Son culture produced a variety of unique artifacts, mostly in bronze, some of which entered a regional trade network. These include the famous bronze drums as well as bronze bells decorated with a geometric pattern. The bells have been found in Vietnam, Peninsular Malaysia, and Cambodia with two more being discovered in 2003 at Pursat, Cambodia. A further eighteen, reportedly from western Cambodia, appeared on the Bangkok art market the same year.

Dong Son drums are more widely distributed, and all share similar decorative motifs. The most prominent aspect of the drums is the flying bird and a "star" on the tympanum. Several scholars concur that the drums were created in northern Vietnam where the greatest concentration of drums is found. They probably served as symbols of authority, conferred upon other regional chiefdoms as emblems of power. Early Malaysian chiefs may have been using their ability to obtain rare and valuable objects such as the drums to demonstrate their power. If proven correct, this idea has far-reaching implications for the current models of the development of intraregional trade networks and requires a reassessment of our understanding of the sophistication of Southeast Asian chiefdoms prior to Indian contact (Loofs-Wissowa 1991; Miksic 1999c, 76; Jacq-Hergoualc'h 2002, 76).

Chinese sources indicate that the peoples of Peninsular Southeast Asia had been in contact with India since the 3rd century C.E. (Miksic 1999c, 77). Regrettably, the Indians did not record their earliest contacts with Peninsular Southeast Asia, but it is abundantly clear that trade between the two burgeoned during the first millennium C.E. Recently, evidence has come to light suggesting that prestige goods were produced in Peninsular Southeast Asia. The site of Khao Sam Kaeo has surrendered evidence of the local manufacture of glass bangles and semiprecious stone beads made from imported raw materials. Such is the quality of the product it has been suggested that these items were made by or under the tutelage of experts from India, where a long tradition of manufacture existed (Bellina and Sila-panth 2006).

From Chinese sources we know that, from the third to the mid–twelfth century C.E., official permission was required should a citizen of China wish to travel abroad (Miksic 1999a, 82). Restrictions were also placed upon foreigners wishing to enter China, and only diplomatic missions and religious travellers were allowed into the interior, others being restricted to the coastal trading areas. Although it imposed restrictions, China did wish to attract and interact with foreign nations. This was driven by the desire to acquire exotic trade goods as well as to legitimize the rule of the emperor.

The Chinese received many foreign delegations through the centuries from "nations" wishing to establish trade relations or seek the protection of the emperor. Often the emperor would officially recognize the rulers of foreign lands and bestow gifts upon them, thereby increasing the foreign ruler's prestige. Although the foreign ruler was, in effect, submitting to the

Chinese emperor, the prestige conveyed by such recognition would provide him much power in his own realm (Miksic 1999a, 82).

Internal Chinese politics often had dramatic effects on the trade relationships with polities located around the Southern Seas. In the early third century China was fractured by the formation of three imperial states after the collapse of the Eastern Han dynasty. These states, the Wu, Wei, and Shu, controlled different parts of the country. Southern China below the Yangtze was dominated by Wu (221–280 C.E.). Western China was under the control of the rival states, which severed Wu access to the lucrative Silk Road, which brought trade goods overland from as far away as the Mediterranean Sea. This political geography forced the Wu to explore wider maritime contacts (Wheatley 1961; Miksic 1999a; Jacq-Hergoualc'h 2002). It is likely that indigenous Southeast Asian traders began to visit China as early as the 5th century C.E. (Miksic 1999).

In the late 6th century, the rulers of the Sui dynasty (581–617 C.E.) sent envoys to a polity on the Malay Peninsula. It is likely that these early trade envoys were interested in courting the polities of the Southern Seas as entrepôts on the route to India (Wheatley 1961; Miksic 1999c; Jacq-Hergoualc'h 2002). Later it became clear that the lands around the Southern Seas could, themselves, offer valuable products. The indigenous wealth of these areas became more important, and the Southern Seas polities began exploiting and exporting their own resources.

RELIGION

There is no doubt that religions from India were highly influential in the early centuries of the first millennium in Malaysia. It is likely that the adoption of these foreign religious practices had political motivations.

By the 5th century C.E. the Mahayana school of Buddhism began to appear in the Malaysian peninsula although this is contested by some who feel it did not appear until the eighth century (Jacq-Hergoualc'h 2002). This branch of the religion, known as the Greater Vehicle, appeared as a divergent school of Buddhism at the beginning of the Christian era. The Malay Peninsula, during the 7th century, came under the influence of Sri Vijaya, a polity based in Sumatra. There were two forms of Buddhism practiced by the people of Sri Vijaya, but Mahayana became predominant and may have been adopted by the people of the Malay Peninsula as Sri Vijaya's political power grew (Jacq-Hergoualc'h 2002, 183).

The arrival of Buddhist beliefs was due in large part to maritime trade links between India and Malaysia. It is possible that the Buddhist beliefs were grafted on to existing animist religions with roots in the prehistoric period. Vestiges of these beliefs remain in ancestor worship and other aspects of Malay Buddhism.

Hinduism was the other major religion practiced in the peninsula. Miksic's (1999h, 92) contention that "Malaysian evidence for the worship of Hindu deities and construction of shrines for Hindu religious practices is only present for the period after the beginning of the 11th century C.E." is contested by Jacq-Hergoualc'h (2002, 133). The latter cites a Ganesha statue from Satingpra, which probably dates to the late 6th century C.E., and a sculpture of Vishnu is thought to have been made circa 400 C.E. (O'Connor 1972, 32). These scholars are also at odds regarding the predominance of these religions. Miksic feels that Hinduism was far less influential than Buddhism in Malaysia during the early period. Nearly thirty Hindu shrines have been discovered on the peninsula, and representations of Vishnu and Siva seem to demonstrate that Hinduism was established from an early date in the region. The practice of Buddhism is also attested to by several remains that can also be dated to this early period, but these are much less common than the Hindu remains (Jacq-Hergoualc'h 2002, 135, 141). One such Hindu temple, which may date to the 7th century, was discovered atop Gunung Jerai, a 1217-meter peak near the Bujang Valley of south Kedah (Miksic 1999h, 92).

There is evidence of Hindu shrines or *candi* around south Kedah between the Gunung Jerai mountain and the Muda River valley (Miksic 1999i, 94). Within an area of about 350 square kilometers, eighty-seven, early historic religious sites have been reported. In many cases it is difficult to determine whether the remains were Buddhist or Hindu. There are twelve *candi* located on mountain tops, a feature which Miksic (1999i, 94) suggests may derive from prehistoric Malay beliefs regarding the sanctity of high places.

Figure 3.1. Site 22, Candi Pengkala in the Bujang Valley (photo courtesy P. Bellwood).

It is equally likely that the mountain sites were chosen as representations of Mount Meru, home of the gods in the Hindu religion. The remains of Hindu temples thus far located comprise an enclosed sanctuary (*vimana*), which would have housed a sacred image, surrounded by an open gallery (*mandapa*) covered by a roof. There is also often evidence of a drain exiting from the *vimana*. This would have carried away the liquids used to bathe the sacred image and is a feature commonly found in Hindu temples in India. Although these were clearly based on Indian models, the Malay *candi* have unique local characteristics. The *candi* of south Kedah are thought to date to the 11th century C.E. during the period of south Indian influence under the Cola kingdom (Miksic 1999i, 94).

SOUTHEAST ASIAN AND CHINESE VESSELS

Much of the wealth of the early Malay polities was built upon trade. The ships that facilitated that trade were clearly an important part of the cultures that grew up on the peninsula. What we know of ancient maritime technology we owe largely to Chinese records although archaeological evidence is slowly accumulating (Manguin 1989; 1996). It had been long assumed that the burden of the transoceanic trade fell on the Chinese and Indian merchants. Increasingly the inaccuracy of these assumptions is becoming apparent. The Chinese describe Southeast Asian ships of remarkable size. Known to the Chinese as *kunlun bo*, these multimasted ships could reach fifty meters in length and were able to carry up to six hundred tons of goods (Manguin 1989; 1996).

We know little of the earliest ships that plied the sea lanes between China and Malaysia, but later vessels may be an indication of their form. Chinese ocean-going vessels, junks of the 10th century C.E., came in many forms. Perhaps the most common form was a rectangular vessel with a rounded hull. They were driven by canvas sails hoisted on up to six masts. There were varying sizes but the largest recorded was 1250 tons and could transport up to six hundred people (Dars 1979).

TRANSPENINSULAR TRADE

The geographic location of the Malaysian peninsula, placed as it is between China and India, has been of great interest to those examining early contacts. As the trading vessels going between India and China were forced to confront the peninsula, there has been much debate about the existence of overland trade routes. Those in favor feel that it is likely that ships would stop and unload their cargo and have it carried overland to the opposite coast, thereby saving considerable time in circumnavigation. There is no doubt that peoples have been crossing the peninsula since early times. We possess the earliest account of such a crossing, written in the second century C.E. by a Chinese emissary to Malaysia.

Crossings were feasible, and in at least eleven places trails may have existed through the mountains to the opposite side of the peninsula. Feasibility, however, does not necessarily reflect ease. While we know that the peninsula was crossed as early as 250 C.E., it is not clear whether it was used in commercial transportation.

There are four places where crossings for commercial purposes could have existed. The first is located at the narrowest point of the peninsula, just forty kilometers from side to side. It begins at the estuary of the Tha Thapao River, where the archaeological site of Khao Sam Kaeo is located (Jacq-Hergoualc'h 2002, 44). Another possibility was a route between Takua Pa, an ancient port site to the Bay of Bandon (Laem Pho site). The archaeological remains on either end of this route have led researchers to suggest they were connected by an overland trail. Other research indicates a possible route from the area of Krabi, Thailand, to the east coast of the peninsula. The last possible route lies between modern Kedah (ancient Jiecha circa 5th century C.E.) and Yarang-Pattani (ancient Langkasuka circa 6th century C.E.) (Jacq-Hergoualc'h 2002, 47).

In the early centuries of the last millennium, the passage across the peninsula would have been treacherous. The forests were thick and filled with wild animals. The rivers were, in places, either raging torrents or too shallow to navigate, and the terrain could be precipitous. It is likely that there were routes across the peninsula, but it is unlikely that these were used to convey substantial cargoes to the opposite coast. Much of what was being traded was of a fragile or bulky nature, and the arduous journey across the isthmus would have resulted in the loss of goods through breakage. There is almost a complete lack of evidence for habitation along any of the routes mentioned above. It is more likely that the routes were used to transport the forest products so sought after by the foreign traders to the coasts from their source (Jacq-Hergoualc'h 2002, 50).

It is possible that, in the early centuries of the first millennium, overland routes were favored due to piracy but these fell into disuse by the 5th century (Miksic 1999g). The reduction in transport costs may have stimulated further trade via this route. Consequently, the political entities along the peninsula seem to have grown more sophisticated.

It seems that ships followed a similar route on their way to and from India and China. Crossing the Bay of Bengal on the southwest monsoon they came to peninsular Southeast Asia at a time that afforded them the benefit of the northwestern winds to help them get through the Straits of Malacca. Once around the peninsula, ships were obliged to await the southwest monsoon for the final drive to China (Jacq-Hergoualc'h 2002, 52).

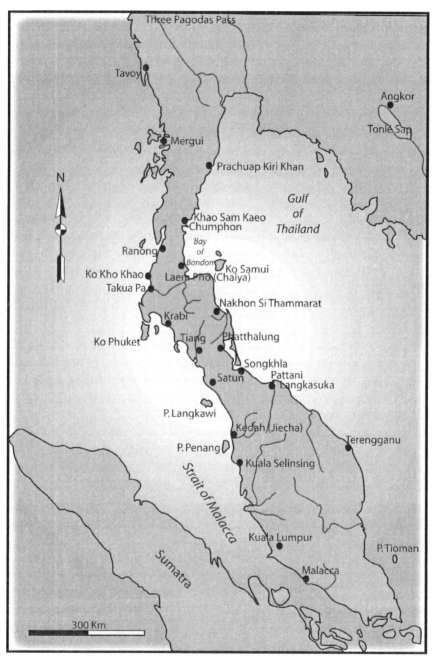

Map 3.2.   Map of Malaysia showing sites mentioned in the text.

For both the Chinese and the Indian traders, it seems peninsular Southeast Asia ceased to be regarded as an impediment to trade rather than a
rich resource to be exploited, and the destination was enhanced by the
presence of safe harbors, congenial populations, and abundant resources
(Jacq-Hergoualc'h 2002, 61). Wheatley (1961, 198), similarly, illustrates
that the Indian traders did not seek always to cross the peninsula but began instead to settle, confirming that "the Peninsula was a local centre for
the diffusion of Indian culture and not merely a barrier over which successive waves of migrants flowed on to found the great kingdoms of Indo-
China and Indonesia."

Wheatley's (1961) research of the Chinese annals suggests that
transpeninsular trade routes did exist. The earliest contacts between China
and Malaysia in the first century B.C.E., recorded in the *Ch'ien Han Shu*,
seem to indicate that goods from China were not always carried through
to the Indian Ocean by Chinese vessels (Wheatley 1961, 12). This suggests
that they may have been transported overland and reloaded on ships
bound for the subcontinent. Later editions of Chinese writings mention
that crossing the peninsula saved travelers about four months on a journey
to India.

It is highly likely that there were routes to cross the peninsula but their
main use was to bring raw materials from the interior to the coasts and perhaps to transport lightweight yet robust goods across the peninsula.
Transpeninsular tracks may well have been used primarily by passengers
seeking to save a considerable amount of time on their way to or from India. Throughout the protohistoric period, there was considerable traffic
along these routes by religious practitioners.

NATURAL RESOURCES

Perhaps one of the most important factors in the sociopolitical development of the Malay Peninsula was the natural resources to be found there.
Once these began to be exploited by local rulers true political development
began to occur.

The natural abundance of the Malay Peninsula stood it in good stead to
become a major source of material desired by international traders. The
forests of this tropical region are home to nearly ten thousand different
species of plants, many of which provided prized products (Dunn 1975,
38). The forests were also home to a diverse range of fauna, including many
bird species, which provided valuable by-products. Products including
spices, aromatic wood, ivory and rhinoceros horn, bezoars stones (concre-
tions found in the gastrointestinal tract of animals), cowrie shells, bird
feathers, and other goods were actively sought for trade.

SETTLEMENT PATTERN

Our understanding of Peninsular Southeast Asia during the early centuries of the first millennium is based largely on Chinese histories. Only a limited amount of archaeological research has been undertaken to explore the accuracy of the information provided in the Chinese annals.

The little archaeological evidence that is available lends support to a hypothesis of sociopolitical development proposed by Bronson (1977). In this model a settlement center is located at the mouth of a major river. This settlement had diminishing control over settlements located farther upstream. Bronson conceives the river mouth center as "A," while "B" and "C" are second and third tier centers located upstream at primary and secondary river junctions. The settlement farthest away from the river mouth, while still involved in the market exchange system controlled by "A" is "D." "D" is where most of the raw materials from the interior are collected for transfer downstream to settlements "C," "B," and ultimately "A," whence they enter the international trade system. The raw materials originate with the producers, "E" and "F." These settlements could be centered on a separate nonmarket exchange system but participate, to a limited degree, in the market system centered on A.

The entire system could be duplicated in an adjacent river basin based on another delta polity identified as "A*." The "A" polities trade the goods that are passed down this system with an overseas exchange partner designated "X," which supplies "A" polities with exotic goods (Bronson 1977).

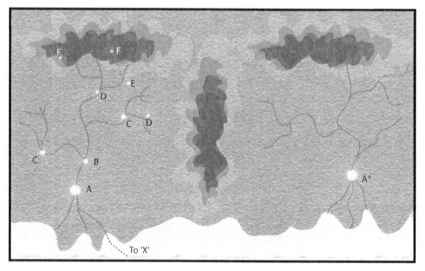

Map 3.3. A hypothesized model of settlement hierarchy and exchange relationships (after Bronson 1977).

Bronson's model is particularly apropos when considering the early polities of Southeast Asia and Malaysia in particular. The system he describes is
bounded by a number of constraints:

> 1: The interfluvial countryside of the drainage basin is sufficiently marshy,
> forested or mountainous to confine all movements of goods to water routes,
> rendering the economic pattern closely congruent with the dendritic pattern
> formed by the main stream and its tributaries. 2: X, the overseas center, is the
> economic superior of A, possessing a larger population and a more productive
> and technologically advanced economy. 3: The basin does not contain enough
> concentrated cultivable land to permit the development of a true peasant soci-
> ety, where wealth is extracted by an elite directly from a land-bound farming
> population, and where revenues derived from trade are consequently of less
> than central importance. (Bronson 1977, 43–47)

Recently, there have been some tantalizing archaeological finds that may
provide evidence for the existence of the system outlined by Bronson. It appears that there are three main clusters of sites that were important from the
first to seventh centuries C.E. On the west coast of Peninsular Southeast
Asia are the sites in the Bernam Valley (southern Perak and northern Selangor) and the sites of the Lkang Valley (Selangor). In the interior of the
peninsula in Pahang another cluster of sites have been found in the Tem-
beling River valley. These early settlements are archaeologically rich, yield-
ing "iron and bronze tools, weapons, bowls and ceremonial objects, stone-
lined chambers and wooden boats"(Miksic 1999f, 66). Further support for
the theory is presented by Allen (1991), who has examined archaeological
data dating to the 17th and 18th centuries from the hinterlands around
Kedah. It is apparent that there were a number of large interior trade centers located on rivers linked to Kedah. These centers are full of ceramics that
originated in Kedah and also have vestiges of Indian-style religious structures. According to historical documentation, the leaders at these upriver
centers were linked to Kedah through a prestige goods network and ruled
over fortified settlements of considerable size. In some cases members of
the "aristocracy" from the primary center were sent to these secondary trade
centers to act as tribute and trade administrators (Junker 2004).

Claudius Ptolemy, a Greek who lived circa 100 C.E. collected information
on the Indian Ocean and South China seas. One of the locations referred to is
the Golden Khersonese, which may well refer to the Malaysian peninsula.
Ptolemy locates a number of trading entrepôts in the Golden Khersonese, including Takola in the upper reaches of the peninsula. At the southern end he
refers to an entrepôt called Sabara while settlements such as Lalonka, Lonkon-
gara, Tharra, and Palanda are mentioned as well. Regrettably the geography of
Ptolemy does not mention either the people or products of the peninsula nor
does it discuss the physical geography of the area (Wheatley 1961, 140).

It is likely that the peoples of protohistoric Malaysia concentrated in the deltas of larger rivers although they were quite dispersed. It is unlikely that their settlements were fortified, at least in the early centuries of the first millennium. Aside from these larger centers it is possible to envisage settlements further inland along streams at the foothills of the central mountain chain and settlements located along the transpeninsular trade routes (Miksic 1999f, 66).

SOCIOPOLITICAL ORGANIZATION

As we have seen, it was, in the past, widely assumed that the peoples of Southeast Asia were transformed from primitive, politically underdeveloped societies through contacts with India. Current opinion based on a wealth of evidence rejects this view, favoring a more balanced exchange of cultural attributes and considered absorption of certain useful traits (Miksic 1999g; Jacq-Hergoualc'h 2002). Nevertheless, the contact with India had an undeniably powerful impact on the various peoples of Southeast Asia. The process has usually been referred to as Indianization, and such was the influence of this alien culture on the peoples of Southeast Asia it is, as Jacq-Hergoualc'h (2002, 73) suggests, probably a mistake to discard the term completely.

It is likely that the political organization of most societies in Malaysia during the early years of the first millennium was at the level of the chiefdom. Regrettably it is not yet possible to accurately describe the transitions from chiefdom to more complex organization based on the archaeological research done to date. It is, however, likely that local chiefs saw an opportunity to reinforce their positions using the traditions and mythology of India. The burgeoning trade between peninsular Malaysia and the subcontinent allowed the rapid adoption of many concepts originating in north India.

The origin of many of the sociopolitical and religious concepts was northwestern India, and it is likely that there was a nearly simultaneous adoption of sophisticated political concepts along the eastern seaboard of India and in Malaysia (Jacq-Hergoualc'h 2002, 94). The concepts did, however, require fertile ground to take root. This would entail a large sedentary, agricultural population at the level of the complex chiefdom. The leaders of these chiefdoms probably began legitimizing their positions through identification with powerful deities such as those represented in the Indian pantheon. The chiefs' positions were further entrenched by the wealth they began to accumulate through their trade relations with foreigners in the early centuries of the first millennium C.E.

It is possible that, during the third century, the peninsula was controlled by a distant neighbor, Funan. According to the chronicles of two Chinese ambassadors to Funan, Fan Shih-man, the ruler of that kingdom, began a campaign to expand the area under his control. The *Liang Shu* tells us that Fan Shih-man "extended his territory for 5-6000 *li*."(Wheatley 1961, 15). The cities mentioned are thought to have been on the Malay Peninsula. Far from being mere vainglorious pursuits these conquests would have allowed Funan to dominate the maritime trade routes and profit immensely (Jacq-Hergoualc'h 2002, 102).

Returning to Bronson's model of socioeconomic organization outlined above we can begin to conceptualize the relationships that may have existed between the various settlements in Peninsular Malaysia. As we have seen "A" level settlements functioned as the apex of the local trade network. Settlements of the "B" and "C" level could be controlled by "A" due to the fact that they were in closer proximity to the capital and their locations were fixed at river junctions. These factors, along with the benefits accrued by "B" and "C" settlements, allowed "A" centers to employ the threat of force to ensure continued cooperation in the exchange network. These lower order centers were locked into a hierarchic relationship with "A"-level settlements. It is not unlikely, according to Bronson (1977), that these mid-level settlements were administered by or even colonies of "A." He feels that, at the very least, the leaders of these communities were bound politically to the center. The only instance in which this relationship may have differed would be if "B"-level communities were the producers of manufactured goods and had access to the larger trade network and control over the settlements further upstream (Bronson 1977).

Bronson (1977, 43–47) feels that the relations between the "A"-level delta settlements and the far upstream locations would "be rather more egalitarian and less consistently coercive than is usual in relations between high- and low-order centres in an ordinary state." This situation reflects a heterarchic relationship whereby settlements at the "D"-level were not completely entwined in a hierarchic social structure. There was a degree of flexibility in the relationship, allowing "D" leverage in certain situations. As Bronson points out, the "A" centers were dependent upon the goods collected by "D" level settlements, and these settlements were not under the direct military or political control of the "A" level centers. Therefore "A" centers were forced to rely on the trade of maritime products and manufactured goods to ensure continued functioning of the regional economy.

"A"-level settlements relied on the existence of an overseas trading partner, "X." The relationship between "X" and "A" was not equal. "A" was nearly totally reliant on the overseas partner for the provision of revenue from import and export taxes, protection fees as well as exotic goods that provided legitimacy to the rulers of "A." These exotic goods were probably crucial in the maintenance of "A"'s relationship with its upstream settlements as they provided their rulers the same legitimacy (Bronson 1977,

46). The Chinese annals suggest that the indigenous peoples of coastal Southeast Asia were interested in acquiring goods that elevated their status compared to that of the inhabitants of the interior. These goods included "salt, rice, iron, and earthenware . . . luxuries such as gold, silver, silks, porcelain and lacquer-ware for the members of the ruling hierarchy; and objects for ceremonial use such as parasols" (Wheatley 1961, 73).

If the "A" level center demanded too much in the way of fees and taxes the overseas trading partner had the option of doing business elsewhere, such as the "A"-level center in the next river valley.

The prevailing opinion among scholars is that these ancient polities were organized as *mandala* (Wolters 1999; Jacq-Hergoualc'h 2002). Each polity had a center, probably near the sea, but the area that it controlled was quite limited. In some cases the center would not even control the entire river valley. The system was based on oaths of allegiance between the rulers of smaller settlements within striking distance of the capital.

URBAN FOUNDATIONS

Chinese historical documents and archaeological excavations have brought to light a number of ancient settlements located on the Malay Peninsula. Regrettably many are now lost to us and we can only speculate on their location, but the Chinese documents do indicate that a sophisticated society existed from the early centuries of the first millennium and that a rigorous trade took place along the coast of Malaysia.

Tun-sun

One of the polities mentioned by Chinese chroniclers of the 3rd century is Tun-sun. Although its location is a mystery, it was likely on the Malaysian peninsula, possibly near P'ong-Tuk or Phra Pathom. This location would have placed the city in an area that may have been dominated by the Mon, but there is written evidence suggesting that it was a vassal of Funan (Wheatley 1983, 15–21; 1983, 213). The Chinese reported that the territory of Tun-sun covered about 370 kilometers (Wheatley 1961, 16).

The political structure is difficult to ascertain. Tun-sun hosted a colony of South Asians including over one thousand Brahmans (Jacq-Hergoualc'h 2002, 102). Tun-sun is mentioned in the 3rd century C.E. in the *Nan-chou I-wu Chih*, a Chinese text in which it is noted that the people of Tun-sun practiced intermarriage with Brahmans from India who were, reportedly, very pious. We also learn that the people of Tun-sun disposed of the dead by allowing birds to consume the flesh. The bones were then burned and placed in an urn and thrown into the sea. Cremation was another common

method of disposal (Wheatley 1961). Although the city was most active in
the 3rd century C.E., Tun-sun is mentioned in the Chinese text the *Liang
Shu* written in the 6th century. This history tells us that the entrepôt was engaged in trade relationships stretching from the Gulf of Tonkin to India and
Parthia (Wheatley 1983, 213). The *Liang Shu* relates a story of an Indian
named Kaundinya visiting Tun-sun. Kaundinya is reported to have received
a divine message that he was to rule Funan and went on to do so (Pelliot
1903a). This story is one of the most famous foundation myths of the later
Khmer empire.

Panpan

Another entrepôt recorded by the Chinese annalists is Panpan, the location of which remains a mystery. It is likely that it was situated on the east
coast near Kelantan or Terengganu (Miksic 1999e). The first mention of
Panpan is in the *Liang Shu*. The Chinese chroniclers leave us the names of
the ruler and a vague idea of its location, saying that the people lived in a
palisaded city by the sea. The Chinese also tell us that it was a great empo-
rium where traders from Dvaravati, Malaysia, Sri Lanka, China, and India
met.

Luce (1925) hypothesized that Panpan was founded by the Funanese
general Fan Shih-man, who named the city to honor his king (Hun) P'an-
p'an. There is some evidence for a connection with this part of the world as
some of the ministerial titles of Panpan were derived from the Khmer language, but there is also evidence of possible Cham, Malay, and Mon in the
recorded titles (Wheatley 1961, 50). Jacq-Hergoualc'h (2002, 107) doubts
that Panpan was ever a vassal of Funan based on his belief that Funan was
nothing more than an aggregate of rival kingdoms and principalities that
did not have the capability of maintaining an empire. He feels that Panpan
was "largely [an] independent city-state-at least until the arrival of Sri Vijaya"
(Jacq-Hergoualc'h 2002, 110). As evidence of this autonomy he cites the
seemingly independent economic relationship with China. Panpan sent
embassies to the Celestial empire in 527, 529, 532, and 534 C.E. and later
in 616 and 635 C.E.

We know something of the rituals of the court of Panpan, in which the
king held audiences on a golden dragon couch, surrounded by his retainers.
The king favored the Indian Brahmans, but there were also Buddhists in the
kingdom during the 6th century. It appears that Siva was widely worshipped
in Panpan as many lingas, the stone phallus representing Siva, have been
found in the area, but Vishnu images are also well represented (Jacq-Hergoualc'h 2002, 128). In the middle reaches of the peninsula, a Ganesha
statue, dated to the 6th century, was found within the proposed realm of
Panpan (Jacq-Hergoualc'h 2002, 133). The coastal area near Nakhon Si

Thammarat is dotted by the remains of Brahmanical temples, further convincing us of the importance of Hindu beliefs (Jacq-Hergoualc'h 2002, 135).

As we have said, Buddhists were also present, although the remains are not as evident. The Buddhist vestiges usually take the form of votive tablets, stupas, and statues. Jacq-Hergoualc'h contends that the early Malaysian Buddhists were of the Hinayana (the lesser vehicle) school and that Mahayana Buddhism (the greater vehicle) was unknown until the eighth century C.E. (Jacq-Hergoualc'h 2002, 148). This transition to Mahayana Buddhism may have been a result of the political domination of the peninsula by Sri Vijaya.

We know little of the international relations of the polity, other than the missions to the Chinese court mentioned earlier. According to the Chinese text *Jiu Tang Shu*, Panpan was bordered by another polity, Langkasuka (Wheatley 1961, 48). Jacq-Hercoulac'h (2002, 114) speculates that the border may have been south Nakhon Si Thammarat, possibly near Songkhla.

Khao Sam Kaeo

Khao Sam Kaeo was probably established in the late first millennium B.C.E. but likely reached its peak between the second and fourth centuries C.E. The site is located in Chumpon Province on the eastern side of the peninsula, near its narrowest part. The site is backed by hills and looks out over alluvial plains. Although there is an area of approximately seventeen hectares delimited by an earthen bank, the site appears to cover up to forty-five hectares if one accounts for areas revealing archaeological finds (Bellina and Silapanth 2006). The investigators of the site feel that the hills surrounding the site may have been used for habitation, while the ancient residents carried out production activities at the foot of the hills near the river. It appears that the site was a center for the production of prestige goods and the detritus suggests that items were made using imported materials. It is interesting to note that this part of the peninsula is devoid of architecture dating to the early centuries of the first millennium, and there is a dearth of exotic trade ceramics dating to later periods. Bellina and Silapanth (2006) wonder if this may suggest that the site was one of the earlier trade entrepôts, in use when sailing technology required ships to hug the coastline.

Langkasuka

Another major entrepôt during the early centuries C.E. was Langkasuka, located near the modern city of Pattani in present-day Thailand. Ban Wat is the modern name of the site where Langkasuka was located, about fifteen kilometers south of Pattani. The territory of Langkasuka may have stretched as far north as modern Songkhla (Jacq-Hergoulac'h 2002, 163). In the early centuries C.E. we learn from the Chinese that the site, founded perhaps as early as the early 2nd century C.E., was walled and protected by towers (Wheatley 1961, 194). The city was entered through double gates, behind which were grand pavilions (Jacq-Hergoualc'h 2002, 162). There are archaeological remains at Ban Wat that may represent those described by the Chinese chroniclers of the *Liang Shu*. This site boasts dense concentrations of artifacts, canals, and the remains of what may have been moats and ramparts (Jacq-Hergoualc'h 2002, 166).

It appears that in its heyday Langkasuka was not actually a seaboard city but located inland, about ten kilometers. The vestiges of canals can be seen connecting the city to the coast. Jacq-Hergoulac'h (2002, 168) speculates that there once existed entrepôt ports of the city-state at the coast and up-river. There is evidence of international trade from the early period, but it is quite sparse. Many bronze coins from China and the Arab world have been recovered at Langkasuka. The reason for Langkasuka's ascendance as a trade center was probably due to its location. The ease of charting a course from the tip of Indochina and the forest products from Langkasuka contributed to its growth (Miksic 1999, 79).

We know little of its history except that it experienced a period of decline due, possibly, to the expansion of Funan's power in the early 3rd century. Later in the mid-5th century Langkasuka returned to its former glory and later still sent ambassadorial missions to China in 515, 523, 531, and 568 C.E. According to Jacq-Hergoualc'h (2002), Langaksuka was still an important center for trade during the 7th century, but by the 8th century it appears to have lost its independence to Sri Vijaya.

Excavations have revealed a brick structure near the former site of Langkasuka. One appears to have been a Buddhist sanctuary in the Indian style. Votive tablets with inscriptions indicate an occupation from the late 6th to 8th century (Weeraprajak 1990; Jacq-Hergoualc'h 2002). We know from Chinese records that Langkasuka was a popular stopping place for Chinese Buddhist pilgrims on their way to India. The votive tablets also indicate a shift in Buddhist beliefs from Hinayana to Mahayana. There is also an abundance of small votive stupas around the site, suggesting local production. Other religious relics include bronze statues of the Buddha, a stone Nandi, and two lingas (Jacq-Hergoualc'h 2002).

Kedah (Jiecha or Qie zha)

On the opposite coast of Malaysia from Langkasuka was south Kedah, a place known to the Chinese as Jiecha and to the Tamils as Kadaram and called Kataha in Sanskrit. This port was used as an embarkation point for journeys to India. Voyagers going to China also stopped here to await favorable monsoon winds. Unlike Langkasuka, Jiecha was not surrounded by land suited to agriculture. Jacq-Hergoualc'h (2002, 198) believes that the people of Jiecha would have relied on shifting dry cultivation rather than on rice.

The archaeological remains at Jiecha comprise the remains of buildings of laterite and brick, which appear to have been rather spartan Buddhist sanctuaries. The inscriptional evidence from the area does not give a clear indication of occupation. Opinion ranges from the 5th to the 13th century C.E., but the structures were probably built sometime between the 7th and 9th centuries (Jacq-Hergoualc'h 2002, 206). Wheatley (1961, 273) believes the site was a recognized stopping point far earlier based upon the finds of seven fragments of a Sanskrit inscription of the 4th or 5th century C.E. (Jacq-Hergoualc'h 2002, 228).

The amount and nature of the archaeological remains and the paucity of agricultural land tend to suggest that Jiecha could never have attained the status of polities such as Panpan or Langkasuka. Jiecha probably did not attain political complexity above a complex chiefdom. The remains of religious structures at Jiecha were probably constructed by foreigners with the permission of the local chiefs (Jacq-Hergoualc'h 2002, 228). Other scholars are of the opinion that Kedah was Malaysia's most significant early trade entrepôt (Miksic 1999e; Shuhaimi 1999c).

The Chinese Buddhist monk, I Ching stopped in south Kedah in 671 C.E. and noted that it was an independent kingdom. By the time of his return voyage, fourteen years later, the polity had fallen under the control of Sri Vijaya. Miksic (1999g, 74) believes that "its suzerainty seems to have been mainly ceremonial as contemporary Indian sources depict Kedah as an important political entity in its own right."

The reason for Kedah's prominence was its location at the entrance to the Straits of Malacca and that it was situated due east of the important Indian trading entrepôts. Advances in sailing technology allowed ships to cross the Bay of Bengal in a direct line forgoing the previous, coast-hugging route. Miksic (1999c, 78) believes that the Muda River provided access to the interior and was used to tranship lightweight, nonbreakable goods. So prominent was Kedah in the mercantile world that the Indians continued to see Kedah, after its incorporation into the Sri Vijayan kingdom, as the center of power rather than the actual capital of Palembang (Miksic 1999c, 78).

The fortunes of Kedah after the beginning of the 7th century are unclear, but it fails to appear in the chronicles of the T'ang dynasty (618–906 C.E.). This does not necessarily reflect a decline in the polity's importance but may indicate that Chinese commercial interest in the region diminished.

The entrepôt port of Kedah was focused around the Bujang Valley, which extends from the mountain of Gunung Jerai and is home to the Muda and Merbok Rivers. According to Shuhaimi (1999a), the settlement in the valley was concentrated on the ridges, foothills, and natural levees. Religious structures were erected on the highest ground. Ten Sivaite shrines were erected in the middle stretch of the Bujang Valley, the dates of which are unclear but were probably quite late.

According to Wheatley (1961, 280), "the settlement attained its apogee as the Peninsular node of the *Sri Vijayan* thalassocracy. At this time it was the chief power on the Peninsula, linked by the persuasive bonds of trade not only with Sumatra and the rest of the archipelago but also with many parts of India."

Kuala Selinsing

Another west coast entrepôt was located near Kuala Selinsing in Perak. The islands off shore from the Selinsing River mouth seem to have been occupied since at least the 3rd century B.C.E. (Shuhaimi 1991; Bulbeck 2004). Today the site comprises a series of mounds in a mangrove swamp near the mouth of the Selinsing River known as Pulau Kelumpang. The inhabitants exploited the rich marine environment, evidenced by the deposition of large amounts of shell. Artifacts found in burials around Kuala Selinsing include stone, bone, bronze, and iron objects, as well as a wide range of jewelery made from nonlocal, semiprecious stone. The workmanship of the beads is quite crude and may indicate locally produced product using imported stone. Gold is also not found in the area, yet there is evidence of goldsmithery at the site.

The pottery is almost exclusively earthenware, but there are some imported ceramics (possibly Iraqi) that are glazed, dating probably to the 10th century C.E. (Shuhaimi 1991). Of interest is a stone seal inscribed with the name Sri Visnuvarman, a name common in south India in the 6th century. Other artifacts of note include Chinese porcelain from the period between 960 and 1126 C.E.

Although this site is rich archaeologically it is not mentioned in any of the histories left to us by the Chinese or Arabs. Shuhaimi (1999c) suggests that Kuala Selinsing may have been a less important trading site than the major ports such as Kedah, but is important in that it suggests that there were trading entrepôts of differing size.

Chitu

The Kelantan River basin was likely home to the trading port known to the Chinese as Chitu, situated just south of Langkasuka (Wheatley 1961). There are, however, no archaeological remains in the valley to support this location. We hear of Chitu, named for the reddish color of the soil in the area, through its contacts with the Sui dynasty (581–618 C.E.), which graced the polity with an ambassadorial mission in 607 C.E. It would appear that Chitu at the time of Chinese contact was a polity, heavily influenced by Indian culture and ruled by a king who was allied through marriage to the local "lords" or "chiefs" (Jacq-Hergoualc'h 2002, 231). It appears that foreign Brahmans were influential in the court but Buddhists were also represented at Chitu. The principal capital, called either *Seng zhi*, or *Shi zi*, was entered through three gates, and was located a considerable distance (one month's travel) up a large river (Shuhaimi 1999b). The walls of the capital were decorated with bodhisattva images, garlands, and bells. Ancillary centers, according to the Chinese, were each ruled by two appointees of the king. Jacq-Hergoualc'h (2002) questions the degree of centralization suggested by this description, preferring to interpret the evidence as depicting a loose association of towns arranged along the lines of a *mandala*. If the Chinese accounts are accurate, the political system in place at Chitu seems well developed as there were administrative bodies governing political and criminal affairs (Shuhaimi 1999b). The Chinese assert that Chitu was a vassal of the Funan "empire." There appears to be a degree of similarity in the court rituals between Cambodia and Chitu. The Chinese historian Ma Tuan-lin, writing in the fourteenth century, in a reference to 7th century Cambodia, says that the king sat in front of a golden disc with rays in the form of flames. An identical disc was described at Chitu (Coedès 1968). Brown (1996) points out that the flaming sun symbol is not recorded as an Indian practice and may reflect indigenous royal and religious imagery. It may be possible that its symbolism dates back to the Dong Son period. Perhaps there is some connection between this flaming sun and the "star" at the center of the Dong Son drums' tympanums.

Thirty oceangoing junks greeted the Sui ambassadors upon their arrival at Chitu. The Chinese envoys presented the sovereign, Li Fo Duo Se, with over 5000 different gifts and received local products in return (Shuhaimi 1999b).

The Chinese ambassadors collected many interesting anthropological details regarding the people of Chitu. We learn that both men and women had pierced ears and wore scented oils. Strict hierarchy seems to have been the rule, as members of wealthy families had gold lockets for which they had royal permission to wear (Shuhaimi 1999b). The staple food of Chitu was rice, supplemented with a variety of meats of various animals.

We learn of wedding and funeral ceremonies, the latter featuring cremation over the river accompanied by drumming and the blowing of conch horns (Shuhaimi 1999b).

Pulau Tioman (Tioman Island)

Tioman is the largest island on the east coast of Peninsular Southeast Asia and its 1000-meter peaks serve as natural landmarks for navigators, as they probably did in the past. There are two known archaeological sites on Tioman, Kampung Juara and Kampung Nipah, located on the east and west coasts, respectively. Both are found in protected bays where ships could safely harbour (Shuhaimi 1999d).

Most of the evidence for the trading activity on Tioman dates from the 10th century. The datable ceramics originate in Guangdong Province of China and date to the period of the Northern Song dynasty (960–1126 C.E.). The other archaeological material we have dates to the 12th–17th centuries C.E. (Shuhaimi 1999).

Laem Pho

Laem Pho was located on the northern shore of the Bay of Bandon. The range of archaeological materials suggests that the site was a major trading point for merchants from all over the ancient world, but it is unlikely that the settlement retained importance for a long period. The potsherds found at the site indicate origins from the Middle East to China. Glass beads are very common, as are Chinese copper coins, some of which date to the 7th century C.E. (Thepchai 1982).

Ko Kho Khao

The sandy island of Ko Kho Khao is located on the west coast of Peninsular Southeast Asia near the mouth of the Takua Pa River. The visible archaeological remains in the area comprise brick structures and evidence of a reservoir. Chinese ceramics and Middle Eastern glass has come to light as have quantities of "Indo-Pacific Monochrome-Drawn Glass beads" (Francis 1991). These are small seed-sized glass beads common in Southeast Asia from circa 500 B.C.E. onward.

The location of Ko Kho Khao, across the peninsula from Laem Pho, has led some to speculate that these sites represented the end points on a transpeninsular route. This idea is rejected by others who doubt that fragile glass and ceramic wares would have been taken across such arduous terrain (Jacq-Hergoualc'h 2002, 292). If the sites were in constant contact, there would be more obvious similarities in their ceramic assemblages than exists (Manguin 1983; Bronson 1996).

Kampong Sungai Mas

Kampong Sungai Mas, located at the mouth of the Bujang Valley, was probably established as a trading port by the 5th century C.E. The port may have only been used up until the 9th century due to the silting of the river mouth (Jacq-Hergoualc'h 2002, 295).

Although we have no documentary evidence, it appears that the dominant religion of Sungai Mas was Buddhism (Shuhaimi 1999d). Based on the ceramic collections recovered from excavations the port appears to have catered to merchants from the Middle East and China (Shuhaimi 1984). It appears that the site was also a bead manufacturing center, as several thousand carnelian beads have been recovered (Francis 1996).

INFLUENCE OF SRI VIJAYA

Although not covered in this survey of early Mainland Southeast Asian polities, the poorly understood political entity called Sri Vijaya plays an important role in regional politics of the 8th century. Sri Vijaya might remain unknown to us were it not for the pioneering efforts of a scholar named George Coedès. Coedès (1918) published a paper that traced the appearance of Sri Vijaya in various inscriptions found in insular Southeast Asia. He then found Sri Vijaya mentioned in texts of the Cola dynasty dating to 1005 C.E. and 1025 C.E. The latter mentioned the Cola domination of the lands now thought to have been ruled by Sri Vijaya. Coedès began to paint a picture of a polity based in eastern Sumatra whose sphere of influence was vast, extending over that island, Java, and up Peninsular Southeast Asia into the territory of Dvaravati. Sri Vijaya's influence waned in the 11th century C.E., but the polity existed from the 7th to the 13th century C.E. Paradoxically, the archaeological evidence for Sri Vijaya is scant, and for this reason it remained largely anonymous for centuries. Although some scholars have called the very existence of Sri Vijaya into doubt (Bronson and Wisseman 1976), the prevailing opinion, supported by more recent finds, is that Sri Vijaya did exist and was able to influence the politics of far-flung principalities.

Sri Vijaya's capital, Palembang, was most likely located on the banks of the Musi River in south Sumatra. The area where Palembang was located is somewhat upstream, but tidal flooding allowed ships of deep draft to access the city (Manguin 1987). It has been confirmed that the Musi River bank was spotted with smaller "hubs" of activity, twelve kilometers upriver from the mouth (Manguin 1992). Chinese ceramics indicate the site was occupied during the 8th and 9th centuries, and the amount of ceramics there suggest that the area of Palembang was a busy harbor. The existence of buildings that may have been used for religious functions has also been reported.

I Ching, whom we have mentioned before, stopped at what is assumed to have been Palembang in 671 C.E. It seems that it was not only a commercial hub but also a center of scholarly learning. I Ching, himself, spent half a year studying Sanskrit (Chavannes 1894). On the return voyage to

China, I Ching lived at Palembang for four years. As we have seen, I Ching stopped at Kedah on his way to India. On the first voyage the Malaysian polity was apparently independent, but by the time he returned he recorded that it had fallen under the dominion of Sri Vijaya (Takakusu 1896). In 695 C.E. Sri Vijaya opened diplomatic relations with China (Pelliot 1904). By the 8th century C.E., Sri Vijaya controlled Ligor, Takua Pa, and the other kingdoms in the northern part of Peninsular Southeast Asia (Shuhaimi 1999c).

Seven inscriptions have been found in the vicinity of ancient Palembang. These are either commemorative stones recording royal beneficence or inscriptions designed to proclaim loyalty to the ruler. From these inscriptions we learn that Sri Vijaya, at the time the inscription was written, was ruled by a king, Sri Jayanasa. Both the name of the polity and the ruler's name are Sanskrit, but it is most enlightening to note that the ruler also held a local title of religious origin (Jacq-Hergoualc'h 2002, 239).

The inscriptions indicate that in 683 C.E. the king launched a military expedition upriver from Palembang. This may indicate that he did not control the interior completely up to that time. He also sent missions to subdue the neighboring island of Java (Wisseman Christie 1995, 265–66). Regrettably these insights into the activities of the Sri Vijayan polity are fleeting; after the end of the 7th century there are no inscriptions. For the later period we are forced to rely on Chinese evidence of diplomatic relations during the first half of the 8th century.

Coedès was convinced that the motivation for Sri Vijayan expansion was not aimed at territorial gain so much as to acquire economic control over the trade flowing through the Straits of Malacca (Coedès 1964b; 1968). Sri Vijaya controlled Kedah by the late 7th century, and Panpan and Langkasuka both came under her control at unspecified dates.

Regarding the political organization of Sri Vijaya, it is difficult to be certain whether the territories claimed to be under its dominion were subjugated militarily or rather chose to be vassals of the Sumatran power. The former is the favored interpretation. As we have seen, Sri Vijaya was sending punitive missions up the Musi River at a point when it was meant to control large swaths of Southeast Asia. Were the polity organized as a complex state, territories in such close proximity are likely to have been secured from the very beginning of its ascendancy. Sri Vijaya should not be depicted as a centralized empire, as it was more likely a polity ruled by a king who was "first among equals" (Kulke 1993). The kings who had become the overlord's vassals represented a constant threat, and the list grew as the areas under domination expanded. Contemporary inscriptions have been interpreted such that the king of Sri Vijaya imposed his dominance over kingdoms and chieftaincies surrounding Palembang but did not depose the rulers (Kulke 1993). To ensure compliance he appears to have installed princes or close allies in these territories. Such a system is consistent with the *mandala* organization.

The Sri Vijayan polity needed a substantial force to ensure the continued fealty of surrounding kingdoms. The *mandala* organization freed Sri Vijaya's military force from colonial obligations. There was no need for huge standing armies in these territories, but a rapid response force could be dispatched to quell any disruptions. There is some indication that Sri Vijaya had a large armed force of about 20,000 men who were sent on an expedition against Java (Jacq-Hergoualc'h 2002, 250). It would be logical that Sri Vijaya used a naval force to deploy its armies to any point in its "empire." The *Orang Laut* or the sea warriors may have served as Sri Vijaya's naval strike force.

Kulke (1993) sees Sri Vijaya's direct sphere of political control as limited, extending only to the "jungles and the mountains which encircled . . . the Musi River system." In adjacent river valleys, polities duplicating Sri Vijaya's political hierarchy existed but were subservient to the more powerful center as is evidenced by the "oath" inscriptions. It is unlikely that there was any desire in Sri Vijaya to solidify or formalize its territories (Kulke 1993, 176). The flexibility of the vassalage system allowed the polity to survive and prosper for many centuries as the physical domination of such far-flung territories was simply impossible.

The preservation of such a vast empire may have been possible through the use of threat of military force and beneficence. The construction of at least two temples in Sri Vijaya's territories is noted in inscriptions of the 8th and 9th centuries C.E. Furthermore there may have been support for the continued dominance of Sri Vijaya by all of the polities involved in trade. With its base at Palembang and naval capabilities, Sri Vijaya could control the sea lanes totally, thereby eliminating piracy. The fact that the entrepôt ports of Malaysia were allowed to continue operating unhindered except, perhaps, for taxation and tribute was another reason why the polity's hegemony went unchallenged (Shuhaimi 1999e, 119). In this manner Sri Vijaya became the main supplier of trade products originating in Southeast Asia, as well as the distributor of goods coming from India, the Arab world, and China. The inscriptions from this period indicate that a bureaucracy existed to run the "empire" on a daily basis, likely a system of officials loyal to the Sri Vijayan monarch who served in foreign capitals (Shuhaimi 1999e). There is even some indication that Kedah functioned as a secondary capital of the Sri Vijayan "empire." A Chinese report of the time states that it was "a double kingdom and the two parts have separate administrations" (Miksic 1999b).

DEVELOPMENTS IN THE 9TH CENTURY

In the period leading up to the 9th century the amount of international trade passing through Peninsular Southeast Asia continued to rise. The importance of ports such as Panpan, Langkasuka, and others began to be eclipsed by larger entrepôt ports.

The reason for this growth may be found in the geopolitics in areas far removed from the Southern Seas. The traditional overland routes that had, for centuries, seen goods flow from China westward were threatened. The Umayyad rulers of the Middle East were overthrown by the Abassids in the middle of the 8th century C.E., and the capital moved several times, being finally established at Baghdad in 752 C.E. The overland trade route was disrupted by this power shift as provincial overlords attempted to break away from Abassid control. The situation was compounded by political unrest farther east in central Asia. Due to an erosion of Chinese control in the region predicated by rebellions against the ruling T'ang dynasty the trade routes grew more dangerous. In the mid-8th century C.E. the Tibetans began to flex their military muscle eventually causing major disruptions to T'ang rule. Even Chang'an, the capital of the T'ang, was pillaged. In 787 C.E. the city of Dunhuang, the place where the Silk Road diverged to circumvent the Taklamakan Desert, was captured (Beckwith 1987). Eventually the Tibetans controlled both the northern and southern routes around the Taklamakan. The area became contested by the Uyghurs, who battled the Tibetans until the 9th century C.E. The result being that the overland route to Europe became too insecure or expensive to traverse and merchants began to look to the alternative sea route.

The sea ports of South China expanded due largely to the trade in products from Southeast Asia. The Chinese began trading ceramics for the forest products of the Southern Seas beginning in the 9th century C.E. At this time numerous kilns appeared in South China to supply the Southeast Asian market (Ho et al. 1990; Ho 1991a; 1991b; 1994).

It has also been suggested that Southeast Asian intraregional trade became more sustained during the 9th century, so much so that cultural influences may be identified. Jacq-Hergoualc'h (2002, 269) contends that temples in Thailand dating to this period reflect Cham influences.

We are less well informed about events of the 9th century in India, and we know little of what was happening to the "empire" established by Sri Vijaya. There is too little archaeological evidence to make any suggestions about the continued interaction with India. Undoubtedly trade contacts between Malaysia and the subcontinent continued, but the necessary research to prove this has not been undertaken. The possibility of disruptions in trade must be considered, however. South India during the 9th century was beset by conflict between varied polities including the Calukya, Cola, Pandya, and Pallavas (Jacq-Hergoualc'h 2002, 272).

There is some evidence of the presence of Indian merchant guilds in Malaysia during the 9th century. Found on the west coast of the peninsula at Takua Pa-Ko Khao, an inscription in the Tamil script records the excavation of a water tank by a royal personage. The tank was placed in the care of a guild of merchants.

As well as south India, we have evidence that Sri Lanka was involved in trade with the Malaysian peninsula. Vessels leaving the Persian Gulf ports crossed to Sri Lanka to offload goods that were, in turn, taken across the Bay of Bengal. During the 9th century, these ships would have landed at Ko Kho Khao and Kampong Sungai Mas, from whence they would resupply and head for Palembang. Ships would then depart Palembang for south China, with a probable stop along the shore of Champa (Jacq-Hergoualc'h 2002, 279).

The power of Sri Vijaya lasted until the incursions by the Cola empire, based in India, began to destabilize the system. The Tamil, who controlled the Cola kingdom, began subjugating the entrepôt ports of Peninsular Southeast Asia in the 11th century. The Cola established Kedah as their main base of operations, where they appear to have exercised some control over the peninsula for about a century.

CONCLUSION

It is clear that the development of the various polities of Peninsular Southeast Asia was due, in large part, to their geographic location between the world's two commercial giants, China and India. Trade between these regions necessitated an encounter with the people of the Malaysian peninsula.

Trading entrepôts developed on either side of Peninsular Southeast Asia as a response to the demand from international traders. At first these merchants came and went with the monsoon winds that powered their ships, but eventually their presence became more permanent. It is apparent that merchants from India resided in Malaysian ports from at least the 5th century C.E. and that their culture was adopted in varying degrees by the indigenous population. Due in part to travel restrictions placed on Chinese merchants, their culture did not have a significant or lasting impact on the indigenous peoples of the peninsula.

It is difficult to comprehend why political entities that had access to such wealth and advantageous positions in an international trade network did not develop into more complex or powerful states. It is possible that the geography of the peninsula discouraged the formation of large, tightly knit political territories. It appears that the polities that developed were not fully evolved states but rather commercially driven entities that had tenuous control of their hinterlands. The territory that the commercial center could claim probably rarely extended beyond the drainage basin in which it was located.

4

The Mon Protostates: Dvaravati and Myanmar

More than any other early polity in mainland Southeast Asia, the entity that has come to be known as Dvaravati is perhaps the most enigmatic. Even after three decades of intensive archaeological research in the heartland of Dvaravati, no indigenous texts have come to light, and the monuments and artifacts are dated relative to similar objects and edifices elsewhere (Brown 1996). Inscriptional evidence is fugitive; less than a dozen inscriptions in the Mon language have been found in Thailand. It is not surprising then that we know relatively little about the development and functioning of the political entity that was Dvaravati.

Dvaravati first came to the attention of modern scholars during the 19th century through the translation of Chinese texts (Beal 1884; Chavannes 1894). These texts mentioned *To-lo-po-ti*, *Tu-ho-po-ti*, and *Tu-ho-lo-po-ti*, names that were translated into Sanskrit-Dvaravati. We know that this polity had an international presence, as it sent a number of missions to the Chinese court, but it is difficult to reconstruct what kind of polity is represented and scholarly opinion is split. Vallibhotama (1986; 1999) has characterized it as a mercantile and maritime state that was divided into two, and Dhida (1999), although seemingly not convinced of the polity's state status, refers to it as such throughout her book on the subject. Wheatley (1983) feels that Dvaravati is best described as a complex chiefdom, and Brown (1996) believes it unlikely that Dvaravati was an empire or even a kingdom. Clearly the issue cannot be resolved until further research is undertaken, but the current evidence appears to favor an interpretation of Dvaravati as a loosely organized political entity at a prestate level. The situation is confused further by the use of the term Dvaravati to describe a school of art and a culture. It is best to consider Dvaravati as a broad term, encompassing all of these things—a culture, comprised mostly of Mon speakers who produced predominantly religious art and lived in large towns concentrated in the Chao Phraya River Valley whose influence extended into other parts of Thailand.

THE BEGINNINGS OF DVARAVATI

It has been argued that, prior to contact with the Indian subcontinent, the communities of the central plains of Thailand were probably autonomous (Dhida 1999, 102). As complexity developed it appears that power was held contemporaneously by more than one settlement, each with its own leader.

The earliest references to Dvaravati date to the middle of the seventh century. These refer to trade missions sent to the Chinese court in 638 and 649 C.E. (Brown 1996; Guillon 1999). The Chinese histories indicate that Dvaravati was located on the central plains of present-day Thailand between the dominions of the ancient Tircul, Sri Ksetra in modern Myanmar, and Isanapura (Sambor Prei Kuk) in present-day Cambodia.

A number of archaeological discoveries confirm the existence of a cohesive cultural group in present-day Thailand dating from the 6th century C.E. The first solid evidence came in the form of coins from Phra Pathom, home to the oldest known Mon inscription (Dhida 1999). These coins are inscribed with the words "*Sri Dvaravatisvara*" (Boeles 1964; Coedès 1964b). As well as an inscription, one coin bears the image of a cow and a calf and another a water pot with floral motifs (Dhida 1999). From this inscription it was inferred that there was a king of a polity called Dvaravati (Coedès 1964b). Early excavations seem to suggest that Nakhon Pathom was occupied for a long period, as the earliest artifacts are said to be stylistically similar to those from Funan (Boisselier 1971). Others argue that it was occupied later and for a much shorter period, from the end of the 6th to the end of the 7th centuries (Guillon 1999). Whether the existence of a "culturally cohesive" group implies political cohesiveness is debatable. It is likely that Dvaravati's political power in the 7th century C.E. was still limited but the culture had been dispersed very widely. The political power of Dvaravati was probably "not . . . co-extensive with the sphere of Dvaravati art" (Dhida 1999, 106–7).

We gain some insight into the organization of social and political power in Dvaravati through a number of inscriptions. These inscriptions hint at the influence of Indian beliefs in Dvaravati both in their contents and in the languages used, Sanskrit and Pali (Dhida 1999, 131–32). They also mention varying royal families, traditions, and local beliefs.

It is clear that the polity of Dvaravati is shrouded in mystery, and trying to decipher the origins of this sociocultural entity borders on the speculative. It is clear nevertheless that the polity was to some degree influenced by the culture of the subcontinent. The preeminent religion seems to have been Buddhism in one form or another, followed closely by Hinduism. The vernacular was written in scripts from the subcontinent, and the motifs in the art certainly originate in India.

THE PEOPLE

Burials are rarely found in Dvaravati archaeological contexts, and we must rely on the inscriptions to try and reconstruct who these people were. It appears that the Dvaravati people were probably Mon speakers. Mon is a language of the Mon-Khmer branch of the Austroasiatic language family. Its closest relative is Nyah Kur, a language spoken today by a few thousand people in central and northeastern Thailand (Diffloth 1984). It is very possible that these people are some of the descendants of Dvaravati populations (Diffloth 1984; Hla 1991; Jenny 2001). Mon speakers were, at one time, found all across what is now Thailand and lower Myanmar. Indeed, there are some indications that the population of northeast Thailand and Thaton in Myanmar were in contact, if not culturally related (Guillon 1999). Vallibhotama (1999) and Dhida (1999) stress that Dvaravati was not solely a Mon entity, however. They feel Mon may have been the official language that served to unite a multiethnic population, including speakers of Khmer, Chinese, and Tai.

The inscriptions found at Nakhon Pathom are the oldest evidence of the Mon language. A schist slab was inscribed with Old Tamil, a language originating in southern India, near the end of the 6th century. Later Mon inscriptions are written in scripts from southeast India (Guillon 1999). The Mon adapted the Indian writing systems to their own language during the 3rd or 4th century C.E. The script they used was probably most often written on palm fronds, and as the text evolved its characters became very circular (Jenny 2001). The inscriptions give no reference to the people in general, and we cannot be sure what the Mon of Dvaravati called themselves but a Khmer inscription indicates that their neighbors called them the *Ramañ* (Coedès 1937–1966).

RELIGION

There is little indication as to how the religious beliefs of the Dvaravati people evolved. It is clear that Buddhism came to be the predominant religion, but it is also apparent that Hinduism was widely practiced. Some have suggested that the religions were practiced along class lines, with the elite preferring Hinduism (Dhida 1999). Evidence of Hindu beliefs comes in many forms including coins bearing auspicious symbols and words. The *srivatsa*, a symbol that takes many forms but is symbolic of fertility and kingship, is widely found on coinage as are images of Vishnu. Other symbols, including the bull, Nandi, Siva's mount, and the *hamsa* (goose), Brahma's mount, are found as well. Similar coins are found at contemporaneous sites across Southeast Asia, including the Tircul sites in Myanmar and also in present-day Vietnam at Oc Éo. Other auspicious Hindu artifacts have been recovered, including an ivory comb from Chansen (Bronson and Dales 1972). The comb had a number of symbols, including a *hamsa*, the sun, a *srivatsa*, an umbrella, the moon, a conch, and two horses, which seems to indicate that the craftsman was inspired by Hindu motifs (Krairiksh 1977). Other objects with clear Hindu association have been found in central Thailand, including statues of Surya (god of the sun), Skanda (god of war), and Vishnu, dating to the 6th and early 7th centuries (Krairiksh 1977; Guillon 1999).

Dhida (1999) concedes that many of the Dvaravati towns may have been ruled by Brahman. U-Thong appears to have been ruled by Brahman, based on inscriptional evidence, from northwest India until the 7th or 8th century. After this period they were forced to relinquish control to another group of Brahman, originally from south India. Although the rulers, including the king(s), may have been Hindu, Dhida (1999, 29) believes that

Figure 4.1.   Found at a Dvaravati site in Suphan Buri (courtesy Fine Arts Department, Thailand).

the populace at large embraced Buddhism, which gradually became the dominant religion. This religious competition, she believes, is represented in a cave relief that shows the Hindu god Vishnu paying homage to the Buddha (Dhida 1999, 29).

Buddhism is clearly represented in Dvaravati in the form of *cakras* or *dharmacakras*. These are representations of a wheel that symbolizes the teaching of the Buddha—the wheel of the law. Cakras are found throughout the Dvaravati territory but are concentrated in the Chao Phraya River valley and in peninsular Thailand. The same design in relief is found further afield, on the Khorat Plateau, indicating a widespread belief in the teaching of the Buddha (Brown 1996).

The pattern is one of mixed religion in a broadly similar cultural milieu. Some scholars have attempted to explain Dvaravati as a culture divided along georeligious lines, some areas practicing Buddhism and other areas following Hindu tenets. Vallibhotama (1986) has suggested that the majority in the western portion of the Chao Phraya Valley followed Buddhism, whereas most people in the eastern part of the valley practiced Hinduism. Others have argued that both religions were equally represented during the Dvaravati period (Wales 1969). In reality there is currently not enough evidence to confidently suggest a division of the territory into Buddhist and Hindu areas. According to Brown (1996), it is unlikely that only one religion was adhered to at one time. He sees Dvaravati as a culture that embraced both Buddhism and Hinduism, the two often mixing.

Although Buddhism dominated the Chao Phraya Valley, its influence on the Khorat Plateau was less secure. Here, the Hindu influence was more

Figure 4.2.   Wheel of Law from Sri Thep, Thailand (courtesy Fine Arts Department, Thailand).

strongly felt. Sites such as Sri Thep, bordering the Khorat Plateau, have surrendered Hindu artifacts, the presence of which is explained by the shifting political allegiance of the town. Wales (1969) thinks that the town was originally influenced by the predominantly Hindu, Funan and later by Buddhist, Dvaravati, and finally, Hindu, Angkor. The northeast seems to have followed a slightly different trajectory in the expression of the Buddhist faith. The *cakra* was the most common expression of the faith in the Chao Phraya Valley, but in the northeast the *sema* or boundary stone seems to have predominated. These stones are found at the cardinal and subcardinal points around ancient settlements or monasteries in the northeast and mark sacred territory. Some of these stones are decorated with *cakra* and some are inscribed. These flat stones are of variable size and are narrow at the bottom and often have a single, pointed crenulation. Brown (1996) thinks that the use of *sema* in the northeast may relate to the prehistoric traditions of the area and the worship of menhirs.

It is clear based on present evidence that Buddhism was the dominant religion, or at least the most expressive, in Dvaravati, but it is less clear as to what kind of Buddhism was practiced. Mahayana Buddhism was certainly practiced in Dvaravati as bodhisattva images have been recovered, but the proportional representation of each school is impossible to determine (Brown 1996). It is likely that Therevada Buddhism dominated in Dvaravati, but there may have been a mixture of Therevada and Mahayana Buddhism at certain sites, especially in the northeast.

The Sarvastivada sect of Therevada Buddhism uses Sanskrit and promotes the belief that a human can reach the stage necessary to enter Nirvana through

Figure 4.3. A *sema* stone from Muang Fa Daed (courtesy Fine Arts Department, Thailand).

Figure 4.4. A golden Buddha head found at U-Thong, Thailand (courtesy Fine Arts Department, Thailand).

meditation, merit-making, and the performance of benevolent deeds. Should one choose not to enter Nirvana but stay behind and teach others the path to Enlightenment he becomes a Bodhisattva. Dhida (1999, 204) believes that this sect originally held political power in Dvaravati. The king was a *Phra Bodhisattva Avalokitesvara, Phra Manjusri,* or *Phra Mettraiya Bodhisattva.*

The Bodhisattva ruler was not, however, the only type of ruler (Dhida 1999, 203). Other rulers subscribing to the Pali canon preferred a different model of kingship, and the ruler was referred to as *Cakravatti Raja* or *Cakravartin.* This model linked religious and political power; the Raja or king was elevated to a semidivine position. The Cakravatti Raja represented terrestrial power and the Boddhisattva the celestial power. It is possible that the erection of the *cakra* had a political motivation, and it has been speculated that they affirm the king's position as the *dharmacakra,* the one who can turn the Wheel of the Law (Dhida 1999, 201).

Of course it is difficult to completely separate Buddhist and Hindu beliefs on kingship, as they spring from a similar social tradition. According to these ancient beliefs the first king was actually a god who, in return for tribute, would deliver an ordered society (Dhida 1999). The religious beliefs of Dvaravati were closely linked to the political organization of the culture.

POLITICAL ORGANIZATION

Dvaravati has been characterized as a kingdom (Coedès 1968, 76), even an empire (Lyons 1979). This opinion is no longer widely supported, and

Dvaravati is now more often described as an early kingdom (Kulke 1986), a fragmented kingdom (Vallibhotama 1986), a complex chiefdom (Wheatley 1983), or a number of hierarchical polities sharing a cultural milieu (Brown 1996; Guillon 1999). It is difficult to say with any certainty what form the political structure of the Dvaravati polity or cultural complex took. Basically, Dvaravati may be viewed in three ways; either Dvaravati was a large unified state, two smaller competing states, or it was comprised of a number of large settlements that controlled ill-defined territories and were in competition with one another. It is difficult to discern why Dvaravati failed to evolve into a more powerful entity than the evidence suggests it did. The more visible states that developed in Southeast Asia were Khmer and Cham, both, largely, Hindu polities. Did the predominance of Buddhism have something to do with the Dvaravati failure to become more unified and powerful? Buddhist kingship is related to karma, while Hindu kingship is related to divine power (Heine-Geldern 1963). Did this hamper the expansion or protection of the Dvaravati polity? It is unlikely that the Buddhist precepts would have prevented the development of an aggressive and centralized state, for it seems one of the primary duties of a Buddhist monarch was to make war (Dhida 1999, 209). According to the Buddhist sacred text, the *Tittiriya Upanisad*, it is not possible for men to engage in warfare without a king (Dhida 1999, 209).

Although Wales (1969) divided Dvaravati into western, central/northern, eastern, and northeastern areas, he believed they were ruled from one capital. Vallibhotama (1986) prefers to view Dvaravati as a fragmented polity with more than one capital in various regions. In his view, the people of Dvaravati may have shared a common culture but, politically, they were divided. He posits the existence of an eastern and a western polity in central Thailand during Dvaravati times. These two rivals were ruled by leaders of differing religious views, Hindu and Buddhist. Archaeological finds from western Dvaravati settlements suggest a Buddhist culture, whereas those in the east seem to have a stronger Hindu influence. Vallibhotama (1986) thinks that this difference in religious orientation indicates a difference in political leadership. Brown (1996, 61), however, believes that this division is untenable and supports Wales's (1969) hypothesis that there is no indication of separate polities under different religious banners.

Dvaravati is often popularly characterized as a *mandala*, a model of a political entity with nebulous, contractive, and expansive limits (Chutintaranond 1990; Grave 1995; Wolters 1999). The *mandala* may be juxtaposed with the unified state in that a number of competing polities existed in a limited area, each centered on a charismatic individual (Dhida 1999, 106). This conception of personality-driven political entities is reinforced by the fact that early Southeast Asian inscriptions seem to equate the power of the state with the power of an individual ruler. Further, there is rarely any definition of political territory in geographic terms before the rise of Sukhothai (Dhida 1999, 106–7).

Several scholars prefer to categorize the protohistoric settlements of the central plains in Thailand as protostates that were socially, economically, and politically self-contained. It was possible for these independent units to form networks with attendant satellite settlements. This view portrays Dvaravati as being comprised of small fortified towns, centered on a palace with small reservoirs and peripheral monasteries, sharing alliances (Kasetsiri 1976, 16; Dhida 1999, 30–31; Guillon 1999, 78). Dvaravati, according to this view, comprised several of these networks that were brought together through economic necessity or advantage. Five separate groups or federations are proposed to have existed during Dvaravati times. The Chao Phraya River Valley was home to three of these federations, in the west, east, and upper valley, and yet another group was located to the east of the valley. The last federation, covering the Pa Sak River valley/Khorat Plateau, was centered on Sri Thep. Of these federations the group located on the coast (which was considerably further inland during Dvaravati times) to the west of the Chao Phraya River were the most influential (Dhida 1999, 33). This group comprised the settlements of U-Thong, Nakhon Pathom and Khu Bua. These sites served as a communication junction for contacts with towns in the east and west. Hall (1976) prefers to depict the relationship between sites as one of core and periphery. He believes that the peripheral sites were located in the western area of the upper Chao Phraya basin. Vallibhotama (1986) divides the Chao Phraya into separate polities, east and west, based on what he thinks was the dominant religion in each.

The political nature of Dvaravati may also be discerned in the art. It has been suggested that the art is locally distinct (Vallibhotama 1986; Dhida 1999), a characteristic which may indicate a lack of centralized power. The strong Khmer elements in the art from sites on the Khorat Plateau has led some to suggest a semiautonomous region within Dvaravati or a Mon intrusion into an originally Khmer territory (Wales 1969). Wales (1974) thinks that the sculpture found at smaller Dvaravati settlements is of poor quality and indicates a provincial relationship with the larger centers that produced higher quality art.

It is the opinion of several scholars that the political entities that existed in the 7th and 8th centuries in Cambodia and Thailand were probably in a constant state of flux, expanding and contracting as events demanded (Higham 1989a; Brown 1996, 11; Wolters 1999). It is also evident that the developmental sequence of the polities that existed in Cambodia followed a far different trajectory than those in Thailand. The former polities appear to have been able to centralize to a far greater degree, beginning in the 9th century, eventually gaining hegemony over the greater part of Southeast Asia.

According to Brown (1996, 47), acceptance of the mandala model to explain the political organization of Dvaravati negates the existence of capitals and provincial towns. Towns that would be considered provincial in a kingdom, those inferior to the capital, are mere nodes in a network of elite individuals that share reciprocal ties with other elites.

SOCIAL ORGANIZATION

It has been suggested that Dvaravati was divided into rulers and the ruled, with some fine degree of hierarchical differentiation among the latter. Those who were ruled comprised rural people, townspeople, craftsmen, tradesmen, soldiers, and slaves (Dhida 1999, 177). This portrayal is, perhaps, a little simplistic, but the broad categories are probably accurate. Perhaps the most exalted, nonelite group were the merchants, whose wealth may have brought them closer to the elite. At the other end of the "governed" class were the slaves and landless laborers or serfs. These people could, as in other Indian-influenced polities, be donated and conscripted for warfare. An 8th-century Mon inscription from Lavo (modern Lopburi in central Thailand) lists servants as part of a donation to attend Buddha images (Dhida 1999, 186). It has been suggested that the slaves and serfs were individuals from foreign lands who were not Buddhists (Dhida 1999, 188). It seems that the slave/serf category was distinguished from another slightly elevated category, the freeman denoted in Mon as "mān."

SETTLEMENT PATTERN

The majority of Dvaravati sites are concentrated on the margins of the central plains of Thailand. Although today it may appear that these sites are landlocked, one must account for higher sea levels during their occupation. Although this argument is yet to be confirmed, it is possible that the location of Dvaravati sites in the past gave them unfettered access to the sea (Vanasin and Suupajanya 1981). Most Dvaravati settlements are located near a river, providing access to food, water, and trade. The rivers also filled the moats that surrounded many of the Dvaravati sites. Given the presence and height of the ramparts at many of these sites, it is possible to speculate that the moats were used for defensive purposes. Many Dvaravati settlements are found on the uplands bordering riverine plains, which afforded flood protection and proximity to terrestrial and riverine communication routes (Guillon 1999, 78).

Groslier (1980) generalized that the oval sites on the Khorat Plateau were Dvaravati foundations and were usually surrounded by one or two moats separated by ramparts. In the central Menam Basin, single moats are most common (Wales 1969, 1). After the 7th century C.E. the oval plan gave way to an oblong and then a more rectangular site plan, but this probably did not occur until the Khmer influence was felt in Dvaravati (Hagesteijn 1989, 18; Guillon 1999, 78).

It is probable that the Dvaravati sites were settlement centers rather than ceremonial locales but we cannot be sure until proper excavations have been undertaken. The fact that we are unsure of the purpose of some of the largest archaeological sites in Thailand is an indication of our ignorance regarding this culture. Nevertheless, it is clear that these were important religious sites as most contain the remains of rather substantial Buddhist monuments both within and outside the moats. Some Mon inscriptions record the existence of "*ra*," meaning small town. These are probably not as archaeologically visible as the larger Dvaravati settlements that we know today recorded as "*dun*" (Dhida 1999, 180). It is likely that the *dun* were protected by a rampart and possibly a moat, whereas the *ra* may have been simple farming or trading towns. Within the larger towns there may have been residential and royal enclosures, the former comprising perhaps ten thousand households (Dhida 1999, 176).

If Dvaravati was a centralized state there should be evidence of a capital. To date, no incontrovertible proof for a supraregional center has been found. Some sites have been promoted as capitals of Dvaravati on the basis of their physical size. U-Thong is one such site, as is Nakhon Pathom, which may have been dominant from the ninth to the eleventh century C.E. Bronson (1979, 325) does not doubt that there was a complex political hierarchy in place during Dvaravati times, citing evidence for interregional trade at Chansen. In a survey of sixty-three sites in the central plains of Thailand, Mudar (1999) found that the majority of sites were smaller than one hundred hectares. Only one, Nakhon Pathom, was large enough, at 602 hectares, to be classified as a primary center. Other categories included very large settlements that covered about 350 hectares and large settlements ranging in size from 101 to 161 hectares. Medium settlements were forty-seven to one hundred hectares, and medium-small settlements were smaller than forty-six hectares. Mudar (1999) has inferred that a combination of the size and location of these sites may correlate to an administrative hierarchy of supraregional centers, regional centers, district centers, and subdistrict centers. Mudar's research seems to indicate the possibility of seven regions in the central basin each averaging 3300 square kilometers. All of this, according to Mudar (1999), suggests that Dvaravati was a state-level polity. Extrapolating population size and agricultural technique, it seems that many of the larger sites relied on other communities to bolster their rice supplies. Many Dvaravati sites appear to have been roughly the same size and strength. It is possible that, from the 9th to the 11th century C.E.,

Nakhon Pathom dominated most of the other settlements of the central plains in Thailand (Hagesteijn 1989, 130). Nakhon Pathom may have been rivaled by sites such as U-Thong, Muang Fa Daed, and Suphan Buri but other sites mentioned in written sources as "capital centers" were not as large as these sites (Hagesteijn 1989, 130). Just as it is difficult to define just what Dvaravati was, it is impossible to assign a boundary to it. Perhaps the best method of determining the extent of the influence of Dvaravati is through its art, especially the distinctive *cakras*. These objects are most commonly found in central Thailand, into peninsular Thailand, and right up to the edge of the Khorat Plateau. On the Khorat Plateau and into Cambodia it is uncommon to find these objects carved in the round, but they are represented on votive tablets, *sema* stones, and plaques. The distribution of these different forms of this cultural and religious marker well illustrates the nebulous and impermanent nature of Dvaravati (Brown 1996, 11).

Recent research in central Thailand indicates that with the advent of the protohistoric period, a two-tier settlement hierarchy developed in the eastern Chao Praya basin. In the case of Chansen, it seems several smaller satellite sites cluster around this larger center, perhaps in a dependant relationship (Onsuwan Eyre 2006, 286).

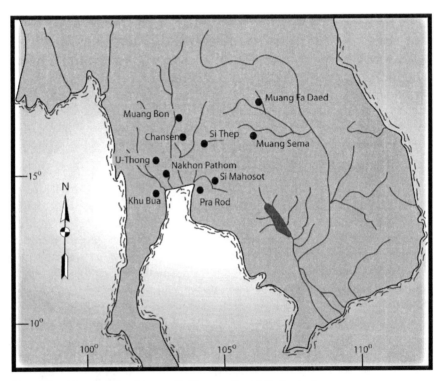

Map 4.1.   Map showing Dvaravati sites mentioned in the text.

With this broad overview of this poorly understood cultural complex we may now turn to examine some of the major settlements of Dvaravati.

CENTRAL THAILAND

U-Thong

U-Thong is located in the Tha Chin River basin in central Thailand. It is one of the larger Dvaravati sites and has been proposed as an early capital by those who prefer to cast Dvaravati as a unified kingdom (Wales 1969; Boisselier 1971). The oval moat that surrounds the site is proposed to have evolved by the 7th century C.E. (Wheatley 1983). The site, noted by the Chinese as *Chinlin*, was certainly of some importance and possesses a number of traits hinting at its significance, including religious structures, fortifications, roads, and irrigation canals. It has been cast as a major port that was a node of distribution serving satellite sites (Vallibhotama 1986, 230). Boisselier (1971) has suggested that the site was first occupied in the 2nd century C.E., and artifacts recovered there are similar to those of Funan and Beikthano (Vallibhotama 1986, 230).

One of the most important artifacts discovered at U-Thong is an inscribed copper plate (Coedès 1958). This artifact gives us an interesting insight into the sociopolitical climate at U-Thong circa the 7th and 8th centuries C.E. Inscribing copper was practiced widely at the time in southern India, but finds such as this are uncommon in mainland Southeast Asia. The earliest inscriptions in the Chao Phraya Basin are written in Pallava, but the U-Thong plate is stylistically different from Pallava. It is best characterized as a "post-Pallava" script, a style that may have been modified by the local inhabitants (Dhida 1999, 99).

The plate records the donation of a linga by Sri Harsavarman, who, according to the inscription, was the grandson of a king Sri Isanavarman. The use of royal names with "varman" suffixes is of great interest and seems to indicate the presence at U-Thong of Hindu rulers. More important in some respects is the possibility that the individuals named are the same as those who ruled in distant Chenla (Cambodia) and coastal Vietnam. There are some problems in identifying Harsavarman with Chenla, as all of the kings with this name who ruled in Cambodia did so after the date assigned to the inscription (Brown 1996, 49). It is, however, possible that the Isanavarman mentioned is he who reigned at Isanapura (Sambor Prei Kuk) during the 7th century. It is known that Isanavarman had a son named Sivadata who is thought to have ruled at Jyesthapura, a city closer to U-Thong. Jacques (1986) has proposed that the Harsavarman of the inscription is Sivadata's son. There are a number of possible interpretations of this inscription. Harsavarman may have been a previously unknown ruler of 7th century Chenla, or he may have been a prince who was made lord over part or all of the Chao Phraya basin. Alternatively, he may have no relationship to Chenla and was an indigenous Dvaravati ruler. The latter is very convenient, as Wheatley (1983) points out; it negates having to explain the presence of a Khmer edict so far from Chenla inscribed on a medium rarely used in that polity. The Mon influenced "post-Pallava" script seems to suggest the plate was inscribed *in situ* (Coedès 1958).

The provenance of the plate and identity of the kings mentioned are important for our understanding of Dvaravati. Was the polity weak in the 7th century, ruled by Chenla kings? Brown (1996) believes that Harsavarman was not a Chenla king but, rather, a king of U-Thong who was related to the kings of Chenla. He strongly supports the notion of two polities in the region with convoluted relationships between the royal families in each, suggesting that they were "interconnected mandala" (Brown 1996, 50).

The U-Thong plate refers undoubtedly to Hindu religious practice, and the royalty are undoubtedly Hindu, using the suffix "-*varman*," or protector. Later finds from the site, however, indicate that it was mainly a Buddhist settlement. It appears that U-Thong's importance declined, and it may have been surpassed by Nakhon Pathom in the last quarter of the 7th century (Wales 1969).

Khu Bua

Khu Bua is a moated site located in the Mae Klong River valley, Ratchaburi Province. A moat over fifty meters wide separates two ramparts and runs two hundred by eight hundred meters around the rectangular site. The site contains a number of structural remains, and more structures are located outside the moat. Nearby lies the former riverbed of the Mae Klong, which has changed course away from the ancient city. Excavations at Khu Bua have brought to light stucco figures (Lyons 1965; Rattanakun 1992), which appear to depict Near Eastern traders. Other stuccos portray kings, courtesans, and prisoners. The most interesting figures are those of *bodhisattvas* similar to those from Ajanta, India. The presence of these stuccos may indicate the practice of Mahayana Buddhism, as opposed to the Therevada and Hindu religions assumed to have dominated Dvaravati (Wheatley 1983, 207).

Nakhon Pathom

Nakhon Pathom, sometimes called Nakhon Chaisi, has often been suggested as a capital of Dvaravati (Dupont 1959; Boeles 1964; Luce 1965; Coedès 1968, 76–7; Wales 1969; Kasetsiri 1976, 16; Wheatley 1983, 199–230; Guillon 1999, 75). Wales (1969) proposes that the locus of power shifted in the late 7th century C.E. from U-Thong to Nakhon Pathom due to the seaward extension of the Chao Phraya delta, which served to isolate U-Thong. The issue of sea levels, however, is not settled, and some scholars dispute that the sites were close to the sea during their occupation (Glover, Vickery pers. com.). New settlements may have been founded in the lower Chao Phraya, Prachin, and Mae Klong basins at this time (Wales 1969). The evidence that Nakhon Pathom was a capital is, at best, tenuous. This assertion has been made solely on the basis of two coins mentioning a royal personage at the site and the large size of the settlement (Wheatley 1983).

Whether Nakhon Pathom was a capital of Dvaravati is debatable, but there is no doubt that it was an important site, covering 740 hectares. The settlement boasted a complex of channels that extended beyond the city (Boisselier 1969; Vallibhotama 1982). The rectangular, moated site is centered on the Phra Pathom stupa. Excavations suggest the site was settled during the 8th and 9th centuries (Indrawooth 1984). A shallow occupation layer surrendered a variety of artifacts including bronze, tin, and iron. The remaining structures hint that Therevada and Mahayana Buddhism was practiced during different times (Dhida 1999, 111).

Sri Mahosod

Another important Dvaravati site in central Thailand is Sri Mahosod, located in the Bang Pakong basin. This moated site appears to have been occupied since the late prehistoric period and contains pottery reminiscent of Iron Age pottery from the Mun River basin on the Khorat Plateau (Pisnupong 1992). Lying above this Iron Age material are artifacts dated to the 6th to 8th centuries C.E. It is likely that a water tank at the site dates to this period as its decorations are stylistically datable to the 5th or 6th centuries C.E. (Pisnupong 1993). By around 750 C.E. it seems the inhabitants were using the Khmer language as the vernacular (Brown 1996, 59).The site remained active in trade up until at least the end of the first millennium C.E., but by this time it had probably been absorbed by the Khmer empire (Higham and Thosarat 1998, 179). The city reached a maximum size of 108 hectares, and the site contains the remains of roads, irrigation canals, and defensive walls (Vallibhotama 1986, 230). The art of Sri Mahosod is rather informative as there are distinct similarities to the art of U-Thong (Vallibhotama 1986; Brown 1996, 56). The site also seems to have hosted both Therevada Buddhist and Hindu communities (Wales 1969).

Three kilometers from Sri Mahosod lies Sra Morakod, another Dvaravati period site (Pisnupong 1991). This site has two phases, the first of which is Dvaravati spanning the 6th to 9th centuries and the second phase covers the 9th and 10th centuries.

Muang Phra Rot

Muang Phra Rot is also located in the Bang Pakong Valley and may have been a major node in Dvaravati transportation routes (Boisselier 1968). The site, which covers over ninety-four hectares, contains ceramics spanning the Dvaravati period (6th to 11th centuries). Similar ceramics were also found in surrounding, smaller sites. It has been suggested that this indicates the site's importance as a focus of trade (Sulaksananont 1987).

Chansen

Chansen, located in Takhli district, north of Lopburi, dates from the Dvaravati period. During excavations in 1968 and 1969, the site revealed abundant pottery confirming this dating. The site is square in plan with rounded corners and a ditch surrounding it. It appears that Chansen was occupied since the middle of the first millennium B.C.E., and seven phases of occupation have been identified terminating circa 1200 C.E. (Bronson 1979).

Ban Khu Muang

Ban Khu Muang is located in Singburi Province, near the Chao Phraya River, and covers 48 hectares. This moated site contains the remains of many ancient brick structures, and excavations have revealed pottery, in the deepest deposits, similar to that discovered at Oc Éo, Vietnam. Based on this evidence it is likely that the site was occupied by approximately 300 to 500 C.E. There is a Dvaravati component on top of this which contains stamp decorated pottery and iron weaponry (Higham and Thosarat 1998, 183).

U-Taphao

As was the case at Sri Mahosod, it appears that U-Taphao was first occupied during the Iron Age. The site is located on the banks of the U-Taphao River and is surrounded by a moat and large rampart. Excavations there have revealed Dvaravati coins, ceramics, and sculpture, including a *dharmacakra* found outside the city walls (Wilaikaeo 1991). An inscription in Pallava script, pronouncing the dharma or teaching of the Buddha, was also recovered. Nakorn Noi and Nang Lhek are two smaller Dvaravati period settlements that may have been satellite towns to U-Taphao.

Sab Champa

Sab Champa is located up the Pa Sak River Valley from U-Taphao on the edge of the central plain. The site covers fifty-eight hectares and is surrounded by two, low earthen walls and a ten-meter high inner wall. The moat around the site is cut into the basal limestone on which the site sits. Inside the walls there are the remains of three brick temples. The statuary and other artifacts recovered indicate the site was occupied from the 6th to 8th century C.E. and probably was occupied until the 9th century.

Lavo

Lavo (or Lavapura) is also known as Lopburi. According to Dhida (1999), Lavo was established as a circular, moated settlement in the Lopburi River basin in the late 6th century C.E. Excavations at the site have shown that a stupa at Wat Nakhon Kosa was constructed in typical Dvaravati style and was decorated with stucco of the 8th and 9th centuries (Jermsawadi and Charuphananon 1989). Inscriptions from Lavo reveal that the inhabitants used the Mon language, and we may assume from the art that they were Buddhists. The three inscriptions so far discovered are all written in Pallava. The oldest inscription dates to the 7th century C.E. (Dhida 1999, 125).

It is possible that Lavo was mentioned by the Chinese monk I Ching. Vallibhotama (1987) speculates that I Ching's *"To-lo-po-ti"* actually refers to Lavo. It is also thought that Lavo was powerful enough to be independent from any other Dvaravati settlement and remained so up until the 11th century C.E. There is also some indication that Lavo influenced towns in the northeast (Dhida 1999).

Phong Tuk

Phong Tuk is located to the northwest of Nakhon Pathom in the Mae Klong River basin. The remains of this settlement comprise ruined stupas and *vihara*, or religious halls. Artifacts of interest include a bronze Buddha statue that postdates the 6th century C.E. and a Byzantine-style lamp of a similar age or older.

Sri Thep

Sri Thep is located on the western periphery of the Khorat Plateau in the Pa Sak River basin. Today the site covers almost five kilometers and is surrounded by two wide moats. The inner moat is circular and the outer moat is more rectangular, suggesting the city was enlarged at some point (Vallibhotama 1986, 231). The city appears to have been occupied from at least the 6th century and excavations have uncovered evidence of a late Iron Age occupation as well (Tankittikorn 1991; Dhida 1999, 131).

Sri Thep is an interesting settlement due to its location on what may have been the hinterland of Chenla and Dvaravati. The iconography and inscriptions indicate that the predominant religion was Hinduism, and Vishnu statues have been recovered from the site (Vallibhotama 1986, 231; Dhida 1999). This influence may have come from the east, and there are other indications that Sri Thep may have adopted many aspects of contemporary Khmer culture. The discovery of an inscription mentioning one of the early Chenla rulers, Bhavavarman, confirms the relationship with the

Khmer (Weeraprajak 1986). Buddhism did, however, make inroads at Sri Thep as numerous artifacts of that religion have been recovered, including a *dharmacakra*, bronze Buddha figures, votive tablets, and *sema* stones. The ruins of a structure believed to be built for Mahayana Buddhist rituals is located outside the city walls and dates to the 8th and 9th centuries (Higham and Thosarat 1998). Wales (1969, 82) theorizes that there were two periods of Hindu predominance at Sri Thep separated by a Buddhist period. He proposes that during the 5th and 6th centuries the settlement was controlled by Funan. When the power of this polity waned, Buddhism took hold for several centuries, but Hinduism was reestablished with the ascendancy of the Khmer in the 11th century. Although there was considerable Khmer influence at the site, it appears that the inhabitants of Sri Thep were Mon with strong ties to Lavo (Dhida 1999). It may be portrayed as a town that linked the central and northeastern regions of Dvaravati, a settlement of considerable power that probably influenced towns in the Mun and Chi catchments.

Dhida (1999) has proposed that an inscription found at Muang Sema in northeast Thailand may refer to the territory controlled by Sri Thep. The inscription mentions the polity of Sri Canasa, which would mean that the name of Sri Thep at that time was Canasapura. The Bo Ika and the Sri Canasa (in Khmer language) inscriptions mention that there was a polity on the periphery of Dvaravati, namely Sri Canasa, which had adopted both Buddhist and Hindu religions (Dhida 1999). This proposition has yet to be proven.

The apparent importance of Sri Thep, revealed by archaeological excavation, is often juxtaposed with its apparent isolation. It is well positioned to facilitate trade from the central plains to and from the Mun/Chi Valleys and perhaps even over the Dangrek Mountains into Cambodia. To this obvious trade corridor a route from the Gulf of Siam, northward into the Mun Valley, and then east to Sri Thep is also possible (Dhida 1985).

Some scholars have proposed that Sri Thep was an Indian settlement, based on the quality of the sculpture found there, but are puzzled that such an important settlement was omitted by Chinese annalists (Czuma 1980). A Buddhist votive tablet dated to the 8th century found at Sri Thep is inscribed with Chinese characters (Brown 1996, 37).

NORTHEAST THAILAND

The Khorat Plateau may be considered as a buffer between the polities of the central plains of Thailand and those east of the Dangrek Mountains in Cambodia. For this reason, it is an area of importance for our understanding of Dvaravati. It should not, however, be viewed as a marginal area. It has been proposed "that during the Dvaravati times, there was a larger population in the north-east than in central Thailand" (Vallibhotama 1970). It has been suggested that the area comprised indigenous chiefdoms that were influenced by Hinduized Chenla in the 6th century C.E. and later by the Buddhist polities of the central plains (Vallibhotama 1976; 1979). The sociopolitical landscape of northeast Thailand suggests the influence of varied cultures, and it is difficult to be sure that Dvaravati exercised any political control over the area. Any examination of the northeast must consider the different influences brought to bear by central Thailand and the Khmer of Cambodia, and it is probably best understood as "an interface between the two cultural areas" (Brown 1996, 20).

Vallibhotama (1976; 1979), based on archaeological evidence to date, divides northeast Thailand during Dvaravati times into five areas. The Mun River valley is divided into three areas, including the lower, middle, and upper reaches. The fourth area is the Chi River valley, and the last is the Mekong River valley. The development of what appear to have been large urban sites did not occur until quite late, probably around the 9th century in the Sakhon Nakhon valley (Vallibhotama 1984, 124). The Mun and Chi may have seen urban development earlier, and there are far more sites in these valleys. Vallibhotama (1984) carried out a survey of sites in the Mun and Chi catchments, identifying over seventy moated sites, and subsequently divided all identified sites into four types: (1) unmoated mounds exceeding five meters in height, (2) settlements with a single moat over twenty-five meters across, surrounding one to three mounds, (3) triple-moated settlements, and (4) fortified settlements surrounded by earth walls and moats. Vallibhotama does not link all the moated sites to the Dvaravati period but believes that their appearance corresponds to the advent of iron smelting technology. Iron appears widely in Southeast Asia circa 500 B.C.E., significantly predating the Dvaravati polities.

Northeast Thailand has not only been influenced by Hinduism but also Buddhism, and there is a connection between northeast and central Thailand. The connection is clearest in the use of the Mon language in inscriptions and the presence of Dvaravati-style art in the northeast. Vallibhotama (1976) has suggested that Sri Thep may have been a gateway for this cultural flow from central Thailand.

Muang Sema

Muang Sema is an oval site covering 280 hectares, surrounded by a moat and wall. It is best known for a large reclining Buddha dating to the Dvaravati period. It is also the location of the Hin Khon inscriptions, written in both Mon and Khmer. Vallibhotama (1984) has suggested that Muang Sema may have been part of the Sri Canasa polity circa the 10th century C.E.

Muang Fa Daed

Muang Fa Daed is a 270-hectare site located in Kalasin Province. The site was probably enlarged over time (Indrawooth et al. 1991), but it was undoubtedly an important center during the Dvaravati period. The site is particularly noted for the number of *sema* stones recovered. Of particular note are those depicting soldiers along a city rampart (Diskul 1956). The *sema* stones and the remains of fourteen religious structures suggest the site was an important religious center. The stucco decoration on these structures betrays an association with similar stuccoed structures in central Thailand (Fine Arts Department 1968).

Excavations at Muang Fa Daed have revealed a pottery kiln, evidence of iron smelting, and bronze smoking pipes (Indrawooth 1991; 1994). The discovery of inhumation burials and associated artifacts, including glass beads, suggest that the site was occupied from the Iron Age.

SOUTHERN THAILAND

Southern Thailand has, for centuries, been an economic, cultural, and religious crossroads. The area has seen the influence of many polities/cultures including China, Arabia, India, Sri Lanka, Java, Cambodia, and central Thailand. It is held that the inhabitants of peninsular Thailand spoke Mon (Stargardt 1985; Veeraprajak 1986), although the inscriptional evidence for this is not solid; inscriptions are generally written in Pali, Sanskrit, Tamil, and later Khmer. The hegemony of Dvaravati culture in peninsular Thailand is not well defined, although it is apparent that there was significant influence on the area from central Thailand. Chinese texts assert that a polity, possibly near Chaiya (Yamamoto 1979), named T'an-ling was a vassal of Dvaravati (Brown 1996, 41). There is, of course, artistic evidence for Dvaravati's influence on the peninsula, but it is not uniform. Brown points out that Dvaravati art is found on the northern peninsula down to Petchaburi. There is very little found between this point and Chaiya, far to the south (Brown 1996, 42). It is possible, as Brown points out, that Dvaravati had incidental influence or wavering control on the peninsula.

Ko Kho Khao

Ko Kho Khao is an island off the Takuapa River in peninsular Thailand, which appears to have been an important locus of trade during the Dvaravati period. Certainly many foreign artifacts have been found at the site, including Arab and Chinese ceramics (Ho et al. 1990).

Of great interest is a recently discovered water tank near the site that is mentioned in an inscription written in Tamil. This inscription is cited as evidence for an Indian commercial settlement on the peninsula during the 9th century C.E. (Coedès 1924b; Wheatley 1983, 297). The tank was placed under the protection of an Indian mercantile corporation called the Minigrammam from South India.

Khao Sam Kaeo

Khao Sam Kaeo may slightly predate the Dvaravati period as most of the finds there date to 1st to the 5th centuries C.E. Two notable early finds include two Dong Son drums. Nonetheless, the site is informative for the period under review, as it appears to have been a major manufacturing center on the peninsula. Production also extended to etched carnelian and onyx beads (Thepchai 1989).

Satingpra

Satingpra is a moated settlement covering 144 hectares in peninsular Thailand, the name of which may derive from Khmer, where "Sating" is a corruption of "Stu'ng" ("river") and "pra" a corruption of ancient Khmer "vrah," meaning sacred or royal (Vickery pers. comm.). Satingpra's location in an arid region made the construction of hydraulic works necessary (Stargardt 1986, 224). The investigators of Satingpra have divided the sequence into four phases, the first of which spans from 300 B.C.E. to 200 C.E. What Stargardt calls "Urban Phase I" is of interest in considering the sites' role in Dvaravati. This phase lasted from the 6th century to the 9th century C.E. Although it appears that the inhabitants of Satingpra had been engaged in international trade since the 2nd century, the settlement only became an urban center circa the 5th and 6th century C.E. Satingpra is distinguished by canals that bisect the settlement, and canals may have played a role in trade across the isthmus. There are many water tanks around the site, and the center is dominated by a citadel with three-meter-thick walls. Stargardt feels that there may have been "a central coordinating authority" in the construction of the canals based on their uniformity (Stargardt 1983, 138). Inside the moats the remains of a 6th century Vishnuite sanctuary were discovered. Stargardt feels that Satingpra relied heavily on agriculture to stimulate early trade, exchanging surplus for forest products, which were then traded for other commodities. Later, during the 8th to 11th century C.E., industry turned to iron and tin smelting and kendi (an Indian-style ceramic pot) production (Stargardt 1986, 34).

Khuan Lukpad

Another important peninsular site is Khuan Lukpad, where evidence of local glass ornament production has been recorded (Veraprasert 1992,

188). There are also indicators that semiprecious stones were worked at the site, including carnelian, chalcedony, and quartz. Of great interest in illuminating international trade is the presence of carnelian seals with Mediterranean motifs, as well as inscriptions in the Pallava script dating between the 6th and 9th centuries. It may be that the settlement was engaged in the production of exotic items for trade in Southeast Asia, in effect copying goods that were formerly imported.

NORTH

Haripunchai

The settlement of Haripunchai or Haripunjaya (Lamphun) was located in the Ping River valley in northern Thailand. Nimmanhaeminda (1967) has proposed that this far northern site is related to the Dvaravati complex. Although scant evidence links the site to Dvaravati, Indrawooth (1994) has stated that the pottery from this site has strong parallels with Dvaravati-period pottery from sites to the south that date to 6th to 8th century C.E. Other pottery and artifacts can be dated to the 10th century C.E. with Dvaravati links. It should be noted that there is very little to suggest a strong relationship with Haripunchai and other sites considered to belong to the Dvaravati cultural complex. No *cakras* have been found, and there is scant evidence for the presence of Hinduism. There is, however, evidence to suggest that the settlement was predominantly Mon (Brown 1996, 62). Historical chronicles indicate that the city was founded in 661 C.E. and fell in 1292 (Di Crocco 1991). Ceramics from the site indicate that it was occupied from the 4th century B.C.E. through the 4th century C.E., and a figurine at the site is similar to those found at other Dvaravati sites (Di Crocco 1991).

THE MON OF LOWER BURMA (MYANMAR)

In his book, *Burma*, published in 1950, D. G. E. Hall (1950, 7) wrote "the early history of Burma is obscure." Unfortunately, little has changed since then. We still have only the most basic outline of events that took place during the early centuries of the first millennium. We do know that from this period the delta areas of the Salween and Irrawaddy rivers and parts of the Malay Peninsula appear to have been ethnically Mon. Indeed, according to written and oral traditions, this very area was the heartland of Mon culture, the place from which the Mon derived and went on to gain suzerainty over large tracts of Southeast Asia (Wheatley 1983, 199). These traditions do not seem to equate with the archaeological evidence produced to date. Compared with the evidence of Mon culture in the Chao Phraya delta, the Irrawaddy and Salween deltas pale. Very little evidence of a powerful Buddhist polity has been yet recovered, although there can be no doubt that the area saw significant developments from early in the first millennium C.E.

We know next to nothing of the Mon peoples of Myanmar between the 9th and 11th centuries. It was during this period that the Burmese may have first entered Myanmar, probably from northwest China, and came into direct conflict with the Mon populations. The Burmese referred to the Mon as the Talaing, which Phayre (1967) believed was "obviously connected with the Talingana," a region in Bengal which has been posited as the home of many Indians migrating to Myanmar.

Burmese records contain a myth that claims that the settlement at Tagaung was founded in 850 B.C.E., but these are unreliable, probably being copies of Indian legends (Hall 1950, 7). Buddhist records indicate that Indian influence in Burma was first brought by two brothers who brought hairs of the Buddha with them. The first written record we have for inhabitants in lower Burma were written in the second century C.E. and tell of cannibals inhabiting the area. These were recorded by Ptolemy, but it is unlikely that he himself visited the area. The lower Irrawaddy is mentioned by 9th century Arab geographers who called it *Ramanadesa* (Hall 1950). It has been suggested that the word is derived from the Old Mon word *Rmen*, which is the source of the modern term Mon (Murari 1985).

The Mon inhabited the area near the mouth of the Irrawaddy River and spoke the same language or a similar language to the Dvaravati peoples in Thailand. The relationship between the groups is unclear. Some believe that the Mon in the Irrawaddy delta were ruled by Dvaravati (Hall 1950, 10), but it is possible that the Mon of Myanmar were independent. The surviving oral and written evidence suggests that the Mon of Myanmar or western Mon were ardent Buddhists and that Pegu and Thaton were the heartland of Mon culture (Wheatley 1961). Paradoxically, there is not a wealth of archaeological evidence to support this documentary evidence. Most of the remains from this area indicate a Hindu religious orientation rather than the expected evidence of a Buddhist polity (Dupont 1959, 7–11). The reason for this may be the relatively late arrival of Buddhism and the Mon in lower Myanmar. The earliest epigraphic reference to Therevada Buddhism in lower Myanmar dates to the 15th century. The inscription refers to a Buddhist mission in the 3rd century B.C.E. (Wheatley 1961, 200). Wales (1967) and Coedès (1966) support the 11th century date, feeling that Buddhism arrived as a result of refugees fleeing a cholera outbreak in northern Thailand, but there is no way to prove this was indeed the cause of the exodus.

Thaton, located between the Sittang and Salween Rivers, was situated in the heart of Mon territory. It is one of the most prominent sites in this area. Today traces of the massive walls and stupas remain. The city was surrounded by a quadrangular wall and several brick structural ruins. Coedès's

(1966) supposition of the Mon of Myanmar originating in what is today northern Thailand is supported by the presence of *sema* stones. These religious boundary markers are found mostly at sites in northeastern Thailand and are very similar to 9th to 11th century C.E. Mon and Mon/Khmer *sema* (Moore and Myint 1991). The walls surrounding Thaton and some of the structures are constructed of large bricks, similar in size to those used at Tircul sites (Moore and Myint 1991).

Another Mon site in Myanmar is Hmawbi on the banks of the Salween River. This ancient city is surrounded by three walls encircling an area 2 km long and 750 m wide (Moore and Myint 1991). The city is walled only on three sides while the river provides defense for the fourth. Thagara, one of the southern-most Mon sites in Myanmar, is located on the Tavoy River. This former Mon settlement is surrounded by circular walls (Moore and Myint 1991). The capital of the Mon kingdom is thought to have been located at Hamsavati (Pegu). According to tradition two brothers, Samal and Vimal, founded Hamsavati in 573 C.E. The brothers ruled the kingdom and were followed on the throne by Tissa, who assumed power in 761 C.E. There are no further indications of who ruled after this period. The traditional foundation date in the 6th century is viewed skeptically, and a more likely date is circa 825 C.E (Murari 1985).

DECLINE OF MON

Pagan was founded by the Burmese only twenty-four years after Thaton. The city is usually referred to by its formal name in inscriptions—Arimaddana, or "trampler on enemies" (Hall 1950). Traditionally it is thought that the Burmans began to expand from Kyauksè in the north. Through military conquest they asserted control over most of present-day Myanmar. These people are mentioned in a Mon inscription in 1102 C.E. as the Mirma. The Mirma went on to conquer Taungdwingyi, Shwebo, Mydedu, and Tabayin, even subduing the people of Arakan on the western coast of Myanmar (Hall 1950). Eventually the Burmans conquered Thaton in 1057 C.E. and subjugated the Mon. From the Mon the animist Burmans adopted Buddhism and greatly enriched their art and culture.

CONCLUSION

There can be little doubt that Dvaravati, like Sri Vijaya, the Mon of Burma, and the Pyu, is a little-known entity. We can say with some confidence that the people who inhabited the central plains of Thailand from at least the 4th century C.E. were, largely, speakers of the Mon language. It is quite likely that, with the passage of time, the number of other minorities increased, creating a multiethnic fabric which still was a predominantly Mon society. There were probably traders and religious men from India and perhaps China living permanently in Dvaravati settlements, while other groups such as Burmese Mon and perhaps Pyu people may have lived within the domain of the polity. The people of the peripheral areas of Dvaravati, such as those on the Khorat Plateau, may also have been mainly Mon speakers, but the Khmer influence was very strong. Southern Thailand was also likely mostly Mon-speaking, whether or not they were a part of the Dvaravati polity.

The people of Dvaravati were largely followers of Buddhism. This is abundantly clear in the large amounts of Buddhist art they left behind. The *cakra* is a unique Dvaravati development symbolizing the teaching of the Buddha. These stone wheels commonly sculpted in the round, but also found in relief, are thought by some to define Dvaravati (Brown 1996). It is clear, however, that Buddhism was not the only religion in Dvaravati as there is strong evidence for the existence of Hindu cults. There are inscriptions commemorating the raising of Siva linga and evidence that Vishnu was worshipped. So strong is the presence of Hinduism that it has led Vallibhotama (1986) to propose that there were in fact two separate kingdoms of Dvaravati in central Thailand, one Buddhist and the other Hindu. The mix of religion is apparent also on the Khorat Plateau where the influence of Hindu Chenla was much stronger, although most of the sites there are characterized by the presence of *sema* stones to mark sacred Buddhist territory. It is probably best to view Dvaravati as a mix of religions with Buddhism being predominant. It is not likely that there were circumscribed areas where one religion was practiced and the other was not.

The least understood aspect of Dvaravati is the political organization. So poor is our comprehension that we do not even know what to call Dvaravati. It may have been a single town in a *mandala*, or it may have been the capital of a kingdom, or the moniker may denote an entire kingdom or empire. Based on the available evidence, Dvaravati was probably a loose collection of settlements whose power and control over territory expanded and contracted with time. It is also likely that there was a preeminent settlement in this system, evidenced by the larger archaeological sites visible today such as Nakhon Pathom and U-Thong. These larger settlements may have been the locus of power where the chief or "king" resided in a palace, if we are to judge from contemporary descriptions by Chinese travelers. The distribution of sites and the ranked sizes of these suggest that Dvaravati may have been a unified polity by the end of the first millennium C.E. (Mudar 1999), but the picture of Dvaravati as a unified and stable empire bordering Chenla on the east and the Burmese Mon kingdoms on the west is probably unrealistic. Although one could argue that Dvaravati boasts monumental architecture, coinage, and transportation systems, it is unlikely that these were centrally controlled across the entire area in which we find remnants of this culture. The monumental architecture seems to be site specific, mostly in the form of moats and ramparts surrounding settlements. The coinage does not appear to have been in wide circulation and may have had a restricted or symbolic use. There is scant evidence for interregional transportation routes in the form of roads, but the waterways would probably have been favored during this period.

Regarding the settlement pattern of Dvaravati, we have seen that the sites are usually found close to rivers, which provided a source of water and access to trade routes. Most of the sites seem to have been positioned to take advantage of the rich agricultural lands in the valleys of central Thailand. It appears that the elite occupied part of the city and the merchants and other nonagricultural people lived in other sections. The rest of the population lived outside the walls and moats, working the land. Much remains to be learned of Dvaravati, and future archaeological research may serve to clear the enigmatic mists that enshroud this important political and cultural entity.

With such scant information it is difficult to have any meaningful understanding of the Mon of Myanmar. We are uncertain what form their government took, what the organization of the settlements were, and whether there was any relationship with the Mon in Central Thailand. It is clear that there must have been some form of centralized organization at least at the settlement level, judging from the size and complexity of the earthworks erected at some of the sites. It is probable that a similar political situation existed here as in the Dvaravati settlements, where a central settlement was surrounded and supplied by smaller satellites villages. It is impossible, based on our current evidence, to say anything further regarding the Mon of Myanmar.

5

Pre-Angkorian and Angkorian Polities

Of all the early states in Southeast Asia, that of Angkor, perhaps, most excites the imagination. Deep in the jungles lie magnificent temples shrouded in foliage awaiting interpretation, explanation, and appreciation. The kingdom of Angkor dates from the beginning of the 9th century until the mid-15th century, but its roots go much further back in time and are the subject of much controversy. Little is known of early Angkorian prehistory with only a handful of sites having been excavated. Therefore, our understanding of the emergence of the complex polities of Cambodia is limited. Most scholars assume that Cambodia developed increasingly complex political entities that at some point came into contact with foreign elements. It is through these external sources that we first learn of early Khmer political organization.

Recent research in Cambodia is more focused on the prehistoric period than it was in the past, and the evidence from this research should serve to fill many of the gaps in our knowledge. It should also remove "the notion that the Cambodian state and civilization were transplanted from India" (Vickery 1998, 6). This viewpoint, espoused by authors such as Coedès (1968) and Majumdar (1944; 1963), took hold during the colonial era and has been tenacious. There can be no doubt that India and her culture had a profound effect on ancient Cambodia, but it is increasingly clear that the relationship between these ancient cultures was more symbiotic. Indeed, as Mabbett (1977a) has indicated, the meaning of the term Indianization has changed.

This chapter will examine what is known of the political structure in Cambodia that probably existed prior to the first mention of the territory in Chinese annals. The Chinese first knew of Cambodia as Funan, and some

91

considerable work has been done on this enigmatic polity that was replaced, it seems, by another known to the Chinese as Chenla. The rise of the
more stable state of Angkor will then be explored.

EARLY POLITICAL COMPLEXITY IN CAMBODIA: FUNAN

Stark (2003, 89–90) has noted that archaeological, epigraphic, and art historical evidence indicate that the Mekong Delta was the center of the region's first cultural system with the trappings of a state-level society including: "(1) high populations and urban centers; (2) the production of surplus
food through intensive rice cultivation; (3) socio-political stratification le-
gitimated by Indic religious ideologies; (4) a system of writing at the end of
the early historic period; and (5) a vigorous network of long distance trade."
To this list we may, perhaps, add monumental architecture (a substantial
system of canals) and possibly the use of coinage in exchange. Regrettably
the amount of data we have from the fields mentioned above are limited,
and we know very little of the polity that has come to be called Funan.

Extensive investigations in the Mekong Delta by Vietnamese archaeologists have turned up little evidence for long-term prehistoric occupation of
the area (Pham Duc Manh 1996; Bui Phat Diem et al. 1997; Dang Van
Thang and Vu Quoc Hien 1997; Dao Linh Con 1998). This does not necessarily mean the area was unoccupied prior to the protohistoric period,
however, as the delta environment is subject to annual flooding that may
have obscured many older sites and many sites have likely been submerged
due to rising sea levels since their occupation. Those that have been discovered suggest occupation from at least 2000 B.C.E. and extensive habitation
of the delta after 500 B.C.E.

It is probable that a similar sequence characterized the Cambodian side
of the Mekong Delta, but we currently know very little about either the prehistoric or early historic sites in this region. What we know of the earliest
complex polity in Cambodia stems largely from Chinese historical documents rather than from epigraphic or archaeological materials recovered to
date (Jacques 1979; Vickery 1998). Both Jacques and Vickery are cautious
about relying too heavily on these sources, preferring to use them in combination with inscriptions and archaeological evidence.

Funan is, at best, poorly understood; even the origin of the name is contested. It is generally accepted that it is a Chinese corruption of the local
name of a dominant polity in the lower and middle Mekong Delta perhaps
derived from the Old Khmer word for mountain (*vnam*) (Jacques 1979; Hall
1985). As the origins of the name of the polity are vague so are the centers
of power. Scholars have long speculated as to the location of the capital of
Funan. Coedès (1968) felt that the capital was Vyadhapura, located near Ba

Phnom, a hill in southwestern Cambodia. While many scholars have been content to accept this interpretation (Wheatley 1961; Hall 1982), Vickery (1986; 1998) is skeptical. The capital of Funan was known to the Chinese as T'e-mu (Vickery 1998), a name yet to be identified on the ground. The name of a city called Vyadhapura first appears in a Sanskrit inscription circa 655 C.E. (inscription K.109) (Vickery 1998) that gives no indication as to the location. Vickery, however, feels that Vyadhapura must be rejected as a possible capital of Funan and that the city of this name was probably located at Banteay Prei Nokor (Vickery 1986, 102). It is now widely suspected that Angkor Borei may have been the capital or, at least, among the largest settlements of the Funan period. The lands around this site are scattered with the remains of brick sanctuaries, and stylistically early statuary has come from the region (Vo Si Khai 1998). The earliest inscriptions from Angkor Borei date to circa 611 C.E. (K. 557, K. 600) and 650 C.E. (K. number not yet assigned). The latter inscription informs us that the last known ruler of Funan lived at the capital during the 7th century (Coedès 1966).

The Environment

Although most scholars would concur that Funan had its center in southern Cambodia and Vietnam (Pelliot 1903a; Aymonier 1903; Majumdar 1944; Coedès 1968; Jacques 1986), there are those who feel northeast (Hoshino 1993) or central Thailand (Boisselier 1965) was more likely the center of Funan. It is likely that the polity expanded from the Mekong Delta area and held, at least, hegemony over some of the coastal areas in present day Thailand and Malaysia.

The lower delta region up the Mekong to the Tonlé Sap is subject to an annual monsoon climate characterized by variations from moist to dry and generally subhumid conditions with fairly stable temperatures, typical of an equatorial monsoonal climate (Sein 1979). This type of climate has a considerable bearing on the lifeways of those who inhabit it, as it dictates the agricultural cycle. Of particular importance are the southwest monsoon rains that swell the rivers of Southeast Asia. This water is carried downstream, and the landscape of the lower delta is inundated. Flooding results in an increase in the fish populations and is an important nutrient source for the inhabitants of the area.

The People

Le May (1964, 36) has hypothesized that the people of Funan had little physical contact with Indians. He believes that Funan may have been introduced to and embraced many elements of the culture through an intermediary, perhaps the "Indian states" of the Malay Peninsula or Mon Dvaravati.

He feels that the early Buddhist art of Funan, which postdates the Hindu, is derivative of Mon Dvaravati art, an opinion echoed by Le Thi Lein (2002).

According to a Chinese account, the people of Funan were tattooed semi-savages who wore no clothes (Majumdar 1944). This description notwithstanding, other Chinese histories inform us that the people of Funan paid taxes and had libraries and a writing system based on an Indian script (Pelliot 1903a). The ethnicity of these people is, however, unknown. Vickery (1998) believes that they may have been Khmer based on the widespread use of that language in early 7th century Cambodia, but they may also have been Cham, Mon, or another Mon-Khmer group. Certainly the geographic area usually associated with Funan is home to a majority of inscriptions written at a later period in either Khmer or Sanskrit (Jacob 1979). Malleret (1959) felt that the ports of Funan, at least, were occupied, in the early first century C.E., by Malay peoples.

There is a long history of people speaking Austronesian languages in mainland Southeast Asia, most prominent among whom are the Malay and Cham peoples. The Austronesian family comprises the languages spoken in Malaysia, most of the languages of the Indonesian archipelago, the Philippine islands, Polynesia, the aboriginal languages of Taiwan, and Madagascar. The Cham found their way to the coast of Vietnam relatively late, possibly in the first millennium B.C.E., probably from a homeland in Borneo (Thurgood 1999). Some scholars feel that the Sa Huynh culture may represent the earliest remains of Cham civilization in Vietnam (Bellwood 1995; Higham 2002, 182), whereas others feel that Austronesian settlers inhabited Oc Éo by the mid–first millennium B.C.E., thus implying that Funan was populated by speakers of an Austronesian language (Hall 1955; 1985; Thurgood 1999). According to Vo Si Khai (2003), skulls found at Canh Den (Kien Giang Province) appear to have Austronesian features, and remains discovered at An Son in central Vietnam and Rach Rung in the delta area dating to the 9th century B.C.E. had similar features.

The linguistic affiliation of Funan is difficult to ascertain but, as Vickery (pers. comm.) points out, the Chinese reported that Funan had occupied a place called Tun-Sun somewhere on the Malay Peninsula, which had five kings and a language very similar to that of Funan. While at first glance one may assume this meant that the Funanese spoke an Austronesian language, it is more likely that the people of Tun-Sun spoke Mon, a language related to Khmer. Thus, it is possible to argue that the people of Funan must have spoken a Mon-Khmer language. Several scholars have argued that the Mon language dominated most of Southeast Asia in the early centuries of the first millennium (Boisselier 1965; Loofs 1979; Stargardt 1986).

Vickery (2005) paints a picture of cosmopolitan ports and those of Funan he believes comprised speakers of Mon, Cham, Malay, and Khmer. The dominant population of Funan, in his opinion, was Khmer. As evidence he cites the presence of Khmer inscriptions from Angkor Borei, carved in the 7th century, which "indicate a society with deep-rooted social and religious structures." The distribution of Khmer inscriptions seems to indicate a northward movement, indicating that the southern regions were inhabited by Khmer speakers for some time, the veracity of which may be determined by the current research at Angkor Borei (Stark et al. 1999). It may be that the lower Mekong Delta was inhabited by Mon-Khmer peoples who came into contact with Malay, Javanese, and Philippine traders or shippers who had been engaged in long-distance maritime trade for centuries (Miksic 1984). Miksic (2003) suggests that it may have been this preexisting trade network that sparked the development of the complex polity of Funan, which became reliant on Austronesian shipping, an idea supported by Vickery (1992).

The Mekong Delta has, in all likelihood, been occupied for many millennia. The environment is well suited to hunter-gatherer groups as mangrove forest covers much of the coastal areas, an environment with a very high biomass (Higham and Thosarat 1994). Later populations found the area suitable for the cultivation of rice. That the people of Funan relied heavily on agriculture is clear from Chinese sources which tell of rich harvests (Pelliot 1903a). It is not surprising that harvests were so productive as the area occupied by Funan was well suited to rice agriculture (Ng 1979; Fox and Ledgerwood 1999). It escapes the harshest weather yet receives ample rainfall, and the soils are enriched by the Mekong's alluvium. Stark (2003) has suggested that the three crops of rice per year, noted by the Chinese, may have been possible if it was cultivated according to the season: floating rice, recession agriculture, and rain-fed agriculture. It is apparent that the diet of rice was supplemented with meat including pork, chicken (Malleret 1962), and probably beef (Stark 2003).

Religion

Some indication of the religious affiliation of the Funanese people may be gleaned from Chinese accounts regarding an envoy sent from Funan in 484 C.E. In this year a Buddhist monk named Nagasena was sent by King Kaundinya Jayavarman to seek support from China in Funan's war against the Cham. Nagasena told his Chinese hosts that the god worshiped in Funan was called Mahesvara, a deity that lived on a mountain called Mua-tam (Pelliot 1903a). It is possible that Nagasena was referring to a Sivaite cult, a proposition supported by the fact that the *Liang Shu* (chuan 54, 8b) refers to statuary of Funan as having two faces and four arms. It is possible that the passage refers to the split face found on representations of Harihara, a deity comprising elements of both Siva and Vishnu (Wheatley 1974, 102). Further support for the existence of a Sivaite cult in Funan may be found in the fact that the Cham worshipped the god as early as the late 4th century C.E., and the religion of Chenla, a post-Funan polity, was remarked upon by the Chinese as being Sivaite (Wheatley 1974).

It is likely, however, that the people of Funan practiced a variety of religions, suggested by the very fact that the emissary to China was a Buddhist monk and further attested to by the presence of Buddhist statuary dating from the 6th and 7th centuries C.E. (Stark 2003). There is no doubt that religion played a prominent role in Funanese life, at least among the elite. The earliest inscriptions from the area (K. 600 and K. 611) suggest that substantial donations were made to the temples, and it is also noteworthy that some of these temples were dedicated to indigenous deities. The temples received gifts of "slaves," agricultural produce, livestock, entertainers, servants, and laborers (Vickery 1998).

There is a sizable corpus of religious sculptural material that has been dated to the Funan period. Coedès (1942) felt that the seven pieces of art in the "Phnom Da style" were produced during the reign of King Rudravarman, who probably ruled from Angkor Borei circa 514 to 539 C.E. Coedès used epigraphic evidence, attributed to the reign of Rudravarman, to date the statuary. As the only known Rudravarman was he who ruled at Angkor Borei, Coedès reasoned that the statuary was created during his reign. Dowling (1999) questions this based on the sculptural techniques employed, some of which do not appear until the mid–seventh century (Bénisti 1970). Previously, the Phnom Da style was separated by the next artistic style, the Sambor style (circa 617–637 C.E.), by a century. It would appear that Dowling's (1999) interpretation is favorable as it proposes a more fluid development of Khmer art styles without questionable lacunas.

Political Organization

The transition to complex political organization in the Mekong Delta is yet to be documented. It is likely that Indian culture was embraced by an already complex society, by individuals who perceived the value of certain aspects of Indian culture and political philosophy. Wolters (1999) asserts that there is little evidence to suggest that there were substantial differences between rulers during the prehistoric period and those of Funan. He feels that historians and archaeologists have placed unfair emphasis on the level of political organization in Funan and that the differences were merely in scale. This has occurred due to a lack of evidence from the prehistoric period and an overreliance on Chinese annals. Wolters suggests that the Chinese histories should not be taken at face value but evaluated with an understanding of the authors' cultural background. The Chinese historians, he feels, would have difficulty conceptualizing a state with flexible borders and no dynastic succession but had no other category to place such a political entity. He also feels that archaeologists are reluctant to view pre-Funan society as a state-level organization due to their reliance on economic factors in the definition of statehood.

Hall (1985, 49) is of the opinion that during the first century C.E. the territory that came to be called Funan comprised autonomous chiefdoms along the banks of the Mekong River. It was these chiefs who engaged foreign traders, a move that may have stimulated the development of greater political complexity with all the trappings of power (Hall 1985, 53). Hall believes, based on archaeological, linguistic, and literary sources, that Funan may be called the first Southeast Asian "state" (Hall 1985, 62).

As early as the second century C.E. we have evidence of the development of a supralocal authority in the lower Mekong Delta. A chief named Hun P'an-huang seems to have succeeded in toppling other chiefs and sending his sons to rule their territories (Pelliot 1925).

By the third century we know, from Chinese records, that an individual named Fan Shih-man ruled the Delta region, his power stretching from the Great Lake to central Vietnam and southwards (Wheatley 1961). Fan Shih-man is even said to have sent naval expeditions to raid the polity Tun-sun on northern Malay Peninsula (Wheatley 1961; 1983; Hall 1985, 265). Tun-sun may have been an ethnically Mon polity and is thought to have straddled the isthmus near modern P'ong-Tuk or Pra Pathom (Wheatley 1961). The conquest of polities on the Malay Peninsula may have brought Fan Shih-man's court into closer contact with Indian traders and religious men, as these people had established themselves on the isthmus (Coedès 1968, 40).

By the early third century, the Funan polity had sent its first trade mission to India and an embassy to China (Hall 1985, 68). It is also possible that Funan was known to the Romans, who nominated a port in Southeast Asia as a *nominum emporion* or recognized trading port (Miksic 2003). Although there is little evidence to support the idea, Coedès (1968, 277) and Malleret (1962, 421–54) both suggested that a port known to the Romans as Kattigara may have, in fact, been Oc Éo. The presence of material culture at Oc Éo indicates, at least, that the trade network in which Funan was involved was far reaching. The Roman artifacts found at Oc Éo probably came to the site via India. These include gold and bronze medallions minted under Antoninus Pius (circa 152 C.E.) and Marcus Aurelius (circa 161–180 C.E.), carved carnelian intaglios, and glass beads and bracelets (Malleret 1962, 112). Although the coins date to the second century, this is not an indication that they are contemporaneous with Oc Éo. A coin bearing the image of a Persian king probably followed the same route. A bronze statue of a youthful Pan has been recovered from Vinh Hung near the Vietnam/Cambodia border. Statues in the round have been identified as being of the Gandhara or Amaravati styles, indicating artistic contact with India (Khai 2003, 46).

The politics of the third century in Funan were tumultuous. Fan Shih-man was replaced by Fan Ch'an, his nephew who apparently killed Fan Shih-man's son to take the throne. The death was avenged later by another of Fan Shih-man's sons who killed Fan Ch'an. This individual was, in turn, murdered by Fan Hsun, Fan Ch'an's military commander around 240 C.E. (Hall 1985).

Although it may seem as if Fan Shih-man's son should have been his successor, it is possible that normal succession was passed from uncle to a sister's son. If this was the case, the Chinese interpretation that the nephew was a usurper is mistaken; he was, in fact, merely claiming what was rightfully his (Vickery 1998).

Several scholars (Jacques 1979; Wolters 1979; Wheatley 1983; Vickery 1998) feel that it is unlikely that Funan was a unified polity under central control. It is more likely that it comprised allied settlements and coastal entrepôts that prospered from their location on the trade routes from China to India. It was largely this trade that stimulated the development of a stratified society, with the powerful enriching themselves and attempting to exert their hegemony over the hinterlands (Vickery 1998). The early chiefs of Funan may have been known as *poñ*, a Mon-Khmer term denoting the ruler of a territory comprising several hundred to thousands of people. These political units were self-sufficient and represented a lineage or clan. The *poñ* title was passed to the succeeding generation matrilineally to the ruler's sister's son (Vickery 1998, 19). Chinese visitors probably encountered *poñ* of the coastal areas and assumed they were kings or deliberately falsified their reports to make vassalage seem more impressive (Jacques 1979). The honorifics seem to have been changed at least as early as the fifth century as some of the more powerful *poñ* began adopting the Indian suffix *-varman*. It has been suggested that great wealth was accumulated by *poñ* living near trading entrepôts and it was these individuals that the Chinese concluded were kings (Vickery 1998).

Wheatley feels that there were significant political developments in Funan from the 2nd century onwards when the smaller chiefdoms were consolidated (Wheatley 1983). Early third-century documents indicate that the territories of Funan were headed by different chiefs (Wan Chen n.d.). Such an organization would indicate the existence of a paramountcy during this period. Wheatley (1983, 143) believes that the evidence indicates the existence of a constantly changing network of integrated chieftainships rather than independent centers of power. The earliest historical documents indicating the existence of a polity more complex than a chiefdom date to circa 502 and 556 C.E. The *Liang Shu* states that a certain powerful ruler installed his sons as rulers of subordinate chiefdoms (Wheatley 1983, 121). It is likely, however, that this process could only apply to the most immediate and important territories; other, more distant vassals likely kept their chiefs who at times may have claimed sovereignty. This may account for the alleged existence in Southeast Asia of over one hundred kingdoms reported to the Chinese during the third century C.E.

Wheatley (1983, 144) feels that, although there may have been regular shifts in power relationships, it is possible to discern a persistent "centroid" of political power from just south of the Tonlé Sap Lake to the mouth of the Mekong Delta.

Vickery (1998, 325) is of the opinion that Funan may be conceptualized as a collection of coastal cities whose authority waned the further inland one went. He feels that the political importance of these cities probably shifted based on a number of factors, not least the ability to attract international sea trade. Vickery (1998) hypothesizes that trade was controlled by matrilineal lineages who passed the politically granted rights to trade from generation to generation. When a direct route between Indonesia and China began to exclude the Funanese ports in the 6th century, there may have been a movement inland spurred by the elite. The shift in reliance on trade may have resulted in gradual changes in the supposed matrilineal organization of the society.

Social Organization

It is clear that settlements, such as Angkor Borei and Oc Éo, with their attendant walls, moats and *barays*, or reservoirs, represent considerable investments in labor. The development of these sites occurred over a number of generations. It is clear that such major undertakings needed direction and probably reflect a high degree of political complexity. Stark (2003) notes that the documentary evidence suggests a three-tiered social hierarchy comprising a ruler and his entourage at the top, a class of free commoners, and "slaves" at the bottom. Dega and Latinis (1996) feel that:

> Agricultural production was more of an industry than a mere fulfillment of subsistence needs. The economy included other pursuits such as aquaculture and craft production. Labor organization, logistics, planning, and management must have been sophisticated, including specialization and labor division characteristically representing state-level or complex society. Available evidence indicates the establishment of class distinction, but even power distribution, and the privileged access to wealth. These factors characterize systems composed of institutional hierarchies, or state level polities. The absence of a large military force within Angkor Borei suggests that the city was perhaps part of a larger, unified polity which did not require protection against internal problems or external military threats.

The networks of canals, *barays*, and monumental architecture seem to indicate a centralized authority, and the system of taxation mentioned by the Chinese may have helped pay for these projects (Stark 2003).

Settlement Pattern

Very little is known about the pattern of settlement during the Funan period. Vietnamese archaeologists propose that there were three types of site, including residential, religious, and mortuary. Residential sites are identified by the presence of wooden piles, which probably supported dwelling structures, and other evidence of habitation. Religious sites are denoted by the presence of brick or stone foundations, and mortuary sites often contain burial jars or cremation structures (Ha Van Tan 1986a; Trinh Thi Hoa 1996; Dao Linh Con 1998; Vo Si Khai 1998). The presence of settlements is attested by Chinese travelers in the second century C.E. who describe walled cities containing palaces and houses (Hall 1985).

Three settlements in the area ascribed to Funan are described in inscriptions as *negara* and were probably the most important cities in a settlement hierarchy (Vickery 1998, 23). Other cities are described as *pura*, a Sanskrit term that indicates a place of political authority, although it is thought that these were less important than the *negara*. The next ranking settlement mentioned are *grama*, or towns or larger villages (Miksic 2003).

The Chinese annals state that the capital of Funan was T'e-mu, the location of which is unknown. There are at least two locations that are strong possibilities, one being the settlement of Angkor Borei and the other a location at the foot of Ba Phnom (Coedès 1968). Nagasena informed his Chinese hosts that the capital was near a mountain named Mayentiram. Coedès felt that this, most likely, referred to Vrah Vnam, the ancient name of Ba Phnom. Vickery (1998) prefers to place the capital at Angkor Borei, located near a hill known as Phnom Da, which could well have been the mountain Nagasena referred to. There is no strong evidence at the base of Ba Phnom to suggest it was a city of major importance, whereas there is ample evidence at Angkor Borei.

Wheatley believes, based on information dating to circa 245 C.E., that by the middle of the 3rd century there were a number of settlements that controlled tracts of territory around them, settlements that could be classified as proto-urban (Wheatley 1983, 121). The location of these settlements remains a mystery, although some of the names survive in inscriptions including Vyadhapura, Tamandarapura, and Samudrapura. The latter may have been the name of Oc Éo but this is uncertain (Wheatley 1983, 125). Wheatley (1983, 145) has suggested that there may have been a three-tiered settlement hierarchy, at the top of which was a paramount capital, surrounded by chiefly seats, with the bottom tier comprised of villages.

Funanese Hydraulics

There is evidence in southern Cambodia and Vietnam of the existence of a network of ancient canals (Paris 1931). These are currently being investigated as a component of the Lower Mekong Archaeological Project (Bishop, Penny et al. 2003; Sanderson et al. 2003; Stark 2003). Although many of the canals are just five to ten kilometers in length, the network is dominated by a channel running from Angkor Borei southward past Oc Éo to Da-noi, which may have been, in turn, connected by canal to Giong-da (van Liere 1980; 1988; Wheatley 1983). The latter settlement was close to the coast, linked to the sea by other wide canals. Oc Éo is transected by the Lung Gieng-da, a channel that was twenty meters wide and two meters deep (Manguin n.d.) and extended northeast for about twenty kilometers to Trap-da and to the southwest toward Ta-kev. This site is located near the coast at the intersection of the main Lung Gieng-da channel and another that ran at right angles to it (Wheatley 1983, 37). All of the main channels appear to have smaller canals providing access to them, and many of the archaeological settlements in the delta region have smaller canals radiating from them.

The purpose of these canals has been debated, and the explanations have run from their use in irrigation, drainage, desalination, aquaculture, and transportation (Malleret 1960; Groslier 1962; Wheatley 1983; Dega and Latinis 1996). There is little solid evidence for the first of these suggestions, although it cannot be dismissed outright. Although at certain times there is an abundance of water in the area, at others it is quite dry, and irrigation channels may have been essential for agriculture. Conversely, there are some areas that are prone to flooding all year round, and drainage canals would have opened more land to agriculture. During the Funanese period the sites were closer to the sea, and it may be argued that the purpose of the canals was to desalinate the water closer to the coast, thereby allowing rice agriculture. While it is not possible to disprove this argument, it seems unlikely that such an effort would have been expended to desalinate a limited amount of land. The soundest explanation for the canals is that they served as transportation routes, bringing goods to and from the Funan settlements. The very fact that coastal sites and major inland settlements were linked is suggestive of a trade and communication network (Wheatley 1983).

The ancient canals surrounding Angkor Borei share a similar morphology, usually with a raised embankment on one side. There are two very prominent canals leading from Angkor Borei to the coast, called Paris canals 1 and 2. These were first identified by French researcher Pierre Paris in 1941. The ancient canals range in width from three to four meters up to twenty-five meters and sometimes follow natural water courses, at which points they tend to meander. Some of the canals were quite shallow and wide, leading Stark and her coresearchers to suggest that they were likely used for transport and communication up until the fifth or sixth century C.E. (Stark 2004). Luminescence dating of the canal suggests that it was dug, or at least reexcavated, between the first millennium B.C.E. and the

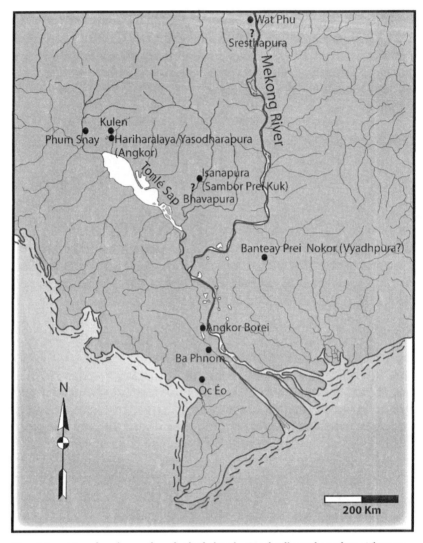

Map 5.1.   Map showing archaeological sites in Cambodia and southern Vietnam.

middle of the first millennium C.E. This dating scheme overlaps with the radiocarbon evidence from Angkor Borei suggesting an initial occupation in the fourth century B.C.E. (Bishop, Sanderson et al. 2004).

Channels are also found on either side of the wall surrounding Angkor Borei. These moats are approximately twenty-two meters wide and two to four meters deep. It is unknown what the original purpose of the moats was, possibly symbolic/religious, defensive, or perhaps utilitarian. They may have played a role in water supply and control and have been utilized for transportation.

Other hydrological features include water tanks and *barays*. The largest of these measures one hundred meters by two hundred meters. There are two large *barays* to the east and south of the ancient city wall, and others are found further from the old city. The morphology of most *barays* is similar to that of Angkorian *barays*, rectangular, although some are square. The *barays* were excavated down several meters, and the earth removed was used to raise earth embankments around the tank. It is estimated that the *baray* surrounding the ancient city of Angkor Borei had the capacity to hold approximately 350,000 cubic meters of water. Recent research on the *baray* and the site indicate a late date for their creation, and they may not have existed prior to the 17th century C.E.

Aside from *barays* and smaller tanks, there are many pools at Angkor Borei, most less than two thousand square meters in size. Although most are located within the city walls, there is a significant number outside it as well. Many of these are lined with rock, laterite, or brick, which differentiates them from the *barays* and canals. Often these pools are found in close association to an abandoned mound or ruined temple foundation. The majority of temple ruins and pools are found in the southern section of the city.

Oc Éo

Based upon the evidence provided by archaeology to date, it would seem that Oc Éo was a trading entrepôt. Nevertheless, some Vietnamese archaeologists have recommended caution in interpreting this evidence. Ha Van Tan (1986a) points out that assigning the material discovered at Oc Éo to the Funan civilization is premature "when we do not know what Funan was." This said, there is strong evidence that the site was occupied during the period usually attributed to Funan and conforms with Chinese accounts of what Funanese settlements looked like.

The excavators of Oc Éo have concluded that the city was established early in the first century, just south of a low, three-peaked hill, called the Bhnam Ba-thê. The site was probably occupied until circa 300 C.E., when it may have been abandoned for a short period. In the latter half of the fourth century the site began to see the appearance of an Indian influence, which appears to have lasted until circa 700 C.E. when the site may, again, have been abandoned. It was during this time that the moats around the city of Oc Éo are thought to have been dug (Manguin n.d.). These five moats, separated by ramparts, delimit an area of about 450 hectares. Chinese annals

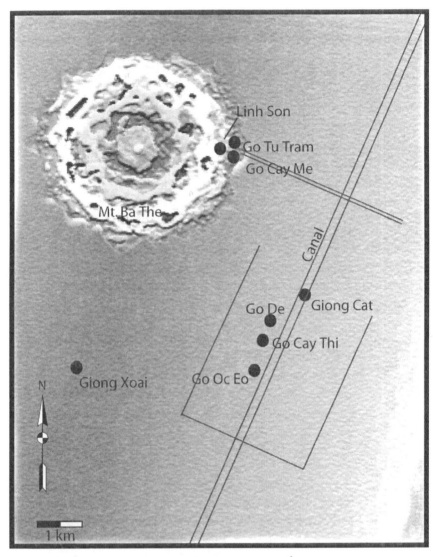

Map 5.2.   Map showing archaeological sites around Oc Éo, Vietnam.

(*Liang Shu* chuan 54 f.7) report that settlements in the region had ramparts that were palisaded and the moats accommodated crocodiles.

Malleret (1960) excavated Oc Éo in the 1940s and discovered the remains of at least two, large brick structures, which may have been surrounded by wooden houses. A gabled dwelling is represented on a stone mold used to make decorative architectural elements. Abundant evidence for a thriving settlement was found during the excavations including evidence of potters, glass-smiths and gold, bronze, and iron craftsmen (Malleret 1959; 1960; 1960–1962). Other hints of life at Oc Éo are found on ceramic sherds from the area, one showing musicians playing a harp and cymbals (Tan 2003, 111).

Recent excavations in southern Vietnam have brought to light scores of brick foundations around Oc Éo, which often contain gold plates embossed or etched with images of Vishnu, *chakra* wheels, lingas, or Garudas. These brick structures comprise a square brick column in which the plates are placed (Le Xuan Diem et al. 1995). At Cat Tien, Lam Dong Province, the remains of brick structures were found to contain many gold plates and images of gods, goddesses, religious symbols, and small lingas (Le Thi Lein 2002).

Similar plates have been recovered from Go Thap in Dong Thap Province (Dao Linh Con 1995), where eight graves containing over 350 gold plates were found. The local production of the plates is attested by the discovery of rectangular stone molds at Nhan Nghia in Can Tho Province and gold working tools at Oc Éo itself (Malleret 1960).

The majority of the structural remains around Oc Éo seem to be Hindu, but there are the remains of a Buddhist stupa at Co Xoai. Le Thi Lein (2002) notes that the remains bear resemblances to those found at U-Thong, a Dvaravati site in Thailand, dating from the 7th to 9th centuries C.E. There are also gold plates bearing Buddhist images from the delta region. It is likely that Buddhist influence came to the area much later and the majority of the Oc Éo culture was Hindu (Le Thi Lein 2002).

Archaeological investigation at Oc Éo has been most productive, although somewhat hampered by the destruction of the site through looting. Vietnamese researchers have found common features at over ninety sites surrounding Oc Éo, of which twenty have been excavated (Khai 2003, 46). They are found over a large geographic area from Ho Chi Minh City to the southern extent of Vietnam. Finds include the remains of pile dwellings, stone and brick structures, and cremation graves. (see map in Khai 2003, 39). The residential sites comprise structures with wooden floors, wood and domestic pottery, animal bones, and botanical remains including rice grains. These sites date from between 170 B.C.E. to 540 C.E. (Khai 2003, 52).

The presumed religious sites comprise foundations of brick or stone which can be dated from the 5th to 8th centuries C.E. Many of these architectural features are associated with religious statuary such as linga or statues of Indian deities as well as ceramics.

Burials attributed to the "Oc Éo culture" are found on low mounds and usually comprise a square burial pit ranging from over a meter to 3.5 meters and attaining a depth of just over one meter. The pit is often lined with bricks and filled with white sand, human ashes, and grave goods including gold leaf, coins, gemstones, and, infrequently, statuary. The gold leaves are impressed with anthropomorphic, zoomorphic, and botanic images. The coins found at Oc Éo are stamped with a "rising sun and temple" and have been found at U-Thong and other sites in Thailand, as well as at the Pyu sites Halin, Beikthano, and Pegu (Mitchiner 1982). The upper part of the burial is sealed by sticky clay or rubble. Although a majority of graves are square, some "funnel-shaped" graves have been identified (Le Thi Lein 2002; Khai 2003, 61). Most of the graves found date from the 3rd to 6th centuries C.E.

Excavations have produced thousands of pot sherds and ceramic vessels, among the most common of which are globular pots with a neck and pouring spout on the side. These are commonly known as kundika or kendi and are found throughout the delta and beyond. Dating from the latter half of the first millennium C.E., they may have been used in rituals (Tan 2003, 111). Other interesting vessels include stem cups, which may have been used for drinking in ritual ceremonies. Temple sites seem to contain a greater number of fine wares, whereas residential sites contain coarse earthenware pots. Tan (2003, 115) believes that the pottery tradition of Oc Éo developed from prehistoric origins.

ANGKOR BOREI

The city of Angkor Borei, in Takeo Province, Cambodia, is located on a slightly raised escarpment (two to ten meters above sea level), nearly surrounded by low-lying delta which, during the rainy season, is inundated (Stark 2003). The most prominent geographical feature near the city is Phnom Da to the west, which rises 170 meters above sea level. The site has long been promoted as one of the earliest centers of a state-level polity in Southeast Asia. There is little doubt that the site has been occupied since antiquity, and there is now evidence that it was settled circa the 4th century B.C.E. (Bishop, Penny et al. 2003).

Some of the earliest inscriptions in Cambodia (K. 557, K. 600), dating to circa 611 C.E., come from the site. The site is covered with the remains of brick structures and an imposing wall and double moat surround the ancient city. Radiocarbon dates and coring indicate that the site has been occupied since the 4th century B.C.E. (Stark 1998; 2003; Stark et al. 1999), a date that corresponds with those from Oc Éo and the Funanese period (Dega and Latinis 1996). Evidence suggests that the site was an important center into the 9th century C.E., with a possible population peak in the 6th and 7th centuries. Sculptural works have been dated to the early 7th century (Coedès 1931; Dowling 1999), and brick monuments have been dated by thermoluminescence to the 10th century (Stark 2003).

The ancient city was advantageously located for the exploitation of natural and agricultural resources. Old alluvial deposits provided excellent soils for agriculture, and the city's location near the Mekong, Bassac, and other smaller rivers provided limitless supplies of water. It appears that these natural resources were further augmented through the construction of canals and *barays*. These factors may have allowed for the production of an agricultural surplus that may have been complemented by fish and forest products such as wood, resin, and wildlife by-products.

Angkor Borei is surrounded by a massive wall, constructed of earth piled on a brick core measuring approximately 2.4 meters wide and 4.5 meters high (Stark and Bong 2001; Stark 2004). Archaeological investigations suggest that the wall was constructed in stages that may have originated, first, with an earthen embankment that surrounded the settlement (Stark 2003). The earth was apparently held in place by packed soil and rubble. The earth was most likely taken from the areas on either side of the wall, creating ditches, which were later filled with water. An estimated 350,000 cubic meters of soil were excavated from the moats and close to a 160,000 cubic meters of soil were used in the walls, which are nearly six kilometers in circumference (Dega and Latinis 1996). Radiometric dates indicate that the site was occupied from the fifth or fourth century B.C.E., and it appears that the moats may have been constructed from the 1st to 3rd century C.E. It appears that there may be variation in the design of the wall at Angkor Borei, as French descriptions of the wall indicate a width of approximately 1.0–1.2 meters wide (B.E.F.E.O. 1933). The core is comprised of eighteen to thirty vertical courses and four to nine horizontal courses of large rectangular bricks. Against this core the rubble and soil were packed. There are further bricks over the top of the wall, presumably to prevent erosion of the packed soil. The wall averages about twenty meters in width, the top of which may have been used as a road or even occupation area (Dega and Latinis 1996). No guardhouses, gateways, or bastions are apparent along the ancient wall, which may indicate that the wall was not designed for military purposes. Its military usefulness is diminished due to the fact that the wall is cut and the city transected by the Angkor Borei River. In order to defer flooding within the city, the banks of the river inside the city are raised and reinforced with large blocks of laterite and granite. It is possible that the wall served to protect the city from seasonal flooding, as well as providing a raised "ring-road" and dwelling area. This assumption is supported by the irregular form of the wall which is roughly D-shaped (Stark 2003). Chinese accounts of Funan describe palisaded settlements (Pelliot 1903a, 254), and according to Stark (2003) the wall around Angkor Borei was originally constructed of earth and this may have "supported a wooden palisade at some point during its usage."

The first major archaeological investigation to be undertaken at Angkor Borei has been the Lower Mekong Archaeological Project (LOMAP) which seeks to understand the emergent complexity in the region between c. 500 B.C.E. and 500 C.E. More than 151 possible archaeological features have been identified by the LOMAP investigations inside the walled area of Angkor Borei, including more than one hundred water control features such as reservoirs, pools, and natural ponds. More than thirty mounds comprised of ancient brick have been identified, the largest of which was seventy meters by thirty-two meters (Stark 2003). Radiocarbon dating indicates that Angkor Borei was probably settled around 400 B.C.E., predating the earliest Chinese accounts of the area by five hundred to six hundred years (Stark et al. 1999; Stark 2003).

Excavations undertaken at Angkor Borei have revealed the presence of a cemetery. Local people discovered eleven skeletons in extended burials, as well as deposits of ash which may represent cremation graves (Stark 2003, 98). Scientific excavation has revealed a further eighteen burials in an area of only two meters by three meters. Most of these burials were inhumations, but some appeared to be secondary burials, as the bones were bundled. Many of the individuals were buried with either pig crania, globular red earthenware jars, or a combination of these items (Stark 2003, 99).

Viewing Angkor Borei in a regional context, it appears that the site was surrounded by many hundreds of smaller sites, many with religious architectural remains. Stark also feels that several of these sites were connected to Angkor Borei via canals, as ceramic collections from these sites can be compared to Angkor Borei's ceramics and suggest that these outlying settlements were occupied no later than the 4th century C.E. (Stark 2003, 98).

DECLINE OF FUNAN

There are a range of theories, including environmental change, conquest, or loss of economic power due to external factors, that account for the decline of the power of Funan. Malleret (1962, 355, n. 4) felt that alterations in the coastline may have isolated Oc Éo, leading to a decline in trade, and Hall (1985, 72) has suggested that increases in rice production elsewhere in Southeast Asia meant that Funan lost export revenue. These theories are not widely supported as there is little evidence for dramatic changes in the coastline (Miksic 1977), nor is there solid evidence that Funan was a large-scale rice exporter or that it faced any competition if it was a supplier of rice (Miksic 2003).

It is possible, according to some authors, that the mismanagement of resources played a role in the decline of the Funanese polity during the 6th and 7th centuries. This, complemented by the possible usurpation of power by competing polities, the evolution of new trade routes between India and China, and decreased demand for the goods produced around Angkor

Borei, contributed to the collapse of the polity. These authors posit that the large-scale construction undertaken may have been another contributing factor to the decline. They suggest that the large number of bricks used in wall and temple construction fueled a huge demand for clay, fuel, and labor, which took its toll. Clear-cutting for fuel and for the creation of agricultural fields may have devastated the forests (Dega and Latinis 1996). As the area around Angkor Borei was depleted, the cost of obtaining fuels and other resources increased—a situation which may have reached a level where economic stress and difficulties with raw material acquisition and production resulted in the partial or total collapse of some associated industries (Dega and Latinis 1996).

By the late 4th century C.E. the caravan routes across central Asia were no longer viable and the Chin dynasty was forced to seek alternative trade routes. This opportunity seems to have been seized by polities on the Malay Peninsula and in the Indonesian archipelago. Ho-lo-tan/t'o in western Java and Ko-ying in the Sunda Strait began trading directly with China, apparently bypassing Funan (Hall 1985; Hagesteijn 1989). In the 5th century the Buddhist pilgrim Fa Hsien and an Indian prince named Gunavarman found that there was no need to break their travel between China and India on the Isthmus of Kra or in Funan (Hall 1985). This situation was exacerbated during the 6th century when technological changes in sailing craft greatly increased efficiency, allowing trading ships to shift from coastal routes to a direct path across the South China Sea to southern China. The change in shipping routes may have effectively cut Funan off from its economic lifeline, contributing to its collapse (Vickery 1998).

The last king of Funan mentioned by the Chinese histories is Rudravarman, after which Funan disappears from the Chinese histories and is replaced by a polity known to them as Chenla. This polity, whose communities were led by individuals bearing the title *poñ*, was thought to have extracted its wealth from agriculture, possibly supplemented by intercommunity *overland* trade (Vickery 1998). Based on the inscriptions left from this period, Vickery (1998) and Hall (1985) feel that the peoples of this new polity were undoubtedly Khmer.

Further evidence of the decline of Funanese power is found in the fact that, in 449 C.E., embassies of the Chinese emperor bestowed titles upon the rulers of several Indonesian coastal polities while ignoring Funan (Hall 1985, 72). Forty years after recognizing the polities of insular Southeast Asia, the Chinese recognized the ruler of a polity called Linyi on what is now the Vietnamese coast (Hall 1985). In the late 6th century the Cham, found in central, coastal Vietnam, profited from trade with China and were better placed to communicate through a shared language with the Javanese and Malay who had come to control the sea lanes at this point (Miksic 2003).

There is evidence from Angkor Borei that the site was in decline by the 5th or 6th century C.E., as there are substantial changes in the environment and hydrology around the site which may indicate that the people changed their subsistence strategy (Bishop, Penny et al. 2003).

Some scholars (Coedès 1968; Hall 1985; Khai 2003) believe that the polity of Chenla began to assert military pressure on Funan and that, in the mid–6th century, T'e-mu was invaded resulting in the decline of the Funan kingdom and the beginning of Chenla. The Hsin T'ang Shu states that the capital of Funan was moved in the late 6th century from T'e-mu, after that city's fall to Chenla (Wheatley 1983). The new capital was called Na-fu-na, possibly the Chinese transliteration of Naravarangara (Coedès 1943–1946), which may correspond to the site of Oc Éo (Khai 2003:69).

Hall (1985) believes that new rulers of the delta either destroyed or failed to maintain the extensive hydraulic networks of Funan. As a result the lands were depopulated as the agrarian population moved upriver toward the Tonlé Sap lake. Vickery feels that the argument for a military conquest of Funan by Chenla is built on weak evidence, writing "that research conducted in a materialistic spirit on the Chinese records of relations with the early Southeast Asia has revealed that by the 6th century Funan was in irreversible economic, and therefore political, decline, and that no conquest theory is required to explain its disappearance" (Vickery 1998, 42) and that continuity in inscriptions with Chenla kings showing respect to Funan rulers is indicative of a gradual and peaceful transference of power (Vickery 1996; Vickery n.d., 32).

It is clear that by the early 7th century there was a shift in population away from the coastal areas (Malleret 1962, 355). Other changes are also discernable, notably the appearance of Khmer in inscriptions, the disappearance of coins, and a marked increase in the Siva worship (Vickery 1998; Miksic 2003). Miksic (2003, 31), who feels that the inhabitants of Funan were likely Mon, suggests that the fall of Funan saw a gradual transference of power and loyalty to the dominant Khmer. He writes, "the Mon of the lower Mekong may have felt more attracted to the new Khmer civilization, and opted to join it." Vickery (1996, 3) is of the view that "Chenla was simply a continuation of Funan, under the same group of chiefs, not a different polity which displaced Funan by conquest, and certainly did not represent the descent by a Khmer population into an area inhabited by non-Khmer." This idea seems to be supported in some respects by the Chinese record of a request from Champa in 643–644, for the T'ang emperor to send military assistance to fend off attacks by Funan. The fact that the name Funan was still being used at this late date may be indicative of continuity.

Data collected by the LOMAP suggest that at least one canal was abandoned during the 5th or 6th century C.E., leading Stark (2004), among others, to hypothesize a major re-organization at this time. They are careful to stress that this does not necessarily mean depopulation of the area, which may have occurred later, during the seventh century C.E. Even if the population of the area was reduced considerably, the site of Angkor Borei was probably not abandoned, but there may have been changes in the way the landscape was utilized for agriculture.

CHENLA

In studying Chenla, historians are not forced to rely so heavily upon the Chinese histories, as there are more primary sources dating to this later period in the form of inscriptions, usually commemorating the foundation of a temple. These are usually written either in ancient Khmer or Sanskrit with the occasional terms in the Mon or Cham languages (Vickery 1998, 83). It appears that those who inscribed the stones were well versed in the proper use of Sanskrit, suggesting that they may have undergone formal training with Sanskrit scholars. Although the corpus of inscriptions is more plentiful than those dating from Funan times, they comprise only 140 steles in Khmer with a further ninety or so in Sanskrit (Vickery 1998, 84).

Tsein-lâp was the name given, by the Chinese, to a polity that was contemporaneous with Funan and may, at some point, have been a vassal of it. The Chinese pronunciation has since been altered, and the polity is now generally known as Zhenla or Chenla. It may be best to think of Chenla as the most powerful polity among several competing chiefdoms or perhaps kingdoms in Southeast Asia during the 7th and 8th century. Eventually the polity of Chenla came to eclipse Funan and dominate its territory as well as the lands of northern Cambodia. Coedès (1964a; 1968) and Majumdar (1944) believed that Chenla had its locus in the area of the middle Mekong River. The capital, Coedès felt, was located near a mountain called *Ling-kia-po-p'o*, interpreted as Lingaparavata, where Wat Phu is located in southern Laos. Majumdar places the capital at Sresthapura, somewhere near Wat Phu. Vickery (1994), however, stresses that it is not necessary to look any further than within the borders of present day Cambodia for the heartland of Chenla. The locations of inscriptions naming rulers such as Bhavavarman and Citrasena-Mahendravarman suggest that these individuals inhabited what is now northern Cambodia. The territory covered by Chenla and the names of its earliest rulers are difficult to ascertain. Coedès (1964) proposed that Srutavarman and Sresthavarman were the names of two early rulers of Chenla, based on a mention in later 10th and 12th century inscriptions. Jacques (1986) and Vickery (1998) on the other hand, believe these two to be mythical figures. The first solid evidence referring to Chenla's rulers cites two brothers, named Bhavavarman and Citrasena-Mahendravarman, sons of an individual named Viravarman. These princes

came from an area to the south of the Dangrek mountain range, which today forms the border between Cambodia, Thailand, and Laos. There is disagreement over the location of the early capitals of these rulers. According
to Jacques (1986), Bhavavarman ruled the eastern portion of his father's
realm from Sambor Prei Kuk near Kompong Thom, while his brother controlled the western areas reigning from an unknown location. Upon
Bhavavarman's death in the late 6th century, Mahendravarman ruled the region from Sambor Prei Kuk until his death, probably in the early 7th century. Vickery (1998) suggests that Bhavavarman ruled from a city called
Bhavapura, near Kompong Thom (Jacques 1972), and that Mahendravarman ruled from Sambor Prei Kuk. Mahendravarman's son, Isanavarman (r.
616?–635? C.E.), also ruled from Sambor Prei Kuk during the 7th century
when the city was called Isanapura. Either way, this interpretation of the rel-
evant inscriptions is a departure from the traditionally accepted understanding of the location of Chenla, which Coedès (1964) placed in what is
today the border between Cambodia and Laos. Jacques's placement does
not contradict the Chinese annals, which simply place Chenla southwest of
Linyi in Vietnam. The Chinese records further imply that there was continuity in the location of the capital at Sambor Prei Kuk at least until the
reign of Isanavarman (Ma Tuan-Lin 1876 in Vickery 1994). Vickery (1998,
21) believes, based on the distribution of inscriptions, that 7th century
"Chenla controlled the area from Ba Phnom to Kompong Thom on a north-
south axis, probably not extending much farther eastward, but including
everything up to the Mekong and Tonlé Sap on the west, and extending
across those rivers into Kompong Speu, Takeo and Kampot." It is known
that, in the latter part of the 6th century, both Mahendravarman and
Bhavavarman dispatched expeditions, presumably, to enlarge their territory.
The inscriptions claim conquest to the north and south of the Dangrek
mountains and covering the territory from the Mekong to the Chao Phraya
Rivers (Vickery 1998).

Isanavarman was followed on the throne by his son, Bhavavarman II (r.
637?–mid 600s C.E.). Little is known of Bhavavarman II's reign. Traditionally the last king of Chenla is said to be Jayavarman I (r. 655/57?–680/81?).
Jayavarman followed Bhavavarman II on the throne, but it is possible that
there was a dynastic break as no connection can be made between this king
and his predecessors (Vickery 1998). Jayavarman I reigned the longest of
any of the Chenla rulers, and it is apparent that he was aggressive in expanding the territory under his control. He is portrayed in inscriptions as a
warrior-king, master of the earth (Wolters 1974, 375). The territorial in-
tegrity of Chenla seems to have been upheld through the reigns of all these
rulers, although not all agree that it was a united polity (Jacques 1986).
Jayavarman is likely to have moved his capital from Isanapura, but it is not
clear where it was moved to. Banteay Prei Nokor is a possible location, but

this site is also claimed as an early capital of Jayavarman II (Jacques 1990) and only excavation will determine the occupation of the citadel. After Jayavarman I's reign it seems that Chenla was gripped by political strife. At this time the Chinese chronicles record that the polity was split into two—Land Chenla to the north and Water Chenla to the south. The accuracy of this assertion is unclear, and it may be that there was a more complex disintegration, with some of the polities conquered under Jayavarman attempting to establish their independence (Wolters 1974).

Religion

The deities of the Chenla period that are known to us are a mix of Hindu, Buddhist, and indigenous personalities. The local gods comprise *vrah* and *kpoñ*, who are, respectively, male and female. Although the *vrah* appear to have a local origin, Siva, Vishnu, and the Buddha were included in their numbers indicating an integration of the religious traditions. Vickery (1998, 149) believes that most localities had their own deities, and these *vrah* and *kpoñ* could have Indian-derived names.

It is likely that Siva worship was prevalent in Chenla, and we have evidence of Siva cults dating as early as 604 C.E. Siva was most often represented in the form of a linga, usually enshrined in a temple structure. Siva represents a complex combination of ideals, at once a personal god and the absolute god and the light of the universe. To his worshippers, Siva is the god responsible for universal creation (and destruction). The god was probably very closely linked to the king, and it is possible that the linga represents the unification of the deity and the king (Haendel 2004).

It is also apparent that the cult of Vishnu was prevalent in Cambodia from the mid–first millennium C.E. There were several different Vishnuite sects in Cambodia, the most prominent being the Pancaratra. The central tenet of the Pancaratra sect was the creative aspect of Vishnu. Strict adherents would perform rites five times a day in honor of the god. In temples Vishnu was often portrayed in anthropogenic form although many of his avatars were portrayed as well. Vishnuites and Sivaites saw their respective deities in the same light. Both were identified with "the Absolute Brahman. He is unique and multiple, transcendent and immanent, he is the universal self, and the individual self" (Haendel 2004).

In the early Chenla period, before rigid hierarchies appeared, the temple may have served as a communal meeting place in the smaller communities, a place where community issues were discussed and the indigenous Khmer gods attended to (Vickery 1998, 308). Many of the later Chenla temples (post-Isanavarman) remain standing today, as they were commonly built of brick, usually in the form of one to three towers that housed a sacred image. It is clear that the temples served several functions aside from their obvious religious importance. They were social gathering places for the elite and fulfilled economic roles. Many craftspeople were assigned to work for temples as were scores of agricultural laborers (Vickery 1998, 292). The amount of goods produced seems to have far outweighed the needs of the temple staff. The production of a surplus of both food and craft goods was a useful political tool. Vickery (1998, 309) claims that often temples specialized in the production of various goods, including rice, fruits, and crafts, that were used in exchange and for enhancing the prestige of the local rulers. Gift exchanges and marriage alliances probably allowed the rulers of nascent polities to expand their control. Thus, through the guise of religious merit the local chiefs could entice the elite to make donations to the temples, thereby enhancing the chief's political power.

Vickery (1998, 163) has illustrated that the Indian concepts of religion were corrupted in different ways in early Cambodia. A good example of this is the fact that women acted as high level officiants in temple rights. These women, entitled *klon mratañ*, apparently were associated with the principal official of the temple in ritual or perhaps scribal roles. There is even some indication that they may have functioned as principal officials in some instances.

It does not appear that during the Chenla period there was a wholesale adoption of the religions of India. The inscriptions appear to suggest that Indic deities were absorbed into the indigenous pantheon and that some of the Khmer gods began to be given Sanskrit names. Vickery (1998, 170) suggests that the idea of "Khmer Hinduism" may be a valid concept in that the religion was adapted to fit the needs of the Khmer rulers. It does not appear that the Khmer of Chenla explicitly thought of themselves as Hindu, nor is there any evidence that a caste system was extant. It also appears as though the suffix, *-isvara*, accorded to many deities, was a Khmer invention, and these *-isvara* were placed in a pantheon of gods with Khmer names (Vickery 1998, 170). This trend seems to be illustrated further during the Angkor period when Hinduism was more firmly entrenched. The concept of *kamraten jagat*, a divine appellation sometimes affixed to a royal title, seems to be a Khmer invention or, perhaps, a modification of a preexisting protective cult (Jacques 1985). Vickery (1998, 140) feels that the gradual supercession of Indian religious iconography over the traditional pantheon was due to the elite attempting to establish a lasting political and economic dominance.

There is strong evidence that Buddhism also played a role in Chenla. Both Mahayana and Therevada Buddhism were practiced in Southeast Asia, but the former was more prevalent. Rarely was Buddhism adopted by the royal family, but it was likely practiced by some members of the elite.

Political Organization

The political make-up of Chenla is difficult to determine but great strides have been made in our understanding of Chenla (Jacques 1988; 1990; Vickery 1998). Based on Chinese sources, it appears that Chenla was a unified state or *kuo*, but analysis of primary and secondary sources may contradict this interpretation. Vickery (1996) believes that, based on the available evidence, it would be more prudent to call Chenla a "chiefdom" rather than a state. It is only under Jayavarman I that some of the attributes of "statehood" appear.

That Chenla was a politically complex structure is not in doubt. As we have seen, by the late Funan period the paramount rulers had come to be known with the suffix *-varman*, an Indic term. By the early 7th century, inscriptions detail a number of hierarchical levels, each with a Khmer title rather than an Indian derived honorific, a fact that leads Vickery (1998) to suppose that the system had been in place for centuries before the inscriptions were written. The ancient Khmer used the title *poñ* (possibly the *fan* of Chinese accounts, which in old Chinese was pronounced *b'iwom*), which may have denoted a ritual chief or head of a clan. These individuals may have been the authority figures in larger settlements (several hundred to thousands of people), and in some instances there may have been more than one *poñ*, although one would have held ultimate power in the settlement (Vickery 1996). It is likely that these individuals were community mediators who resolved disputes but it appears that they could not amass property. The *poñ* were thought to be descended from a female deity known as a *kpoñ* (Vickery 1996, 5; 1998, 22). The title *poñ* was held by males but apparently could only be passed on through a female relative. Vickery (1998, 23) speculates that this system began to collapse during the Funan period, when access to prestige goods through trade may have enriched certain *poñ*. Vickery notes that a number of strategies allowing the *poñ* families to control land were attempted. These strategies included alliances through marriage so the joined families could control a supraterritory. None of these attempts appears to have endured however. It is likely that some *poñ* of Funan had succeeded in breaking with tradition, adopting the suffix *-varman*, and thereby allowing patrilineal descent rules to come into use (Vickery 1996). It is clear that the term *poñ* disappeared from inscriptions by the 8th century, indicating a shift in the political structure of Chenla. It appears that this rank was replaced by the honorific *mratāñ* (Vickery 1998, 24). Also of interest is the shift away from indigenous religion. *Kpoñ* were replaced by gods with Indic names (Vickery 1996).

According to the Chinese histories the polity of Chenla was, in the beginning, a unified entity. These same histories indicate that there was political turmoil during the reign of Isanavarman and the polity ruptured into two parts, usually denoted as Land and Water Chenla. Analysis of genealogies of the pre-Angkorian period indicates that a rather more serious fragmentation of Chenla may have occurred, with the formation of many smaller polities (Dupont 1943–1946). The diversity of the political landscape during the 7th century is illustrated in the inscriptions. It appears that certain individuals were using honorifics that were usually reserved for the gods and kings. One such individual, reigning between Isanavarman and Jayavarman I, is Salagramasvami who claimed the title *vrah kamratan añ sri* and was, in all likelihood, the deserved owner of the title (Vickery 1998, 140).

Vickery (1998, 336) suggests that Isanavarman was a paramount with no more than formal superiority in some areas. While the king's authority was strong in a core area of Kompong Thom and Prey Veng, it may have been weaker in the south and north and his dominion may not have been contiguous. There are anomalies in the inscriptions that indicate that vassals of Isanavarman may have been separated by more independent polities in which his name was invoked but where political appointments and decisions were undertaken by local lord or kings (Vickery 1998, 339).

During the 8th century it appears that there was ongoing political consolidation within Cambodia. We know of a city or territory called Aninditapura, the location of which is unclear (perhaps between present-day Kompong Thom and Kompong Cham (Vickery 1998, 384). The rulers of Aninditapura seem to have been allied with the rulers of Sambhupura (perhaps near modern Sambor) and the so-called –*aditya* kings, whose territory is also thought to have been near Sambor Prei Kuk (Vickery 1998). It would therefore appear that the consolidation may have been one whereby strong rulers, the proximity of whom is remarkable, agreed to support the lineage of Bhavavarman, Mahendravarman, and Indravarman. It is possible that this system was preserved under Jayavarman I, with the exception of Sambhupura, but may have faltered upon his death.

Vickery (1994) suggests that, by the time of Isanavarman, Chenla controlled large swaths of territory, perhaps in a patchwork, from coastal, eastern Thailand to the coast of Vietnam and that this control persisted into the reign of his son Bhavavarman II. Bhavavarman II, it seems, controlled the area from Takeo Province, in Cambodia, to eastern Thailand and from Phnom Bayang in the south to, at least, Phnom Hanchey in the north (Vickery 1998, 342). Even so, Vickery (1998, 367) is of the opinion that Isanavarman's realm was not a state but more likely a complex and very large chiefdom, in which the most important political appointments were reserved for family members and it was still necessary to include vassal territories in his realm, the loyalty of which he could not assure. The investments in art and architecture during the late Chenla period are cited as further evidence of political stability (Briggs 1951; Coedès 1964b; Vickery 1994), as are the inscriptions which demonstrate "similarities of language, style, and content in the pre-Angkor corpus are much greater than the areal differences, indicating that, in what the Chinese called 'Chenla' there was at least a common base of administrative, cultural and political practices, with, as would be expected, local variations, both spatial and temporal" (Vickery 1998, 132).

It appears that there was a serious drive to centralize the political structure of Chenla during the reign of Jayavarman I. It has been proposed that Jayavarman I, like his father, Candravarman, came from northern Cambodia and was unrelated to the earlier dynasty with its capital in Kompong Thom (Vickery 1998, 342). Later inscriptions mention a *-pura* called Candrapura, which seems to have been in the north. Clearly, the origins of this line are obscure. We know little of Candravarman, but it seems Jayavarman's reign began in around 655 C.E. and lasted about twenty-six years (Vickery 1998, 335). The capital is also unknown but may have been at Sresthapura (probably located somewhere between Siem Reap and Kompong Thom), Vyadhapura (possibly in Kompong Cham at Banteay Prei Nokor, according to Vickery, or Ba Phnom, as Coedès believes), Naravarangara (possibly Angkor Borei as suggested by Coedès in Vickery 1998, 352) or Purandarapura (possibly in Siem Reap Province, in the opinion of Jacques in Vickery 1998, 334–36).

Vickery (1998, 368) feels that Jayavarman I began to centralize his power, bringing religious foundations under his control by discouraging private foundations, eroding the power of the *poñ*, and intervening in the economic business of the elite. He also began to appoint individuals outside his family to, seemingly, important positions, including military specialists. A major shift in administration is evident in the fact that Jayavarman reorganized the domains of local chiefs and apparently the authority of these individuals. This is also the first time imprecations appear in the inscriptions, warning against the desecration of the royal foundation (Vickery 1998, 26).

Jayavarman I probably died around 681 C.E. and was followed on the throne by a woman named Jayadevi who took the title *vrah kamratan añ*. It is thought that Jayadevi was the daughter of Jayavarman I (Jacques 1988, 64; Vickery 1994, 201; Higham 2002, 42). It is likely that Jayadevi ruled over much of the area that now comprises modern Cambodia with a consort or ally, Napaditya, from circa 681–705 C.E. After Napaditya's death she governed alone until circa 720 C.E. (Jacobsen 2003). The trend toward centralization, begun by Jayavarman I, seems to have been continued by Jayadevi. Noteworthy is the fact that geographical boundaries in her inscriptions ceased to be described in terms of personal dominions (Vickery 1998, 368).

Social Organization: Chenla Titles and Ranks

Inscriptions were not the exclusive domain of the paramounts during the Chenla period. Individuals with the title of *poñ* or *mratañ*, who appear to have held status below "royalty," also erected inscriptions, but it is clear that their power was, at most, local (Vickery 1996). The honorific of *poñ* is thought to derive from the Funan period and may have been the title that the Chinese transcribed as *fan*. The term fell from usage at some point around 719 C.E. (Vickery 1998, 190). The title was held only by men and was used with a given name which was usually of Indic derivation (Vickery 1998, 193). That the title *poñ* could be a signifier of considerable rank is illustrated by the fact that Isanavarman I's son held the title (Vickery 1998, 198). Vickery (1998) hypothesizes that *poñ* was an indigenous term originally applied to chiefs of settlements, and as a supralocal authority came into being the title was ascribed to those holding high political office within the polity.

Another rank title was *mratañ*, a term that came, eventually, to supercede *poñ* and continued in use until the reign of Suryavarman I (r. 1002–1049) (Vickery 1998, 190). The term *mratañ* does not seem to have an indigenous origin. It appears to have been a conferred title as opposed to *poñ*, which Vickery (1998:203) argues was ascriptive. It appears that *mratañ* was used for people who ruled major settlements, *-pura*, not that *poñ* were excluded from holding the title of *mratañ*. This does seem to suggest, as Vickery (1998) notes, that *poñ* and *mratañ* may have been of similar rank, but their functions were certainly different.

In studying the titles of Chenla, Vickery (1998, 207) concludes that gods and humans may have been ranked in a single hierarchy as certain ranks could be applied to both. At some point in the 7th century, chiefs or kings began to apply the title *vrah kamratan añ* to themselves (Vickery 1998, 209). Perhaps in an attempt to differentiate themselves from the *poñ*, some chiefs had begun to call themselves *vrah kamratan añ*, a title usually reserved for male deities. This may have allowed these individuals to abandon the circumscription associated with *poñ*, who were seen as local and ritual leaders (Vickery 1996). Other inscriptions of the 7th century mention, in hierarchical order, the people who had been assigned to a specific temple or religious foundation. After the *poñ* came female "officiants," followed by entertainers, specialized workmen, and, lastly, at the bottom of the hierarchy people called *kñum*, or agricultural laborers, sometimes interpreted as slaves. It appears, at least during Chenla times, that this term is better understood to mean "client" or "juniors" rather than slaves (Vickery 1998, 306).

Prior to the arrival of Europeans in other parts of Asia, research has shown war was the most common means of acquiring "slave" labor (Watson 1980; Reid 1983; Scott 1983). These captives were rapidly integrated into the socioeconomic system of their new society to become laborers, artisans, warriors, and traders (Junker 2004). It is possible that the *kñum* represented captives integrated in such a way into the Chenla social system.

It is possible to identify different classes of people—the elite, comprising the paramount ruler and his officials and aristocracy, and those who were ruled (Vickery 1998, 257). The nonelite classes are given rather cursory treatment and are mentioned usually only as part of a donation to a religious foundation. We may infer something of the economy from these inscriptions, however, particularly that land ownership existed as elites are recorded as donating property for use by a temple.

The elites made the donations and often listed, as part of their largesse, numbers of individuals assigned to serve the god. There are some instances of what one would assume to be individuals of rank being named in donations. These people, who were responsible for ritual functions, were usually female, in some instances the relations of *poñ or mratañ* (Vickery 1998, 271) and often held the title *tañ*. Inscriptions citing these people were more common in the earlier Chenla period, and Vickery (1998, 219) hypothesizes that this may reflect a move away from local elites founding temples and installing their female relations as officiants. Below these people were entertainers such as singers and musicians, whose given names were either Khmer or Sanskrit in origin. Below this group were craftspeople usually identified as *kñum*. There are other groups below these, the functions of which are unclear. The last group named in inscriptions were usually field hands, people who most often had very simple Khmer names (Vickery 1998). There is much debate over whether this last class represented "free" individuals or a class of slaves. It is tempting to suggest that, because they are listed among the donations to a temple, they were deprived of free will. As Vickery (1998, 230) states, we cannot know the true status of the *kñum* without understanding the whole structure of Chenla society. Vickery (1998, 112), at least, believes that there was some room for social mobility, claiming that craft specialists could attain high rank.

Vickery (1998, 260) feels that the predominance of female names in foundation inscriptions and especially the fact that many have associated children named with them may reflect a matrilineal tendency in early Khmer society. This supposition is further enforced by evidence of matrilineal descent in early royal inscriptions (Vickery 1998, 261–70).

Individuals who cannot be considered to have been of the ruling stratum include *kloñ*, a title that may be roughly equivalent to chief or overseer of laborers (Vickery 1998, 251).

The inscriptions are silent regarding daily events, and we have no knowledge of markets, or the collection of taxes. It would appear that Chenla functioned without the use of coins, as these are not mentioned and are unknown archaeologically. Much has been made of the Khmer mastery of irrigation and its role in the rise of Angkor (Briggs 1951; Sedov 1978; Claessen and Skalnik 1981; Stargardt 1986; Zuylen van 1991; Stott 1992), but it is interesting to note that the inscriptional evidence from Chenla seems to indicate very little central control over irrigation (Vickery 1998, 306). Local communities appear to have controlled the irrigation networks under the supervision of their chiefs. According to Than (1982), during the rainy season rivers were diverted using canals to fill tanks or create dams to trap water for distribution to the rice fields.

Settlement Pattern

It is very difficult to ascertain any evidence for settlement patterns during the Chenla period; indeed many of the major centers are lost to us. There may have been an administrative unit called a *nagar*, which may have been at the top of the hierarchy although most of the capitals bore the title *-pura*. The *pura* were large settlements and perhaps the most politically important. *Pura* were ruled by *mratan klon*, *kurak klon*, and *kurun*, officials who were known by the Sanskrit suffix, *-svami* or *-isvara* (Vickery 1998, 24). We do know that the capitals were usually named after the ruler, Bhavapura, Isana-pura, etc. and that these names were often applied to describe the polity as a whole (Vickery 1996, 10). It is likely that there were other major centers throughout the territory controlled by Chenla, and some of the names are known to us, including Indrapura, Vyadhapura, and Jyesthapura. Some light is shed on the matter by a Chinese history, the *Sui Shu*, with reference to early 7th century Cambodia, which states that there were thirty towns in Chenla with over one thousand inhabitants. A later history referring to the 8th century claims that, in the territory to the east of "Water Chenla" (prob-ably corresponding to southeastern Cambodia), there were many small towns that were called "kingdoms" (Wolters 1974, 371). Wolters (1974, 370) believes that, in the northwestern part of what is now Cambodia, there existed a number of principalities that were eventually conquered by Chenla. These, he says, were relatively close together, their capitals less than one hundred kilometers apart, yet they were politically distinct until they were subjugated.

Northwestern Cambodia witnessed the rise and conquest of a number of small polities during the 7th century. Military excursions were first under-taken by Bhavavarman I during the late 6th century, but he was unable to subjugate the principalities permanently and they were able to dispatch in-dependent emissaries to the Chinese court by 638 C.E. The territory was re-conquered by Jayavarman I in the mid- to late-7th century, but again it ap-pears that it was necessary for Jayavarman II to reconquer the area in the 8th century (Wolters 1973).

Vickery (1998, 73) feels that, during the 5th and 6th centuries C.E., chiefs or perhaps royal individuals erected a number of inscriptions in the border areas of modern Thailand, Cambodia, and Laos. He calls these individuals "the Dangrek chieftains" in reference to the mountain chain that separates these countries. Mentioned in these inscriptions is a Prince Citrasena, prob-ably the same Citrasena mentioned by the Chinese in the *Sui Shu*. It is also likely that this individual is known as Citrasena-Mahendravarman. The inscriptions have traditionally been seen as evidence that the early kings of Chenla descended from the border areas of Cambodia and overthrew the Funan polity. Vickery (1998, 79) prefers to interpret the evidence in the reverse—that the Chenla princes mentioned in the inscriptions actually pushed northward and that they were making attempts to establish authority over a wider area. Whether this attempt was successful or not is unclear, but Vickery believes that the evidence should be interpreted as military expeditions rather than the establishment of a wider empire. That Chenla was engaged in expanding its area of control seems to be confirmed by the mention in Chinese histories. Certain territories which sent missions to China (circa 638 C.E.) reported aggression by Chenla in the mid-7th century (Wolters 1974). The locations of the polities mentioned are unknown, but Coedès speculated that they were in the Mun River basin (see ref. to Coedès in Wolters 1974, 374).

Wolters focuses his attention on northwestern Cambodia in search of the territories mentioned by the Chinese. One such territory is transcribed as Wu-ling, a corruption of Miu-liang or Malyang, a place name first appearing in the epigraphy in 893 C.E. A later inscription from the 11th century places Malyang in the south of Battambang Province. Another polity mentioned is Fu-na or Vanapura, which Wolters (1974, 361) feels was in western Cambodia, south of the Dangrek mountains near the Chup Smach Chom Tup passes. Also mentioned by the Chinese are *Chia-cha* (Gajapura) and *Seng-kao* (Sangko), but the location of these is purely speculative.

Wolters (1974, 370) asserts that the people of these principalities were ethnically Khmer based on the fact that Khmer language inscriptions dating to the first half of the 6th and 7th centuries have been found in the territories they occupied. It is also apparent that the northwest was not isolated politically or economically. There is evidence for the absorption of Indian culture in the names of rulers and cities, as well as in the art. It seems that these polities were able to assert their independence after the military incursions of Bhavavarman I and Citrasena-Mahendravarman and were able to send embassies to the Chinese court prior to their final subjugation by Jayavarman I, which probably had occurred by the middle or end of the 6th century C.E. (Wolters 1974, 373).

During the 7th century, China received sixty-nine different diplomatic missions from twenty-four different territories in Southeast Asia (Brown 1996, 16). It appears that during the 8th century considerably fewer missions were sent to China. Smith and Watson (1979) suggest that this may suggest an absorption of the smaller polities by expanding powers. Alternatively, the necessity of being recognized by the Chinese court may not have been as important in the 8th century. This explanation seems unlikely as Champa and Chenla both continued to send missions. The purpose of these missions is unclear, but economic gain through the establishment of trade relations is certainly one likely benefit. Others include prestige at being recognized as a viable political entity by the Chinese emperor (Brown 1996, 17). Wolters (1974) is of the opinion that Cambodia, in the 7th century, comprised a number of semiautonomous chieftainships whose rulers did not necessarily feel themselves to be a part of a larger, supralocal political entity. The enduring domination of a large territory was only accomplished under Jayavarman I.

Brown (1996, 11) has illustrated the difficulty in drawing definite boundaries between the polities of the 7th and 8th century. This is illustrated by the appearance of *cakras* (wheels of law), symbols mostly associated with the Dvaravati kingdoms of central Thailand, in areas peripheral to Dvaravati proper. This symbolism is found in the Malay Peninsula and on the Khorat Plateau, and *sema* stones (boundary markers) are found throughout the Khorat Plateau and into present-day Cambodia. These symbols clearly indicate that drawing distinct boundaries around these early polities is impossible. That the area west of the Dangrek mountains was under Khmer control, at least temporarily, is indubitable. Inscriptions left by Mahendravarman on the Khorat Plateau (Jacques 1989) and later Chenla rulers (Coedès 1924b) are clear testimony to this fact.

EARLY POLITICAL COMPLEXITY IN CAMBODIA: RISE OF ANGKOR

The period during which Jayavarman II came to power is difficult to interpret as there are few records that give insight into the structure of the politics and social world of late Chenla. It has been suggested that there was political disintegration after the death of Jayavarman I, but it is very difficult to confirm this based on the epigraphic evidence. Vickery (1998, 390) argues that the lack of evidence for the reemergence of smaller polities, and the apparent florescence of art and architecture at the time, suggest stability rather than disintegration. The division suggested by the Chinese historians may reflect the rise of a new center of power, Sambhupura, perhaps near the confluence of the Mekong and the Kong, San, and Srepok rivers. This polity was, apparently, able to assert its authority over some of eastern Cambodia, although it appears they were not related to the rulers of Chenla. The level of political complexity attained by Sambhupura is not clear but that it held some autonomy seems indubitable (Vickery 1998).

Toward the end of the Chenla period, with the accession of Jayavarman II, the geographical concentrations of the inscriptions seem to indicate a shift northward, to the area where Angkor was to flourish (Vickery 1998, 315). This northward shift is curious as the area is not as well-suited to rice

agriculture as are the southern provinces. There were other, contemporaneous developments in northern Cambodia including the rise in power of the
Sambhupura polity. The city was located near Sambor on the Mekong, and
it is presumed that its territory encompassed the northeastern territories of
Cambodia, rich in forest products and ores (Vickery 1998, 316). According
to Vickery (1998, 317), 8th-century records indicate that there may have
been a drive to populate the north and northwestern portions of Cambodia, specifically Battambang, Banteay Meanchey, and Siem Reap Province.

An 11th century inscription called the Sdok Kak Thom has, in the past,
been interpreted to say that Jayavarman II returned from Java after having
been kidnapped during a Javanese raid on Cambodia (Coedès 1964a).
Scholarly opinion now seems to indicate that the original interpretation of
Java may be misleading (Jacques 1986; Vickery 1998). The current opinion
seems to be that Java may, in fact, refer to Champa, often referred to as
"chvea," with whom the Khmer were battling during the period in question
(Vickery 1998, 387). It is possible to infer that Jayavarman II's political ca-
reer began in southern Cambodia, possibly with a base at Banteay Prei
Nokor (Coedès 1968). According to the traditional interpretation of the period, there appears, as has been noted, to have been a movement northward
to the area around Angkor, where he established a capital called Hariharalaya (Roluos). Vickery (1998, 405) has suggested this move may have been
prompted by movements of the Cham capital. In the mid-8th century the
Cham capital was moved southward to Panduranga (near Nha Trang)
where it stayed until the 870s. The Khmer capital was apparently moved
again to a place called Amarendrapura, possibly located in the northwest of
Cambodia (Vickery 1998, 394). Finally Jayavarman II is thought to have occupied the Kulen mountains north of the Angkor area, establishing a capital called Mahendraparavata.

This interpretation has been revised by Jacques (1972a, 1990), who feels
that Jayavarman first established himself at a city called Indrapura (possibly
Banteay Prei Nokor) and from there expanded his influence over Vyadhapura (possibly near Prey Veng), Sambhupura, Wat Phu (Laos), Aninditapura (possibly in the Angkor region), eventually establishing a capital at
Hariharalaya near Angkor. Jacques (1990) feels that Jayavarman II then expanded his realm and established Amarendrapura as the capital (possibly
in Battambang Province) but eventually abandoned this city and founded
Mahendraparavata.

We know, from later inscriptions, that Jayavarman II proclaimed himself
Cakravartin atop Mount Mahendra in the Kulen mountains in 802 C.E.
(Wolters 1973). The title and associated ceremony has been given great
weight and is often used to mark the birth of the state in Cambodia. The
concept of *kamraten jagat ta raja,* or *devaraja* in the Sanskrit, is sometimes
taken to mean that the kings became living gods (Briggs 1951; Giteau 1957;

Coedès 1964a; 1968; Hagesteijn 1987). Jacques (1985) has surmised that the concept was more Khmer than Indian in that the *kamraten jagat ta raja* was a protective indigenous god who was summoned to ensure the safety of the realm. The *kamraten jagat ta raja* was a separate entity from the king and "lived on" after his death (Coedès and Dupont 1943–1946, 110). *Kamraten jagat* seems to be an innovation of Jayavarman II, but the title may have its roots in the title of *vrah kamraten añ*, which was used as an honorific for gods and kings in the 7th and 8th centuries (Vickery 1998, 424). After this ceremony Jayavarman II moved his capital back to Hariharalaya not far from where Angkor was to be established.

It is unclear when Jayavarman II died, but it is evident that the Khmer were a force to be reckoned with in the later years of his reign. In 838 C.E. the Cham requested assistance from the Chinese to resist an attack by the Khmer. If Jayavarman were alive at this time, it probably meant that he controlled the northern reaches of Cambodia, which gave him access to coastal Vietnam via the mountain passes (Wolters 1973:29). If Jayavarman were dead by this date, it illustrates that he had succeeded in building a strong and stable realm encompassing the greater part of Cambodia that enabled his successor, a mere child, to undertake raids on foreign dominions. Jayavarman II's consolidation of power and the elimination of other, seemingly independent *-pura*, set the stage for further centralization in the Angkor period. It seems that there was an overhaul of the political system under Jayavarman II in that the title *poñ* is finally eliminated and *mratañ* nearly so, to be replaced by *mraten klon*, designating the heads of "provincial" *-pura* (Vickery 1998, 407).

Political Organization

According to Vickery (1998, 28), political power and the consolidation of territory was on the increase during the 8th century, evidenced in the size and opulence of royal religious foundations. Jayavarman II's base was probably Vyadhapura (possibly Banteay Prei Nokor) in Kompong Cham Province. From this base he widened his control, first over Bhavapura, in Kompong Thom, and then over Sambhupura. After Battambang was subdued he moved to Siem Reap (Vickery 1998, 29). "Cambodia, in its Chenla and Angkor periods, appears as the prototypical inland agrarian state, an example of the Asiatic Mode of Production in a very nearly pure form" (Vickery 1998, 257).

Examining the transition from the Chenla to the Angkor period, which begins circa 802 C.E., is difficult as there is a lack of reliable primary sources. There is only one inscription which dates from the end of the 8th century to the late 9th century, a period of momentous change in Cambodia (Vickery 1996, 15). This peculiarity has led some to suggest a period of political instability (Coedès 1968). Vickery posits that the continued development of artistic and architectural styles is evidence of a stable political climate. According to Vickery, the political climate may have been stable and consolidated to such an extent that edicts proclaiming domination and wealth were unnecessary.

It is interesting to note that the first evidence for recognition of a supraterritorial entity in Cambodia appears in 868 C.E. The country is referred to as "kamvudesa" in both Khmer and Sanskrit (Vickery 1996).

There may have been a shift in the social status of *kñum*, individuals assigned to undertake manual labor at religious foundations, from the 9th century onward (Vickery 1998). During the preceding Chenla period the social status of these individuals is unclear, but during the Angkor period it appears that they come to be regarded more as slaves.

Royal marriage patterns seem to change in the 9th century. Prior to this period high-ranking females generally married lower-ranking males. Jayavarman, however, took all his wives from low-ranking families, which Vickery (1998, 408) suggests may represent a greater centralization of power.

CONCLUSION

It is clear that much research remains to be undertaken if we are to begin to understand ancient Cambodia and the developments that led to the rise of the complex polity at Angkor. What we know derives heavily from epigraphic and historical sources, which may have been embellished and often do not inform us of everyday events. It falls to archaeologists to fill in the picture of events that led to the state in Cambodia.

It is likely that these events began long before the establishment of Funan. While this polity appears to have prospered and may have been responsible for large engineering works such as canals, it is unlikely to have been anything more than a complex chiefdom. It is probable that Funan held no permanent control over its dominion and is likely to have relied heavily on treaties and agreements.

The Chenla polity appears to represent a progression in political complexity. Although probably best characterized as a polity with flexible borders, along the lines of a *mandala*, Chenla seems to have been a more centralized political unit than that of its predecessor. A dynastic tradition was established and power centralized, for most of the time, at Isanapura. Although difficult to confirm, it appears as though the Chenla polity was able to expand its sphere of influence in a more lasting way than was Funan. Due to a lack of evidence, it is impossible to accurately interpret the political organization of Chenla and whether it possessed the attributes of a true state-level polity. Judging from the data available from the later polity of Angkor, it is likely that Chenla was not a true state. There is little doubt that it was a highly complex political entity that held sway over a substantial geographic area. As we have seen, this is a trend which continued into the Angkorian period. The level of complexity from the 9th century onward is apparent in the ever more grandiose religious monuments and water control projects on the Angkor Plain.

6

Champa

The Cham are an ethnically distinct population found throughout modern Vietnam and Cambodia. The Cham speak a language that belongs to the Austronesian language group. The majority of Austronesian languages are found in island Southeast Asia and throughout the Pacific. The Cham are in this way unique, and their ability to survive in Southeast Asia is due in part to their early political and economic strength. Champa refers to a protohistoric kingdom, founded by at least the 4th century, along the coast of Vietnam. It is known largely from Chinese records and sparse inscriptions and, more recently, archaeological evidence. Champa is best thought of not as a unified polity but as a collection of smaller domains that shared linguistic and cultural traditions. Taylor (1992, 153) describes Champa as "an archipelagically-defined cultural political space." Each river valley may have defined the political domain of a different monarch or chief, with the capital located at the mouth of the river and villages stretching upriver. The coastal monarch's control of these villages in the hinterland may have rested on his ability to form alliances (Hall 1992, 253–54). The kingdom of Champa stretched along the coast of Vietnam from Hoanh Son in the north to the vicinity of present-day Ho Chi Minh City. It is likely that the influence of this primarily coastal polity was felt far inland and probably encompassed various ethnic groups who spoke languages related to Cham, such as the Jörai, Cru, Edê, and Raglai peoples, as well as the Austroasiatic groups, the Ma, Sré, and Stieng (Dharma 2001).

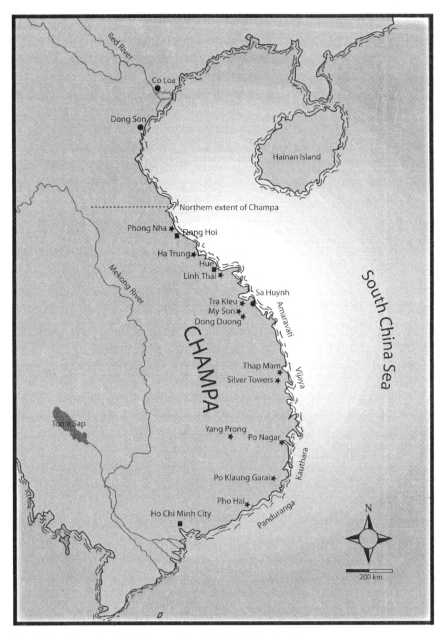

Map 6.1.   Map showing Champa sites (indicated by stars).

ORIGINS

The roots of Champa are probably to be found in the Sa Huynh culture. Sa Huynh is a site in Quang Ngai Province that has rendered a number of clay jars containing human remains, bronze and iron implements, and semi-precious stone jewelry (Parmentier 1924). Since the discovery of the first jar burial sites, others have been found and it is now possible to elucidate a developmental sequence of this culture's mortuary tradition. In the mid-second millennium, Sa Huynh people interred their dead in painted jars with stone tools. Near the end of the second millennium B.C.E., the style of painting changes and bronze tools begin to appear. By the beginning of the first millennium C.E., iron and glass began to accompany the carnelian and agate beads in Sa Huynh burials (Ngo Si Hong 1991). Jar burial sites related to the Sa Huynh culture have been unearthed all along the central coast of Vietnam.

One of the more recognizable Sa Huynh artifacts are the two-headed animal and globular earrings. This style has been found at sites as far away as Thailand, the Philippines, and the Indonesian archipelago (Fox 1970; Majid 1982; Ha Van Tan 1986b; Glover 1989). Some of the Sa Huynh burials include glass, carnelian, and agate beads indicating involvement in an overseas trade network with India. Chinese contact is confirmed with the presence of coins in Sa Huynh burials that date to 9–23 C.E. Weapons and other artifacts of Han origin have also been found (Southworth 2004, 212).

EARLY POLITICAL COMPLEXITY IN VIETNAM: LINYI

The Chinese historical record indicates that there was a rebellion by people who spoke an Austronesian language to the south of the Je Nan commandery (present day Hué). The revolt resulted in the foundation of a polity the Chinese called Linyi (Dharma 2001). Over time, the polity grew more powerful, extending northward to Hoanh Son and southward as well, apparently absorbing settlements that had embraced the Hindu religion. The area north of Linyi was inhabited by proto-Vietnamese speakers who managed to stave off successive attempts by Linyi to conquer them in the 4th, 5th, and 6th centuries C.E. (Dharma 2001). Linyi for all its apparent pluck still paid tribute to the Chinese emperor, although it did try to free itself from this obligation on a number of occasions.

It is unclear whether the people of Linyi and Champa were one in the same. Certainly by the 4th century it seems the people of Linyi were speaking Cham (Coedès 1939). The territory encompassed by both did eventually come to be called Champa. Vickery, however, feels that it is likely that the people of Linyi were originally Mon-Khmer speakers based on the use of the term *Fan* to describe local leaders in Chinese accounts. This is the same term used for leaders in Funan, which was also likely to be a Mon-Khmer population. These Mon-Khmer speakers may eventually have merged with the inhabitants of what is now northern Vietnam (Vickery 2005, 17).

It appears likely that the polity of Linyi had its genesis in rebellion. The area known by the Chinese as Xianglin comprised part of the Han dynasty's Rinan commandery, which stretched as far south as the Hai Van Pass. The imposition of a rigorous tax regime during the 2nd century C.E. may have led to widespread rebellion in Xianglin and the formation of Linyi. By 248 C.E., Linyi felt strong enough to send a force north to attack Rinan and the Chinese provinces Jiuzhen and Jiaozhi (Southworth 2001).

It is very difficult to determine, based on the evidence available, which territories are referred to when Linyi and Champa are mentioned in the Chinese annals or even in the epigraphy of central Vietnam. Some believe Linyi was not located in present-day Vietnam. Hoshino (1999, 61) feels that it was more likely to be found in southern Laos or northeastern Cambodia, interpreting the *Sui Shu* to mean Linyi was located near the present site of Wat Phu on the Mekong River, rather than near central Vietnam. Southworth (2001, 335) believes that the confusion stems from a poor understanding of the separate lineages that ruled the territories to the south of the Chinese commanderies. During the 5th and 6th centuries it is possible to identify some individual rulers, such as Gangaraja, who ruled the area of the Thu Bon Valley, and Fan Yangmai, identified with Linyi and Bhadravarman and who may have held domain over both territories. It is not until the 6th century that we can say the territories south of the Chinese were largely brought under the control of one man, Rudravarman. Even so, as Southworth (2001, 241) notes, it is unsure how far the name of Champa can be extended outside the Thu Bon Valley (in which My Son is located) up until the 8th century C.E. This tends to lend support to the model of political organization suggested by Hall (1992, 253–54), in which individual polities had sovereignty over a single river mouth and valley. The extent of any monarch's power beyond this realm would likely have been dependent upon his ability to form alliance networks or upon the economic success of the polity. This supposition is further supported by Chinese references to ten kingdoms located about one hundred kilometers south of Linyi along the coast of Vietnam. This reference also would seem to indicate that Linyi was located in the vicinity of the Thu Bon Valley (Southworth 2004).

The earliest known Sanskrit inscription from Southeast Asia is eponymously named Vo Canh. The inscription appears to be written by a descendant of one Sri Mara and proclaims that his wealth should be used for the happiness and use of all. Who Sri Mara was remains a mystery, but he has been identified with the founder of Linyi (Maspero 1928). Coedès (1940) preferred to identify Sri Mara with Fan Shi-man of Funan (circa 230 C.E.). This view is indirectly supported by Filliozat (1968) and Jacques (1969, 123).

The Vo Canh inscription was originally thought to date from the 3rd century C.E. based on paleographic comparisons with inscriptions found in southern India (Bergaigne 1888; Bhattacharya 1961, 223–24). Others felt that the style was more similar to northern Indian styles and should be dated to the 4th or 5th century C.E. (Sircar 1939, 55; Gaspardone 1953, 479–81). A heated debate over the origin of the inscription has raged for over a century (Buhler 1886; Maspero 1928; Sastri 1936). As Southworth (2001, 202) notes, "despite this protracted debate there remains little reason to doubt the original dating and palaeographic arguments of Bergaigne."

Finot (1902) believed that the Vo Canh inscription was erected by rulers or the elite of the Champa polity and that its presence indicates a unified Cham kingdom around Nha Trang. Southworth (2001, 213) notes that no inscription up to the 5th century, including Vo Canh, mentions Champa or any unified regional polity.

Our understanding of Champa is clarified by the records left to us by the Chinese military expedition to the area in 605 C.E. The Cham capital was located at Trà Kiêu, not far from the famous Cham temple site of My Son, a Hindu center since the 4th century (Dharma 2001). Based on present evidence it appears that the influence of India spread northward from the southern coast (Boisselier 2001).

The geographic location of Vietnam has meant that it has had continuous contact and influence from its northern neighbor, China. As early as 221 B.C.E. the Chinese have sought to expand their territory and subjugate what is now Vietnam. Qin Shi Huangdi, the emperor or China at this time, was the first to exert a strong influence in northern Vietnam with his conquest of southern China and northern Vietnam. The collapse of the Qin state led to the independence of the former Chinese commandery, or military province, of Nan Hai. The Chinese eventually regained control of Nan Hai in 111 B.C.E. with the conquest of the area by the Han empire, which established three commanderies—Jiaozhi, Jiuzhen, and Rinan—reaching as far south as Dong Hoi. It is likely that these territories were left to their own devices and were incorporated in China only in name. The area regained complete autonomy between 9 and 23 C.E. but was brought under Chinese control, except for some rebellions which were thoroughly quashed by the Chinese. Rebellions in these commanderies were to become common, occurring roughly every half century from 43 C.E. to 192 C.E. The last of these rebellions had lasting repercussions and led to the creation of a polity known to the Chinese as Linyi. It is likely that Linyi was located in the former Han commandery of Xianglin. The survival of this polity can be attributed, in part, to the collapse of the Han dynasty in 220 C.E. China was

divided between three competing empires. The southernmost of these was
the Wu, situated in the Yangtze River valley. The Wu court received embassies intended to establish trade relations from Linyi, Funan, and another
unidentified polity known as Tangming. The relationship between Linyi
and the Wu was not always friendly, and in 248 C.E. the polity was em-
boldened to raid Wu commanderies in northern Vietnam. Later Linyi con-
spired with Funan sending embassies to the Jin court in central China. Linyi
and Funanese raids on Wu territory continued until the collapse of the Wu
and the accession of the Jin. The Jin emperor recognized Linyi as an independent polity and thus opened a fruitful trade relationship with Linyi in
late third century C.E. Records of the Jin empire provide us with a glimpse
of the political geography of Southeast Asia at this time. No less than thirty
"kingdoms" located to the south of China sent embassies to the Jin court at
this time. This seems to indicate the existence of a complicated network of
polities in Vietnam and Cambodia, in which Linyi and Funan were perhaps
the predominant players. Another important kingdom was Xitu, the southern neighbor of Linyi. Chinese histories record that Xitu had ten smaller
kingdoms as dependencies. The fact that so many polities were able to send
independent embassies to the Chinese court indicates that neither Linyi,
Xitu, or Funan held hegemony in the region.

The situation seems to have changed during the fourth century as Linyi
began to attack its Jin trading partner—a policy which led to the polity's de-
feat in 420 C.E. and again in 446 C.E. at the hands of Chinese armies. The
latter invasion saw the complete subjugation of Linyi with the sacking of its
two principal centers.

The Chinese invasion of Linyi in 446 C.E. resulted in a shift of power to
the area of the Thu Bon Valley in Quang Nam. The decline of Linyi as a trading center coincided with a number of other events, including an increase
in trade between India, Sri Lanka, and China and the ascension of
Guangzhou as the major trading port of southern China. The area of Thu
Bon was geographically well situated as a port of call due to the nature of
the trade winds (Southworth 2004). The Chinese chronicles continued to
refer to this part of the world as Linyi.

Although the Thu Bon Valley became an important center at this time, we
know little of its history. During the late 6th century we see the first reference to Champadesha in an inscription at the temple complex of My Son. It
is likely that this polity was also referred to as Linyi by the Chinese, as we
have a record of the Sui emperor sending armies against Linyi and capturing two citadels, one of which is very likely to have been located at Trà Kiêu
in Quang Nam.

The polity centered on the Thu Bon Valley came to prominence by the
seventh century C.E., but we have little detailed information regarding Linyi
at this time. The glimpses we get are usually revealed in Chinese histories or
inscriptions. We do know that Linyi prospered during the seventh and

eighth centuries C.E. from trade with the Tang empire, and dozens of trade embassies were sent to the Chinese court from 650 to 750 C.E. (Southworth 2004). After the mid-eighth century the prosperity of Champa began to decline due to events far to the north. Rebels in northern China captured the economic centers of Chang'an and Luoyang, effectively ending trade with the south of China. This was compounded by the sack of Guangzhou at the same time by Persian sailors. This epoch marks the end of the use of the name Linyi in Chinese records. After the mid-eighth century the name "Huanwang" is used to describe this polity that likely had its capital in Quang Nam. The polity of Huanwang appears to have been one of considerable import as we have evidence that its armies attacked China in the late eighth century C.E. We have inscriptional evidence from 774 and 787 C.E., indicating that invaders attacked the southern Vietnamese coast, destroying Hindu temples at Phan Rang and Nha Trang. These shrines were rebuilt in 799 and 784 C.E. respectively by kings from Panduranga and Kauthara. The existence of these southern kingdoms suggests that the polity of Champa was not unified under one king. The kingdoms of Champa, nevertheless, grew rich from international trade.

ENVIRONMENT

Champa occupied what may be described as southern and central Vietnam, comprising coastal plains, deltas, and the Truong Son Mountains, which run the length of most of modern Vietnam. The majority of the country comprises mountainous terrain reaching one thousand meters, occasionally interrupted by passes. The geography is important to an understanding of the development of the Cham polity, as the mountains, in places, reach the sea. This, naturally, inhibits communication and trade in a north-south direction. The mountains also served to isolate the Cham from their neighbors to the west.

The northern portion of Vietnam has a tropical climate, whereas south of the Hai Van Pass, in the middle of the country, the climate is subtropical. The coastal areas experience two "seasons." The summer sees high temperatures, eased by monsoon rains in August and September. This is followed by a "winter," which is cool and dry.

All of the rivers in Vietnam flow either east or west, into the South China Sea or the Mekong River system. The mouths of the largest rivers in Vietnam flowing to the coast are home to millions of inhabitants and have been occupied since antiquity. The Mekong also empties into the South China Sea via a vast delta in the far south of Vietnam. Although not as large as the Mekong, the rivers of coastal Vietnam are more than capable of supporting a large human population on the fertile alluvial, fresh water supply, and the rich fishing grounds at their mouths.

PEOPLE

That the Cham speak an Austronesian language is beyond dispute, but what is far from clear is when these people arrived in central Vietnam. There is some indication that the presence of Chamic peoples may stretch into the remote past. Sa Huynh is an important archaeological site in central Vietnam. The sand dunes there have surrendered burial jars that bear a resemblance to burial traditions in western Borneo, Sarawak, and the Philippines (Harrisson 1968; Fox 1970). The jars at Sa Huynh were interred around 1000 B.C.E. or earlier, and other sites seem to indicate that the tradition continued elsewhere to at least 500 B.C.E. (Ngo Si Hong 1991).

The material culture, including bicephalous animal and globular ear ornaments, from the Sa Huynh culture sites is also found in the Philippines and on Sarawak (Ha Van Tan 1977; Fox 1979; Majid 1982). While the people of Sa Huynh probably made these artifacts, they were also engaged in a trade network that stretched as far as India, as evidenced by the presence of semiprecious stones and glass beads. These finds, dating to the mid- to late-first millennium B.C.E., represent the earliest trade between the subcontinent and Southeast Asia (Southworth 2001). The Sa Huynh culture sites occupy the same area that was to be home to the Champa polities, and there have been attempts to link the two. Several locations have been suggested as "interface-sites," based on ceramic similarities between Champa period settlements and Sa Huynh occupations and the presence of Sa Huynh material beneath Champa settlements (Ngo Si Hong and Thinh 1991; Ngo Si Hong et al. 1991). Although there is no absolute evidence for a transition, it is likely that Sa Huynh represents a mainland extension of the Austronesian language family, and is a probable precursor of the Cham culture (Southworth 2001, 98). It may be argued that the settlements at Sa Huynh represent the first landfall of Cham speakers on the mainland (Bellwood 1993, 51). From whence these people came is a mystery but it is likely that their origins may be found in insular Southeast Asia.

It is likely that the Cham language was used colloquially while Sanskrit was employed for important religious edicts and foundation inscriptions. Southworth (2001, 224) has suggested that Cham, written in scripts derived from southern India, was used for "a wide range of documentary, religious and literary purposes."

RELIGION

The Dong Yen Chau inscription from central Vietnam testifies to the existence of indigenous religious beliefs among the Cham. This inscription, written in the Cham language, probably dates to the late 5th or early 6th centuries (Lombard 1987). The evidence, both monumental and paleographic, suggests that Hinduism was the predominant religious system.

The most significant religion in early Champa appears to have been Saivism. Siva was worshipped in the form of a linga. The Cham king Bhadravarman installed linga in his kingdom at the end of the 4th or beginning of the 5th century (Bagchi 1930).

There can be little doubt that Buddhism played a central role in Linyi/Champa from a very early date. The invasion of Linyi in 605 C.E. yielded a booty of gold tablets and Buddhist texts written in the Austronesian language (Wang Gungwu 1958, 64). Mahayana Buddhism, brought by monks who stopped in Cham ports whilst traveling between India and China, appears to have flourished in Champa after the 8th century. The temples at Dông Duong are a testament to the presence of the religion.

The major Hindu temple complex was located at My Son. These were usually dedicated to Siva. Temples erected by the Cham outside My Son in the mid-seventh century C.E. are more often Vaishnuite.

SOCIAL AND POLITICAL ORGANIZATION

The Vo Canh inscription suggests that the societies of central Vietnam in the 3rd century C.E. were matrilineal (Southworth 2001, 204). Southworth notes that modern Austronesian groups in Vietnam are similarly structured, which demonstrates the strength of the indigenous beliefs in a community that had adopted the trappings of Indian culture. The peak of Champa's glory came from the 8th century when it covered the largest geographical area of its history. The polity appears to have been divided into five regions or principalities, Indrapura, Maravati, Vijaya, Kauthara, and Panduranga (Dharma 2001).

SETTLEMENT PATTERN

It has been suggested that each river valley represented a distinct political domain (Hall 1992). At the mouth of each river a market/trade center served as a clearing-point for goods collected from the interior. A string of villages along the river were connected politically to the market/trade center and acted as collection points for goods collected in the hinterlands. Southworth (2001) notes that this pattern is similar to the theoretical model proposed by Bronson (1977) in which a polity develops from settlements based at river mouths. Commercial interaction between the coastal settlements binds the polity, and it extends itself into the hinterland primarily through commercial contact up each respective river valley. This premise is supported by the fact that all of the early Sa Huynh artifacts have been discovered near large rivers (Ho Xuan Tinh 1993, 85). An understanding of the settlement pattern in Champa is hampered by the paucity of research that has been undertaken. While we know the dimensions of some sites such as My Son and Dông Duong, others are as yet undiscovered or unresearched. Wheatley is of the opinion that, during the early centuries of the last millennium, the settlements of Champa probably resembled a "matrix of chieftainships integrated into a continually changing pattern of chiefdoms" (Wheatley 1983, 397). The majority of Cham sites are found in the Thu Bon Valley in Quang Nam Province, central Vietnam.

According to the *Shuijing Shu*, a Chinese history compiled by Li Daoyuan in the early 6th century C.E., the Chinese carried out an invasion of Linyi in 446 C.E. One of the fortified towns mentioned was Qusu at the northern edge of Linyi's territory. This city was surrounded by a nine-meter-high brick wall that was over two kilometers in circumference (Pelliot 1904). It is likely that Qusu was located on the Gianh River near modern Ba Don in Quang Binh. Qusu was probably located about two hundred kilometers by road from the eponymously-named Linyi, the capital of the polity which was probably located near the modern city of Hué (Aurousseau 1914, 12; Stein 1947, 27, 71, 76). The site of Long Tho, south of the Huong River (near Hué), is a likely location for the ancient capital (Parmentier 1909, 512; Southworth 2001, 274).

The capital, as described by the Chinese chroniclers, moved after its destruction and, in 605 C.E., is likely to have been located in the Thu Bon Valley (Southworth 2001, 275). The information derived from the Chinese sources is important for our understanding of the settlement pattern of Linyi/Champa. Rather than representing a movement of one political center as the Chinese records imply, it is more likely that "they should be considered not as a sequence of 'capitals', each replacing the former, but rather as a series of essentially co-existing and autonomous urban centres, each based on a strategic river system, and each competing with each other for economic advantage and political supremacy" (Southworth 2001, 275).

INTERNATIONAL RELATIONS

The empire was surrounded by Funan to the west, the Viet to the north, and the Chinese, further north still. Champa, as we have seen, paid regular, if begrudging, tribute to the Chinese from an early date. Its relations with the Viet were strained, as the Cham tried on several occasions to expand their territory northward, only to be rebuffed. The Khmer were originally friendly toward the Cham, but this relationship soured after the 9th century and the neighbors became firm enemies. Another source of annoyance for the

Cham were the Malay, who plundered southern Cham settlements near the end of the eighth century. Gradually the Malay and Cham began to engage in commerce and the aggressive nature of the relationship faded (Dharma 2001).

The Cham relationship with the Chinese empire was tumultuous, but there is little doubt that the Cham had regular contacts with the Chinese, at least in the south, from the 1st century B.C.E. Chinese influence in northern Vietnam can be dated as far back as 185 B.C.E. when Ou Lou (Au Lac) became a vassal territory of Nan Yue (modern Guangdong). Nan Yue was eventually subsumed by the Han empire, which took further interest in the southern lands, establishing three "commanderies" in what is now Vietnam. The Han engaged in international trade, and the commanderies in Vietnam seem to have been entrepôts in this trade. It is likely that a trade mission of Emperor Marcus Aurelius stopped in central Vietnam on its way to the Han court in 166 C.E. (Ishizawa 1995, 12). After the fall of the Han dynasty, the former empire was divided between three kingdoms—the Shu, Wei, and Wu. The latter of these assumed control of the former commanderies in northern Vietnam (Pelliot 1903b, 251). Sometime around 230 C.E. the Wu court sent embassies to Linyi, which, in turn, sent a tribute mission.

The good fortune of the Wu court was not to last long. In 263 C.E., the deadlock between the three kingdoms was broken and Wei and Shu were combined as the Jin dynasty. The Wu were left to face the combined force to the north. The southernmost commanderies took the opportunity to throw off the Wu yoke. These rebellious commanderies, Linyi and Funan sent missions to the Jin court in 268 C.E. (Pelliot 1903b, 252). The action came to naught as the Wu eventually regained control of its territories, but Linyi remained recalcitrant. The Chinese histories record raids on its territories in the decade after 271 C.E. by Fan Xiong, a king of Linyi (Xuanling 578–648, 3 and 97; Maspero 1928, 53–55).

It appears that Linyi and Funan shared good relations during the late 3rd century, as Chinese chroniclers record that they assisted one another and both refused to be absorbed by the Jin empire (Xuanling 578–648, 57; Pelliot 1903b, 255). Embassies from both Funan and Linyi are recorded among the twenty-one missions from polities around East and Southeast Asia sent to the Jin court in the late 3rd century (Xuanling 578–648, 3 and 10; Pelliot 1903b, 252). This period also seems to have been a prosperous one as trade between Funan and Linyi flourished. From the beginning of the 4th century this economic relationship began to decline, possibly as a result of the high tariffs imposed by the governors of the Chinese commanderies who controlled the overland trade routes (Wang Gungwu 1958, 296; Southworth 2001). Compounding the problem was the disintegration of the Jin empire. So weakened were the Chinese that, by 346 C.E., Linyi felt able to invade their commanderies in northern Vietnam, demanding that the border between China and Linyi be established at the Hoanh Son massif (Southworth 2001, 296). These incursions resulted in retaliatory raids by Chinese armies, which resulted in tribute missions being dispatched by Linyi to the Jin court in 372, 373–374, and 377 C.E. (*Jin shu* 9 and 97; Maspero 1928, 61).

The peace did not last, as Linyi again attacked the southern commanderies in 405 C.E. The Chinese responded by attacking Linyi coastal settlements in 407 C.E., and after further aggression by Linyi the Chinese definitively crushed the Linyi navy in 420 C.E. (Southworth 2001, 300). This naval victory was among the last for the Jin emperors, as the Southern Song dynasty was established in the same year. The new emperor received a Linyi mission at his court the following year. Although Linyi was subordinated and continued to send embassies to the Chinese court over the next twenty years, it continued raiding the southern Chinese commanderies (Southworth 2001, 301). The Chinese continued to punish Linyi with military action.

Relations with Funan seem to have soured during the 5th century C.E., as Funan requested military assistance in 484 C.E. from the Qi who had replaced the Song dynasty in ruling China. Despite the military setbacks during the early part of the century and the disputes with Funan, the 5th century was one of prosperity in central Vietnam. The trade between India and China was burgeoning, which brought traders to the coastal areas of Vietnam, especially to the Cham settlements of the Thu Bon Valley (Southworth 2001, 302). Competition over this trade may have led to the disputes between Funan and Linyi.

SITES

Coastal Vietnam is dotted with the remnants of Cham civilization. These brick ruins give us insight into the grandeur of the Cham empire. The earliest structures date to the late 4th century, and the Cham continued to erect brick sanctuaries until the 15th century.

Bhadravarman I is known primarily from inscriptions in Sanskrit and the remains of a temple foundation at My Son, erected during the late 4th century. The shrine was dedicated to Siva Bhadreshvara and housed a linga. Destroyed by fire it was reconstructed in the early 7th century by Sambhuvarman (?–629 C.E.) who added a shrine to Lakshmi at My Son. Further temples were added by Vikrântavarman I (r. 653–? C.E.) and II (r. ?–731 C.E.) in the mid-7th to early 8th centuries. There appear to have been significant political changes during the mid-8th century. The Chinese record that a southern polity called Hu Wang existed. For a century from 758–859 C.E., northern Champa is not mentioned in Chinese chronicles (Boisselier

2001). Power seems to have been centered around Nha Trang, where the sanctuary of Po Nagar was erected by Prathivindravarman (r. mid-8th century). This sanctuary was destroyed by the Javanese in the late 8th century but restored by Satyavarman in 784 C.E. The Javanese were aggressively attacking, not only Champa, but the Malay peninsula as well. Although the military strikes were brief, the Javanese had a lasting effect on Cham culture, influencing the artistic styles and perhaps are responsible for the implantation of Mahayana Buddhism (Boisselier 2001, 35).

Later, the power shifted further south to Panduranga. Later still Harivarman (r. 802–c. 820 C.E.) founded sanctuaries at Senâpati Pâr and added temples at Po Nagar. The next king, Vikrântavarman III (r. mid-9th century) added further temples to Po Nagar and built sanctuaries at Mong Duc and at Hoa Lai. In the late 9th century the Cham embraced Mahayana Buddhism, erecting temples at Dông Duong and Rôn, as well as adding sanctuaries at My Son. The capital was established at Indrapura (present-day Quang Nam Province) in 875 C.E. In the years that followed, until 918 C.E., My Son was enhanced by Kings Jaya Simhavarman I (r. c.897–c.904 C.E.) and Bhadravarman II (r. 905–917 C.E.). At this juncture, King Indravarman III took power (r. 918–959 C.E.). He was followed by Jaya Indravarman I (r. 960–965 C.E.), who constructed a shrine at My Son and returned the capital of Champa to Indrapura. The reestablished capital was moved to Vijaya by the succeeding king, Harivarman (r. 989–999 C.E.). Jaya Parameshvaravarman I (r. 1044–1060 C.E.), who followed Harivarman, seems to have belonged to a different lineage and founded a new dynasty to rule Champa. He managed to subdue the people of Panduranga, who revolted and consecrated a linga at Po Klaung Garai and restored Po Nagar. The dynasty founded by Jaya Parameshvaravarman was short-lived, dying out after failed attacks on the Dai Viet to the north by King Rudravarman III (r. 1062–1074 C.E.). From 1074–1081, King Harivarman IV worked to have Simhapura and the temples of My Son restored. His successor, Jaya Indravarman II (r. 1086–1113 C.E.), founded shrines at My Son as did his successor of the same name. King Jaya Harivarman I (1147–1166 C.E.) returned from a foreign country to lead wars against the Khmers, Viet, and hill tribe people of the interior. He also founded shrines at My Son and Po Nagar. The Cham armies, under Jaya Indravarman IV (r. 1166–?), gained short-lived victories in Cambodia, taking Angkor in 1177. The Khmer had their revenge in 1181 retaking their capital and occupying Champa for nearly forty years. The Cham regained their independence only to weather Mongol occupation and constant war with the Viet and Khmer. Temples were founded during this time, such as the shrines erected at Po Klaung Garai and Yang Prong in the late 13th century. The Cham polity finally collapsed in 1471 with the capture of the capital Vijaya by the Viet.

The chronology of Cham sites has been studied since the early part of the last century (Parmentier 1918). Stern (1942) maintained that the inscriptions found with temples may well refer to a structure that was long ago destroyed and bore no resemblance to that which still stood. Instead he dated the structures based on the evolution of stylistic features. While widely used, there are still problems with Stern's technique as it assumes a cultural unity for Champa and does not account for localized traditions (Southworth 2001).

According to Majumdar (1944), the Cham temples were built in the Dravidian style, simple, yet beautiful, towers tapering to the top. Similar towers are known at Sivaite shrines dating to the 7th century C.E. in Tamil Nadu. Majumdar (1944) draws further parallels between the elongated style found at My Son and certain temples of Tamil Nadu, asserting the styles were contemporaneous. While the styles are similar, Majumdar (1944, 151–52) concedes that "the Chams did not blindly imitate the Indian proto-types and added new elements of their own" (c.f. Parmentier 1902).

My Son

My Son, in Quang Nam Province, comprises over seventy brick structures dedicated to Hindu deities, labeled A through N by French archaeologists (Stern 1942). The remains of the earliest shrines of Champa are to be found here in group E. Boisselier (2001, 33) states that the shrines in this group reflect a broad range of influences from Dvaravati, Indonesia, and south India, as well as Khmer. The latter influence is unsurprising given the putative links between the Khmer ruler of the time, Isanavarman I, and the ruler of the Cham (Boisselier 1956; 2001).

One of the most important inscriptions found at My Son is now lost. This 1.69-meter stele in Sanskrit commemorates the deeds of Bhadravarman ("protégé of radiance") and can be identified to the foundation of the Sivaite, Bhadresvara temple at My Son (Southworth 2001, 209). The inscription's primary subject is Siva, but it also mentions Brahma, Vishnu, and Siva's consort, Uma, and may be the earliest such record of these deities in Southeast Asia (Southworth 2001, 215). Based on paleography, the inscription is dated to the 5th century C.E. (Buhler 1886, Tafel VII, X–XI; Sircar 1942, 473, n. 4). One of the most important finds at My Son was a stele (Inscription number C72), inscribed on both sides and attributed to Bhadravarman. The stele, nearly two meters tall and over a meter wide, has disappeared. The Sanskrit text, recording the foundation of the Bhadresvara temple at My Son, is notable as it may be the earliest mention of Visnu, Brahma, and Uma in all of Southeast Asian epigraphy (Southworth 2001, 209, 215).

Dông Duong

An inscription from 875 C.E. indicates that a new dynasty was founded in present-day Quang Nam. The dynasty's founder was Indravarman II, and the capital, Indrapura, was named for him. The new dynasty established a complex of temples, dedicated to Mahayana Buddhism, at Dông Duong. Regrettably these structures were destroyed during the American war in Vietnam.

Trà Kiêu

One of the most important Cham sites is Trà Kiêu, located on a tributary of the Thu Bon river in central Vietnam. According to the archaeologists who worked at the site, it has roots in the Sa Huynh culture but developed its own identity and became a leading settlement of the Cham empire (Nguyen Chieu, Lam My Dung et al. 1991 in Southworth 2001). It is likely that the site had been occupied first at some point during the first or second century B.C.E. (Southworth 2001, 93).

Trà Kiêu has been posited as the capital of Linyi, which it may have been. There is some disagreement over when it may have been identified as such. A Chinese history, the *Shuijing Shu*, compiled in the early 6th century C.E., identified a capital in the vicinity of the Trà Kiêu and may have been at the time the book was written.

DECLINE

During the middle of the ninth century C.E., the Tang emperor attempted to stop trade goods from entering Yunnan and enriching the kingdom of Nan Zhao, which reciprocated by attacking the Red River Delta. The result was the disruption of the trade between northern Vietnam and the Indonesian archipelago and the Arab world. The center of trade moved further north to Guangzhou, which adversely affected the Cham. It is likely that the Cham "empire" survived on trade and that the revenue from these activities was necessary to maintain the complex network of political alliances between the varied polities of Champa (Hall 1985). Once the trade was threatened it was only a matter of time before political alliances unraveled. Champa was, at the time, ruled by King Indravarman who built the Buddhist temple of Dông Duong circa 875 C.E. It appears that Indravarman's realm stretched from the modern provinces of Quang Tri in the north to Quang Ngai in the south (Schweyer 2000). The Cham influence over the northern section of Vietnam began to wane over the next sixty years with the growing strength of the Dai Viet polity. In 982 C.E. the Dai Viet invaded

Champa and eventually occupied the northern portion of the Cham empire for several decades.

In the eleventh century a new Cham kingdom called Vijaya formed in southern Vietnam in modern Binh Dinh Province. Vijaya represents the Cham apex, a victorious kingdom in war against the Khmer to the west. Under king Shri Jaya Indravarmadeva, the Cham vanquished their long-time enemies, the Khmer, capturing Angkor. Regrettably for the Cham the victory was not long lasting, and the Cham occupiers of Cambodia were routed near Angkor. The Khmer King Jayavarman VII swept to victory, capturing Vijaya in 1191 C.E. The Cham did not disappear, however, and regained their independence resisting a Mongol invasion in the late 13th century. The last great event of the Cham kingdom was the invasion of Dai Viet in 1370 C.E., after which the power of the kingdom waned.

CONCLUSION

The relationship between Linyi and Champa is unclear. Some scholars have proposed that Linyi and Champa are different names for the same polity (Maspero 1928; Coedès 1964a). Others feel that the two were politically, geographically, and ethnically different (Stein 1947) or of the same ethnicity but governed by separate lineages and in different areas (Wheatley 1983). Coedès (1964a) believed that Linyi represented the first stronghold of Austronesian speakers in Vietnam, which was formed around 192 C.E. Whether or not this is the case is unclear. Other researchers have shown that Linyi actually existed further north than the area with the highest concentration of Cham (Austronesian) inscriptions (Stein 1947). These inscriptions, dated to the 4th century, are concentrated around My Son and Trà Kiêu. Absorption of Linyi by Champa seems to have occurred at some point and was complete by the early 7th century (Boisselier in Vickery 1998, 49). Another interpretation is that the people of Linyi spoke Cham but may have been politically differentiated from Champa or that the ruling classes of Linyi were Cham speakers (Wheatley in Vickery 1998, 49). In the mid-eighth century the political center of Champa seems to have shifted from the Danang area to Nha Trang (Vickery 1998, 316).

We know of Champa from an Arabic source, the *Kitab al-masalik was 'l-mamalik* written circa 850 C.E. This literary work describes the trade route from the Persian Gulf to China, mentioning both Cambodia (Qmar) and Champa (Sanf). Based on the sailing time from Qmar to Sanf, it appears that the Arab traders were putting to port at modern Nha Trang (Southworth 2001, 36).

Champa was probably the source of a great many forest products and may have even engaged in the trade of finished products. We know that there was a vigorous trade in eaglewood, a fragrant wood derived from trees native to Vietnam (Yule 1875; Southworth 2001).

The earliest inscription in the Cham language dates to the 4th century and confirms the presence of Cham speakers south of Danang at this time (Wheatley 1983). Inscriptions in Sanskrit from the early 7th century indicate that a Siva shrine was dedicated at My Son by Bhadravarman, ruler of Champa. It has been suggested that his capital was Trà Kiêu , not far from My Son (Coedès 1964a).

The Quang Nam area is a center of Cham culture in Vietnam, based on the location of the inscriptions and the Chinese annals. Wheatley (1983, 395) believes that it is safe to argue that the Cham of Quang Nam were known to the Chinese as the people of Linyi. The capital in early times may have been Van-xa, near Hué, and later Trà Kiêu (circa 605 C.E.). There are difficulties with this argument, however, in that the people of Linyi are not described as being Indianized, and the names and dates of rulers recorded by the Chinese do not correlate with the Sanskrit epigraphic dynastic records (Wheatley 1983, 395).

According to Chinese records of the late third century, Linyi was one of several kingdoms located to the south of China. It is apparent that the situation at this date was one of complex interrelationships between small polities. The smaller states probably functioned in a quasi-independent manner, perhaps belonging to a nonbinding confederation headed by the acknowledged preeminent political power. Each of the participating states is likely to have maintained its own trade networks, which stretched into the remote interior where much of the raw material for trade came from.

Some researchers (Stein 1947, 71 and 111) feel that Linyi has no relationship to the polity that left the Sanskrit records and only later were these Indianized peoples conquered by Linyi. By the early 5th century C.E., Stein (1947) believes that the area of Quang Nam hosted the capital of a powerful polity called Amaravati. The territory may have comprised the area from Binh Dinh (then known as Vijaya) to Nha Trang down to Phan Rang (see map 6.1). The Chinese preferred to call the polity Linyi, at least until 758 C.E.

According to Hoshino (1999, 55–56), the *Sui Shu*, written in the mid-seventh century, places Linyi in geographical order before Chenla, indicating that it was closer to Chinese territory in northern Vietnam. Another enigmatic polity, Chitu, which may have been located to the south of Linyi, is mentioned. The *Sui Shu* goes on to say that Linyi was subjugated in the beginning of the 7th century by an army of ten thousand Chinese cavalry and convicts (*Sui Shu* 82, f. 2 verso, in Hoshino 1999, 58). The vanquished king of Linyi, Fan Zhi, fled and established a new capital, the location of which is unknown. The Chinese divided Linyi into three administrative districts and pursued Fan Zhi, eventually defeating him but installing him as ruler under Sui control. It is very difficult to discern where all of the described events took place, and the location of Linyi cannot be firmly established.

Southworth (2001, 243) feels that Champa was not a great territorial empire but is better pictured as a polity with its power focused on the Thu Bon River valley. The rulers of Champa did, however, have the ability to strike quickly and ferociously using their unparalleled naval expertise. This naval power enabled them to establish a network of ports that swore allegiance to the Cham kings.

7

Models of Political Development

Based upon the evidence that has accumulated over the last four decades of research in Southeast Asia, it is widely agreed that the indigenous populations of the region had evolved politically complex societies. Many of the societies that appear to have embraced Indian ideals were likely fairly political advanced, probably to the level of chiefdoms. In this chapter I will clarify the specific attributes of the political forms that have been mentioned.

The assessment of political status among pre- and protohistoric societies is a contentious issue in archaeology, yet it remains one of the most important. Certainly in Southeast Asia our comprehension of the past social and political climate is limited. The primary method of assessing the organization of a prehistoric community is through the analysis of mortuary assemblages. Although imperfect, these data are by far the most revealing of all archaeological evidence. Through the analysis of mortuary remains, we gain insight into the relative worth of the individuals represented in our sample, as well as an indication of how the social unit functioned.

Explicit interest in prehistoric political hierarchy is a mere five decades old. Contemporary researchers struggle to formulate accurate and realistic models of development, but a review of recent literature demonstrates the tenacity of many of the original formulations.

CHIEFDOMS

Chiefdoms are often viewed as being more complex forms of sociopolitical organization than tribal societies but less complex than the state. Yoffee (2005, 23–25) states that:

> The chiefdom began life in anthropological literature (Service 1962; 1975; Carneiro 1981) with several defining attributes: social organization consisted of branching kinship structures called ramages or conical clans, wherein all members are ranked pyramidally in terms of distance from real or putative founding ancestors. Chiefdoms are "kinship societies" (Service 1962:171) because status is largely determined through place in the generational hierarchy of groups and of individuals within the groups. In political terms, chiefdoms contain hereditary and usually endogamous leaders (sometimes called nobility) and centralized direction, especially in matters of ceremony and ritual, but they have no formal machinery of forceful repression. . . .
>
> The chiefdom represented a breakthrough in social evolution in which local autonomy . . . gave way to a form of authority in which a paramount leader controlled a number of villages. Chiefs thus organized regional populations in the thousands or tens of thousands and controlled the production of staples and/or the acquisition of preciocities; the chiefdom was thus the stage preceding the rise of the state. For Carneiro, states were only quantitatively different from chiefdoms—larger, and with more powerful leaders.
>
> Henry Wright differentiated between simple chiefdoms, which are the classically ascriptive sort, with ranks determined according to the distance from common ancestors, and the complex chiefdom in which there is a regional hierarchy with a paramount chief ruling over subsidiary chiefs. These paramount chiefs centralized decision-making authority and they could (and did) mobilize resources to their seats, but they left local communities and subchiefs in place. As Wright put it, chiefdoms are externally specialized in order to get the goods from the various regions to the Paramount's control, but they are not internally specialized (i.e. with a specialized bureaucracy) to accomplish the task. There was a rank difference between chiefs and commoners, with the chiefs forming a sort of "class" and competing with each other for leadership and control of the ritual institutions that could legitimize their status. However, such attempts at control of goods without a permanent, specialized coercive authority meant that rebellions, breakdowns, destruction of centers, and changes in symbolic orientation were part of what complex chiefdoms were about. This inherent tendency to break down caused chiefdoms to "cycle". . . .
>
> For Spencer (1990), the distinction between chiefdom and state had to be emphasized: chiefs, lacking internally specialized enforcement machinery, avoid delegating central authority and rely on the local power of sub-chiefs, while kings (in states) systematize and segment their power so as to undermine local authority. Thus the transition from chiefdom to state proceeds transformationally.

Of all political entities, the chiefdom is perhaps the most contentious. Since the use of the term by Oberg (1955) in a unilineal typology of Central and South American societies, there have been myriad definitions of its constitution. The term was employed by Service (1962) in his consideration of general cultural evolution and was posited as a transitional stage between nonranking bands, tribes, and the state. In this type of society, the chief is the highest-ranking individual and all others are ranked according to their genealogical proximity to him. The relationships between individuals and even lineages emphasize social differences. Although the chiefs occupy an exalted position they lack the power to utilize force in coercing others to follow their will.

The position of chief is a permanent "office" in that it has "ascribed functions and conventionalised attributes no matter who occupies it" (Service 1962, 155). The sanctity of the office is ensured by two types of rules, *tapu* and rules of succession. Tapu sets the chief apart from others, and rules of succession ensure a smooth transition of power (Service 1962, 155). The chief will usually follow sumptuary rules that serve to distinguish him from others. Symbolic ornamentation, dress, food, and sometimes speech are used in this way. Sumptuary rules may also, with time, come to apply to the chief's immediate family, resulting in the adoption of primogeniture (Service 1962, 155). It is not only the chief's family that is ranked, but the whole society with a continuous gradation of ranks from top to bottom. There is no class system in the strict sense; rather, individuals may be viewed as a class unto themselves (Service 1962, 155).

Service (1962) differentiates chiefdoms from less complex polities largely based on the presence of redistribution and specialization. The basis of chiefly power lies in the role of redistributor. All goods produced are rendered to the chief, who in turn distributes them throughout the community. Some of the goods may be reserved by the chief to support craft specialists, the chiefly retinue, and perhaps priests. Specialization in craft products is an important factor in consolidating the office, and symbols that differentiate the chief are frequently employed.

Sodalities, common among tribal societies, are not widely found in this societal form. Their integrative purpose is rendered redundant by the centralizing nature of the chiefdom (Service 1962, 155). There is, alternatively, an increase in the number of sociocentric terms within the chiefdom that define the relationship of the bearer with the chief. Those individuals farthest from the source of power may adopt terms which denote achieved status if such a status is seen to be more prestigious than their genealogical rank. With these terms and titles go the associated paraphernalia and external symbols of social position.

It is widely held that kinship plays a prominent role in chiefdom societies. Ethnographic research has revealed that the conical clan is often a powerful element (Kirchoff 1959), although the chiefdom is not necessarily contingent upon a clan organization (Wason 1994). Indeed, there seems to be a good deal of variation between chiefdoms; in some the chief may be deified (Earle 1991), whereas in others inheritance may be contested (Drennan 1991), and chiefs may even be overthrown (Goldman 1970).

According to Service (1962), the well-developed chiefdom will expand territorially through internal population growth. Usually this occurs as families with low potentiality in the inheritance scheme, such as the youngest brothers, move to the periphery. Firth's (1936, 371) term "ramage" is used to describe this "branching and re-branching of the family structure, acquiring greater autonomy and independence the further they move away from the parent stem." Such fission of local subgroups took place on many Pacific islands and may have played a role in the colonization of new islands. Each local ramage is ranked in relation to the senior ramage, just as members of each ramage are ranked internally (Kirch 1984). The new territories occupied by the subgroups on Pacific islands would have been self-sufficient because their territories included a range of eco-zones.

Chiefdoms may be further differentiated from tribes in that they have greater productivity and larger population densities. The residential group is not the relatively autonomous and self-sufficient economic and sociopolitical unit that it is among tribal societies. There is a tendency for different residential groups to specialize and become increasingly dissimilar. Demographically, chiefdoms have centers that coordinate economic, social, and religious activities. These centers evolve as specialization and redistribution come to characterize a large part of the activity of the society. Given such a central role, the office of chief eventually encompasses social, political, and religious functions (Service 1971).

The fundamentals of religion in the chiefly society may be similar to those among the band level, but the ideology is expanded and formalized. According to Service (1962), the shamanistic practices and local life cycle rituals remain, but ceremonies and rituals serving wider social purposes become more numerous. Ancestors may be deified, their importance determined by genealogical rank order. A priesthood may also evolve to administer the reformed religion, a position that, like that of the chief, is a permanent office.

Fried (1967), whilst acknowledging Service's (1962) theoretical contribution, employs a different terminology in his attempt to understand non-egalitarian society. Beyond the egalitarian form, Fried (1967, 109) proposes a rank society "in which positions of valued status are somehow limited so that not all those of sufficient talent to occupy such statuses actually achieve them." According to Fried (1967), the ranked society may or may not be stratified. A society may strictly limit the positions of prestige without affecting the access of the entire membership to the basic resources upon which life depends.

Although the rank society, like the chiefdom, is structured along kinship lines, the differences between them are significant. An important point being that rank in Fried's model does not exclude the possessor from quotidian tasks. In fact, the position may demand more work as these individuals are expected to contribute more than nonranked individuals (Fried 1967). The division of labor in rank society runs along lines of age and sex, and there is little evidence of craft specialization.

Rank society shares the concept of redistribution with chiefdoms, in that goods flow into a central paramount from which they are redistributed through the various components of the group. The populace supplies the chief with labor, raw materials, and half of their agricultural yield in return for protection, conflict resolution, and supervision of the organization of labor, when necessary. The chief in turn uses the agricultural products to feed his craft specialists and retinue. These groups repay the chief by supplying legitimacy and finished crafts, which serve to consolidate the chiefly office. The paramount may redistribute foodstuffs received from subordinate chiefs who preside over different ecological/agricultural niches. Exchange between individuals, which is the predominant form of circulating goods among egalitarian societies, may still exist, but it is not the exclusive mode of circulation in chiefdoms (Fried 1967).

The original definitions and descriptions of chiefdoms have been both embraced and criticized. Reviewing the literature, it seems that the form has remained largely intact, although many variations have been proposed. Anthropologists are far from agreement on the defining characteristics of chiefdoms, as well as the formative causes. Sahlins (1958) originally believed that productivity was a cause of political complexity and could therefore be used as a measure of the same. He was later to modify his views to suggest that population growth resulted in stratification and productivity (Sahlins 1972). Sahlins saw the chiefdom evolving coincidentally with the public economy where production is, in part, controlled at a level above the basic household unit of production (Sanders and Webster 1978). This allowed the existence of part-time specialists and communal labor forces.

The attempts at refinement of the chiefdom model have not gone uncriticized. Tainter (1978) opposes the expansion of the terminology dealing with chiefdoms, fearing it may lead to an unmanageable number of pigeon holes. Peebles and Kus (1977) agree that chiefdoms are usually characterized by increased complexity of organization, productivity, and population density, as well as institutionalized offices of leadership. They question, however, the suggestion that redistribution is a univariate phenomenon, a causal factor, and a constant correlate of chiefdoms.

REDISTRIBUTION

It had long been assumed that the power of chiefs derives to a large extent from their role in internal exchange, or a redistributive network. In Polanyi's (1957) definition, a redistributive system is one in which there are appropriational movements of produce toward a center and out of it again. Fried (1960; 1967) and Service (1962; 1975) propose that a redistributive economy was a necessary condition for the rise of chiefdoms. Fried (1967, 183) writes, "the move from egalitarian to ranked society is essentially a shift from an economy dominated by reciprocity to one having redistribution as a major device."

More recently, the role of the redistributive economy among chiefdoms has been reevaluated. Service's (1962) emphasis on the explanatory importance of redistribution as a means of provisioning chiefly societies, and his insistence on using it as a defining feature, are not sustained by recent archaeological and ethnohistorical case studies (Wright 1994). The status of redistribution as a consistent component of the chiefdom is questioned by some (Earle 1975), as is the assumption that it is cross-culturally valid. Although it may not be manifest in every chiefly society, there can be little doubt of the existence of some form of economic control by chiefs in most chiefdoms (Earle 1975.).

Earle (1987), in discussing the purpose of internal exchange, sees two alternative explanations, one is managerial and the other control oriented. Under the former, the chief's motives are more altruistic than with the latter. Service (1962, 159) believes strongly in the managerial position, attacking the "tendency in modern thought to see exploitation, wealth expropriation and greed as the causes of the rise of authority, classes and the state." He strongly believes that "sumptuary rules were social and political in origin not economic."

The development of redistributive processes has been alternatively attributed to settlement in diverse ecological regions, which led to community specialization and exchange in staples and regional interdependency (Service 1962; Creamer and Haas 1985). Centralized management would oversee inter- and intracommunity exchange. According to this position, elites attract followers and discourage segmentation by providing managerial services required in a highly productive economy (Gilman 1981).

This argument conflicts with data that indicate that intercommunity exchange of staples is unlikely because communities are probably already self-sufficient (Finney 1966; Earle 1977; 1978; 1987). It is also suggested that staple exchange would occur too infrequently to fulfill need. The expense of such an undertaking would also be prohibitive. Earle (1973; 1987) believes that, in chiefdoms where staple is employed in redistribution, its use is restricted to public feasts and distribution among the elite. The wholesale redistribution of an agricultural yield across several communities is unrealistic as is the concept of interdependent specialist communities.

An alternative model, to one in which the chief's primary role is the coordination of exchange, sees the chief's main purpose as organizing the construction and maintenance of irrigation projects (Service 1962). There is, however, a lack of ethnographic and archaeological evidence to support this model and so it has been largely dismissed (Earle 1987). The only remaining model positing a managerial role for chiefs is that of risk management, in which the chief, storing staples, is capable of assisting in an emergency (Muller 1987). According to Johnson and Earle (1987), when population density is high, management and storage of surplus are necessary. This also provides the chief with the means to invest in other political and economic ways.

Earle (1987) asserts that there are few adherents to the managerial models presented above and suggests that most researchers now prefer an explanation in which elites vie for control of the economy. In the control model, elites ensure the compulsion of others through the monopolization of rare but essential and/or valued items (Schortman and Urban 1996). Whether control derives primarily from staple production or wealth distribution is debatable (Earle 1987). Elite ownership of land (often acquired through conquest) ensures control of staple production. In complex chiefdoms, the paramount may "own" the land and offer its use to subordinate chiefs who support him. These subordinates may, in turn, distribute it among householders (Peebles and Kus 1977) whose produce or labor could then be extracted as a form of rent (Earle 1991).

There is some indication that the nature of internal exchange may differ depending on the level of social stratification. Kirch (1984) believes that less stratified societies would have redistributed goods back to the householders, whereas, in more stratified societies, the goods were used to support the chiefly hierarchy and were not redistributed to the same degree. Earle (1991) also proposes that the system of finance employed by a society may be used as an indicator of its complexity. Those employing a system of staple finance, using food and technological items in payment for services, may indicate a less complex political structure. A society using a wealth finance system in which items (of symbolic value) are obtained, through either external exchange or internal craft specialization, may be characterized as more complex. This is rather a simplistic evaluation, however, because, as Gilman (1991) points out, any system of wealth finance must rest on some form of staple finance. This is well demonstrated in the Hawaiian chiefdoms, where the paramount received sumptuary items from regional elites which were then redistributed to the elite as symbols of rank. In return for the sumptuary items and staples, the paramount would lift the *tapu* on agricultural land for use the next year (Peebles and Kus 1977). Control of land was also pivotal in the development of Copper Age Spain, where the emergence of social stratification coincides with the introduction of intensified subsistence agriculture. Gilman (1991) argues that those who controlled the land extracted rent from the agriculturalists. It is difficult to overstate the importance of chiefly control of land, for, as Creamer and Haas (1985) note, without land a chief lacks an economic power base, which inhibits the ability to establish an independent physical power base.

In order to better understand redistribution, Earle (1977) proposes a categorization of different forms of internal exchange, including leveling mechanisms, householding, share-out, and mobilization. Leveling mechanisms are defined as those which discourage wealth accumulation by individuals or groups. The pooling of produce in domestic units is defined as householding, and share-out is explained as the allocation of goods produced by cooperative endeavor. Mobilization is the "recruitment of goods and services not coterminous with the contributing members," (Earle 1977, 215) as is the case with tribute, taxation, and corvée labor. Mobilization refers to intercommunity production and a public economy, elements found in most ranked and stratified societies.

Describing chiefly societies as redistributive does not consider the scope of the entire economy. Redistribution in its strict sense may not even be a necessary attribute of this type of society. Peebles and Kus (1977) cite evidence from Hawaii (Earle 1973; 1975; Kus n.d.) to demonstrate that redistribution was not the dominant mode of exchange in prehistory. It is further stated that goods that were redistributed went no further than the elite and that redistribution did not serve to unite independent communities in diverse ecological zones. Kirch (1984) concurs with Peebles and Kus's (1977) view of redistribution, stating that in societies with low levels of stratification the chief is more closely bound to the people, resulting in tribute being redistributed back to the householders. In more stratified societies, however, the goods rendered to the chief are more likely to be distributed among elites.

In Hawaii, there is no evidence of environmentally specialized local production units united in a redistributive network in which all goods flowed through a paramount chief. Rather, the paramount received and distributed sumptuary items and food for himself and his followers, specialists, and elites. The precontact societies of Polynesia, although often posited as archetypes of chiefdom society, are a source of contention, with some arguing that chiefdoms do not exist in Polynesia (Kohl 1987; Yoffee 1993).

Sanders and Webster (1978) adhere to the definition of chiefdoms proposed by Service (1962), viewing them as multicommunity societies with internal ranking, common descent, and adoption of the principle of primogeniture. They believe, however, that Service's definition is too specific and describes a particular type of chiefdom, citing examples in which redistribution is not practiced and others which are not organized as ramages (Taylor 1975). They also criticize Service for creating a dichotomy between ecological and societal variables, which they believe inhibits the "explanatory and processual utility of his model" (Sanders and Webster 1978, 276). Searching for a model that will incorporate all chiefdoms, Sanders and Webster turn to Fried's (1967) ranked society, which they embrace with one modification—that it may not be stratified. These authors wish to separate stratified and ranked society, establishing them as separate types. They disagree with Fried's belief that stratified societies are a development of ranked societies, and Fried's assertion that stratified societies usually break down into simpler social forms is similarly criticized. Sanders and Webster (1978) feel that stratified societies cannot break down in the absence of a demographic or ecological disaster and will invariably lead to higher levels of organization.

Dissatisfied with the essentially unilineal nature of cultural evolution inherent in both Service and Fried's models, Sanders and Webster (1978) propose a modified multilineal paradigm in which different evolutionary trajectories relate to variations in the natural environment. They see the environment as the crucial determinant in the evolution of sociopolitics.

Although he agrees with most of the traits that identify Service's (1962) chiefdom, Wright (1984) takes issue with the emphasis placed upon the importance of redistribution and the idea that the chiefdom was a necessary stage of progression to statehood. Recognizing the need for the chiefdom taxon, Wright prefers to define it as a sociopolitical entity in which there is a range of complexity. Simple chiefdoms are those in which control is exercised by individuals from a local elite subgroup and in which there is just one level of control. Wright believes that among complex chiefdoms there exists a "class" of ranked individuals whose members compete with each other for access to controlling positions and stand together in opposition to other people. This type of chiefdom, he says, may cycle between one and two levels of control hierarchy above the level of the local community (Wright 1984).

Wright (1984) concedes that we lack an understanding of the circumstances in which producers would willingly give up their goods to a chief without coercion or reciprocity. In discussing paramountcy, he hypothesizes that, once the position was established, the paramount chief would have taken marriage partners from outside his own lineage, suggesting that these extraneous links may have led to claims of cosmic powers. The aggrandizement of such schemes may have resulted in tribute mobilization.

The centripetal flow of tribute would have served to consolidate the paramount chief's position, making the other office holders permanent political and ritual subsidiaries. Theoretically the two levels of control hierarchy should be evident in the settlement pattern of the complex chiefdom. The centers of subsidiary chiefs should be located to facilitate control with a minimum expenditure while main centers will grow no further than the limits imposed by tribute demands (Wright 1984).

Carneiro, dissatisfied with Service's and Fried's definitions of chiefdoms, proposes his own. According to Carneiro (1981, 45), "a chiefdom is an autonomous political unit comprising a number of villages or communities under the permanent control of a paramount chief." Although he accepts the dual hierarchical definition of chiefdoms, he feels that the division of chiefdoms into simple and complex could not encompass the demonstrated range of variation. He proposes a three-level typology in which "minimal chiefdom" meets the minimum requirements of a chiefdom. A "typical chiefdom" is one that is clearly a chiefdom, with elaborations in many aspects of its political and social structure, but still well below the level of a state. The last category proposed is the "maximal chiefdom," which describes a society that has become large and complex enough to approach the threshold of the state.

In more complex chiefdoms the stability of the paramountcy relies upon the society's productive success; reductions in the upward flow of goods may result in claims of incompetence by lower chiefs. For this reason the paramount would be motivated to streamline production or to increase his potential income through territorial conquest. Such polities exhibit a pattern of centralization and decentralization deteriorating roughly every decade. Regional wars and perhaps the usurpation of chiefly lineages would occur every century or so (Carneiro 1981).

According to Kirch (1984), the chief occupies the central role in the organization of production. He believes that chiefly demands for surplus would have stimulated innovations in agricultural production as well as territorial expansion. The high degree of ritual activity in the Hawaiian islands demonstrates the extent of the demands issued by the paramount. The demands for surplus to be used in ritual led subordinate chiefs to undertake the conquest of territory (Kirch 1984).

Earle (1987) views chiefdoms as political entities that organize regional populations in the thousands or tens of thousands, with a centralized decision-making hierarchy coordinating activities among several village communities. The concept of the chiefdom is valuable, Earle says, because it can be used to define societies of similar scale and organization on a cross-cultural basis.

Earle subscribes to the notion, introduced by Sahlins (1958), that increased polity size and production is a correlate of increased political complexity. He stresses that an increased population stimulates political centralization, which in turn streamlines decision making. Population density will also affect sociopolitical development, and societies of differing territorial size may result in different trajectories.

The hierarchical levels of chiefdoms posited by Service (1962) and Wright (1984) are enlarged upon by Earle (1987), who believes that the number of hierarchical levels is related to polity size and spatial distribution. Leaders of large polities are unable to make all the decisions and require subordinates to take action on less important matters. Although the office of chief may be set apart from the subordinates, the different levels have similar duties.

Earle (1987) believes that the concepts of stratification and ranking have been artificially separated. He argues that structural differentiation (ranking) and economic differentiation (stratification) should be seen as a continuum. The structural or political differentiation in a society cannot be seen as strictly symbolic but must derive from economic control.

Johnson and Earle (1987) argue that either one of two systems of finance existed in chiefdom societies, staple (Earle and D'Altroy 1982; D'Altroy and Earle 1985) and wealth finance (Johnson and Earle 1987). The redistributive system outlined above is what Johnson and Earle (1987) refer to as staple finance. Wealth finance (D'Altroy and Earle 1985; Brumfiel and Earle 1987) is described as the controlled production and distribution of valuables. These values are culturally important in the establishment of individual status.

The concept of the chiefdom, while useful, must be applied judiciously given the range of morphological types. Gibson (1982), in examining Irish chiefdoms, found the number of hierarchical levels and the ability of the chief to enforce his will varied widely.

Rothman (1994, 4), somewhat critical of the step-stage typologies, attempts to divorce himself from the definition of chiefdoms as "tightly defined structural types" and prefers to use the term to describe flexible ranges of organizational variation. The trait lists advanced to identify chiefdoms hamper our understanding of these entities as widely variable social organizations. The complexity of societies should be determined through an examination of the functional differentiation between societal units or subsystems such as households, classes, or villages (Rothman 1994). Rothman sees complexity as having horizontal and vertical axes, the former consisting of the number of units of similar functional type and the latter consisting of the number of hierarchical levels. There will also be a degree of integration or interdependence among the functional units along the different axes. This integration may be economic, social, or political, and a positive correlation is not necessary. Rothman believes that the degree of centralization defines the nature of leadership organizations in the functioning of society.

Feinman (1991, 230) is also critical of the step typology and feels chiefdoms are "a sociopolitical form" not a class or type, saying that "chiefly formations should be associated with a supra-household decision making structure or relatively permanent positions of leadership, but not with marked internal differentiation of such structures."

Renfrew (1974) defines "group oriented" and "individualizing" chiefdoms. The former are societies in which personal wealth in terms of valuable possessions is not emphasized but where a solidarity of the social unit is expressed most effectively in communal or group activities. Among individualizing chiefdoms, a marked disparity in personal possessions and in other material indicators of prestige appears to document a salient personal ranking, yet often without evidence of communal meetings or activities.

This concept is elaborated upon by Blanton et al. (1996), who argue that every society is composed of an "exclusionary" as well as a "corporate power strategy." One of these is more likely to be dominant at a particular time in any given society. The exclusionary power strategy, similar to Renfrew's (1974) individualizing chiefdoms, involves the development of a political system in which an individual monopolizes sources of power. The alternate strategy, which may be likened to Renfrew's group-oriented chiefdoms, involves the sharing of power across different sectors of society. The authors stress that this need not mean a nonhierarchical society, but the behavior of leaders or chiefs is restricted, which negates the monopolization of power by an individual.

The exclusionary strategy and the centralization of power are often thought of as the hallmarks of complex societies (Blanton et al. 1996). It is this misconception which Blanton et al. wish to dispel, arguing that the corporate strategy is able to transcend the scale limitations that are imposed by the exclusionary strategy.

THE EMERGENCE OF "COMPLEXITY"

Theories on the origin of complex society are as varied as the definitions proposed above. There are, however, a finite number of variables that may be posited as causative factors in the emergence of chiefdoms. Gilman (1981) feels that most of the theories on the origin of complex societies center on the services that elites provide in varying situations. It is clear, however, that external stimuli, aspects of culture that have developmental priority and events perceived to be beyond the control of the human population, play a prominent role in many of the theories presented below.

Service (1962) stated that the rise of chiefdoms was related to a total environmental situation that was selective for specialization in production and redistribution of produce from a controlling center. In a cyclical pattern, increased specialization resulted in the evolution of redistribution, which both organized specialization and distributed products. Specialization may develop in a society that inhabits a geographic region comprising several ecological niches, and redistribution develops as a more efficient method of circulating goods than exchange. Redistribution may also result from collectivization of community skills in large-scale cooperative projects, whereby an individual may organize skilled laborers.

Service (1962) believes that the system grew ever more complex, with the redistributor recruiting superior specialists to produce goods for his/her own consumption. These individuals would have been rewarded with a share of the products to be redistributed, such as food and other necessities. Their products were in turn used by the redistributor to consolidate further his/her position through the display of wealth and prestige belongings. With the ability to demonstrate superiority through wealth display, the redistributor may eventually be referred to as a chief. Once this position is a permanent aspect of the society, widespread social inequality will be entrenched. The transformation of the position of redistributor to a hereditary office creates further possibilities of inequality. The status of the chief consequently enhances the status of his/her kin group. In such a situation, an individual's status is dependent upon sanguinity to the chief (Service 1962).

The genesis discussed above pertains largely to those chiefdoms that exist in isolation. An established chiefdom may be the catalyst for the creation of other chiefdoms, termed superorganic development by Service (1962). A tribal society could not compete with a chiefdom, and competition between them would, he argues, result in one of several alternatives. The weaker social group may be expunged from the territory, exterminated, enslaved, sacrificed, or absorbed. Service believes that the last of these alternatives is the most promising avenue for the development of larger chiefdoms.

When a new population is incorporated, the structural features of the larger entity are duplicated in microcosm within the new social element. Each local kin group will appoint its own "chief" who will be responsible for collecting goods to be passed on to the superordinate chief (Service 1962). As we have seen, the territorial expansion of the chiefdom is driven by breakaway factions. These groups tend to come from the lower echelons of the society, far removed from the chief in terms of consanguine relationship.

According to Fried (1967), the development of ranked societies may occur independently or as a result of influence from external groups. These are respectively termed pristine and secondary evolution (Fried 1967). Populations inhabiting areas with an abundance of food, or those in possession of technology capable of increasing production, are the most likely to undergo the former. The demographic outcome of this process is an increase in regional population density and larger residential units. Fried (1967) hypothesizes a drop in infant mortality and an increase in warfare among such societies, the effects of which are a result of ranking rather than a cause.

ENVIRONMENTAL FACTORS

Sanders and Webster (1978) see variation in environmental stimuli as a basic component of cultural evolution. These are split into first and second order factors based upon the role they play in sociopolitical development. Agricultural risk and diversity are first-order factors, whereas productivity, size, character, and location are second order.

Environmental risk may be assessed by examining the environmental parameters, such as temperature and rainfall, which are essential in food production. Areas characterized by frequent fluctuations in these parameters are classified as being high risk. Diversity refers to the proximity and pattern of spacing of different environmental conditions, which may be exploited by a human population, for both subsistence and nonsubsistence resources.

Second-order factors such as productivity may be described as the potential of the exploited land to yield subsistence products for the support of human populations, a factor which affects all the evolutionary processes (Sanders and Webster 1978). The productive potential depends upon the natural environment and the subsistence technology employed. The production of large surpluses above the subsistence level is crucial to the development of complex societies because they allow hierarchical centralization. Due to this nonsubsistence, segregation may reach complex levels and proportions (Sanders and Webster 1978).

Population density has long been posited as an integral factor in the development of complexity, and Sanders and Webster include it in their scheme. They believe that the larger the population, the greater the need for an efficient apparatus of control. A corollary of the size of the population is the "size" of the environment. This concept is similar to Carneiro's (1970) circumscription, in that the size of the environment affects the processes of cooperation and conflict by determining the size, density, and distribution of population on the landscape (Sanders and Webster 1978). The character of the environment refers to a number of factors, especially topographical. These may serve to isolate a society or, alternatively, position a group for optimal communication and transportation. The character of the land will play a role in determining the overall cultural patterning in the environment (Carneiro 1970). The location factor is included in the scheme to account for the position of a culture group in reference to other complex societies which may be influential.

Environmental variability is seen by Kirch (1984; 1991) to be significant in initiating processes leading to the differentiation of chiefdoms. Many of the factors cited by Kirch (1991) in the Pacific are similar to those raised by Sanders and Webster (1978), including isolation, the size of islands, the character of the islands, and potential for agriculture. According to Kirch (1991), the environment was not only integral in the development of complexity but was in some cases adversely affected by it. In the Marquesas, the depletion of wild foods and erosion of arable land, brought about by clearance and cultivation, was caused by rapid population growth. The resulting ecological degradation was compounded by environmental hazards such as drought and acute competition over productive resources.

Similarly, Earle (1991) states that the success or failure of political strategies would appear to be in part determined by the ecological conditions in which a society exists. According to Earle (1991), the adoption of alternative strategies is directed largely by nine environmental conditions:

1. Natural productivity and potential for intensification
2. Regional population density
3. Existence of external markets
4. Natural circumscription
5. Concentration of productive resources
6. Proximity to non-food resources
7. Proximity to avenues of trade and communication
8. Social circumscription
9. Structural preconditions of hierarchy

Earle (1991) highlights two aspects of many chiefdoms that are dependent upon the environment. The first of which is the extraction of a surplus. Many researchers contend that the production of a surplus is a primary condition for the development of complex societies. The production of a surplus is dependent on the natural productivity and potential for intensification, as well as the availability of human labor to work the land and possibly the existence of external markets from which alternate sources of food and exotic goods were extracted. The second factor, a circumscribed environment, is also seen as crucial in the evolution of a complex political apparatus, in that the alternatives of the population are limited and the surplus is consequently channeled toward the center.

These factors alone are not sufficient cause for chiefly development in themselves. The importance of the interaction between the environment and human beings is stressed. Bargatzky (1984 in Earle 1991) hypothesizes that environments are dynamic sets of cultural and natural conditions that are constantly modified and created by human intervention. Differing environments offer individuals varied opportunities for the control of resources and consequently finance. Such a scenario would see environmentally specialized local production units united by a redistributive network. We have seen, however, that the relationship between high environmental diversity, ranked organization, and redistribution is not evident in prehistoric Hawaii, where there were apparently two levels of economy (Peebles and Kus 1977). At one level the local kinsmen participated in a reciprocal trade network, while on another level chiefs participated in a redistributive network, headed by the paramount, in which only sumptuary items circulated.

The role of the environment is well demonstrated in prehistoric New Zealand, where initial colonization by Polynesians led to significant changes in social organization. According to Anderson (1982), new systems of political power and prestige were established as the colonizers were released from the traditional social stratification and sources of wealth. New hierarchies were established, and the legitimacy of these was demonstrated through conspicuous consumption, delineation of territory, and wealth display.

POPULATION PRESSURE

Increases in population have long been proposed as a motivating factor in the development of sociopolitical complexity (Steward 1949; Fried 1960; Sanders and Price 1968). "Population pressure" may be defined as occurring whenever the total needs of a population approach the maximum output that the subsistence system produces (Brumfiel 1976). The basis of population growth, and consequently political development, has been attributed to environmental factors such as favorable agricultural conditions, as it was in Mexico (Wolf 1959). Other variables cited include technological advancements, which increase production allowing population growth (Childe 1951; 1954; Wittfogel 1957; Adams 1966). The relationship between agriculture, population, and political complexity has more recently been examined by Schurr and Schoeninger (1995), who believe that the introduction of maize was linked to population growth and political development in the Ohio River valley. Increased production not only serves to increase population density but also allows the accumulation of production beyond subsistence. Agricultural surplus may consolidate a redistributive network and allow craft specialization (Renfrew 1986). Some argue that technology was a servant of population pressure and that intensification of agricultural techniques is a direct result of population pressure (Boserup 1965). Others see growing populations increasing pressure on energy supplies, which in turn stimulates sociocultural change (Orans 1966; Harner 1970; Kappel 1974). Whatever the preferred scenario, there is little debate that there is a relationship between population and the level of political complexity present. It has been recognized that the larger the population, the more complex the political apparatus will be (Carneiro 1967; Kappel 1974).

Population growth is an important component in many of the unilineal evolutionary schemes in which all societies, depending on the environment, progress through the same increasingly complex stages. The pressure on existing resources results in competition, which in turn produces competitive responses eventually leading to differential access to resources, occupational specialization, and centralized political power (Sanders and Webster 1978). As an alternative to this, Sanders and Webster (1978) present a model in which population growth occurs at a constant rate, which, in their view, is a necessary precondition of all evolutionary trajectories. Circumscription also plays a role in their model, in that smaller geographic spaces are hypothesized to evolve faster than larger ones based on the increasing demand that population brings on resources.

Increasing complexity is also seen by Johnson and Earle (1987) as a correlate of population growth. The risk of an agricultural shortfall in the face of increasing population requires the facilitation of storage and surplus distribution, usually undertaken by an individual. Increasing population may also result in external trade, which requires management.

Increases in prehistoric populations have been attributed to a number of factors, including technological revolutions, ecological factors, and the principles of natural selection. Many processual archaeologists embrace demographic determinism as an explanation of increased complexity. This principle sees the cultural system adapting to external factors in which human beings are acted upon by forces beyond their understanding and control (Trigger 1990).

Kosse (1994), following Darwinian principles, argues that there was a shift in the unit of selection from the individual to the group at some point in the past. Various factors led to selection for increases in the size of the cultural unit. Complexity, according to Kosse, was essentially a consequence of increased unit size and is seen as a means of maintaining functional efficiency within the unit.

Convinced of the role played by demographics, Baker and Sanders (1972) linked the rate of political development to the rate of population growth. According to their calculations, a population could double in size in a century; the resulting increase in numbers would demand a more complex political apparatus. Such a situation is posited for Hawaii, which saw the development of complex chiefdoms. According to Kirch (1984), rapid population growth and intensification of agriculture took place over a 400-year period, resulting in the implementation of social mechanisms for control and distribution of agricultural and other products. Stevenson (1968) also sees population as a concomitant of organizational complexity in Africa.

The role played by increasing populations in the development of sociopolitical complexity among prehistoric societies is not unanimously embraced however. Earle (1991), in reference to a symposium on chiefdoms, states that population growth as a prime mover for cultural evolution received little support among the participants, although he conceded there were situations where it was a major factor. Even in cases where there is evidence of unabated population growth, Earle (1991) does not seem to view demographic pressure alone as a cause of increased sociopolitical complexity. Other researchers have found that there is no evidence of a relationship between population size and centralization (Millon 1962; Carneiro 1967; Brumfiel 1976; Netting 1990).

Even the premise of naturally increasing populations has been criticized. Cowgill (1975) argues that population growth is not a tendency of human populations and that preindustrial societies are characterized by a balance of fertility and mortality rates. Wynne-Edwards (1962 in Brumfiel 1976) argues that, if any population pushed the limits of its energy supply, it would be caught in a downward spiral of overexploitation and diminishing returns. It is on this basis that he argues for selection that would constantly favor a population that established a demographic equilibrium well below the maximum limits set by its food supply. Precisely this situation was documented among the Tupi in South America (Wagely 1973) and Cahokia in the southeastern United States (Muller and Stephens 1990), whose populations remained stable at a level set by their subsistence economy.

The role of population pressure in the development of complexity is viewed by some critics as instrumental only under restricted circumstances. In circumscribed environments, where expansion is impossible, the role of increasing populations in political development is conceded (Carneiro 1967). Without circumscription, populations are expected to segment, although this is not always the case, as is demonstrated in Bronze Age Europe. According to Gilman (1981), broad stretches of uninhabited, but habitable, land existed yet were not utilized. Instead a hierarchical social structure developed, causing Gilman to conclude that "the shift toward social complexity occurs . . . on too broad and diverse a front for the resource circumscription argument to be viable" (Gilman 1981, 4).

Alternative effects of population growth that are often overlooked are the demands placed upon resources and, consequently, the social apparatus. Systems of redistribution and tribute payment would be adversely affected by growing populations. If resources are stretched and subsistence needs not met, tribute may decline, and a chief would be unable to maintain his retinue in the face of an ever expanding populace. There is a possibility that, instead of stimulating further centralization, the result may be the collapse of existing hierarchies.

CONFLICT

A growing population will result in increased competition for resources. This competition may manifest itself in a number of ways, but the rise of complexity is most often associated with competition expressed through warfare. Indeed, the source of conflict is used by some as a measure of complexity. Tribal societies are thought to have engaged in raids for the purpose of capturing mates or for retribution, whereas more complex societies are characterized by conflict over resources, labor force, and wealth (Fried 1967; Carneiro 1970; Johnson and Earle 1987; Tong Enzheng 1991; Redmond 1994).

The correlation between population pressure and increasing warfare was examined by Vayda (1960), who, investigating prehistoric New Zealand, linked rapid population growth to conflict over land. He describes a form of demographic circumscription where, at a certain point, all the valuable agricultural land was claimed, resulting in conflict as the population continued to grow. The forcible annexation of cleared land was economically preferable to clearing new land (Vayda 1960). Competition over agricultural land is also documented by Green (1967), Cassels (1974 cited in Kirch 1984) and Johnson and Earle (1987).

Some scholars attribute warfare as a causative factor in the development or consolidation of social hierarchies (Coser 1956; Webster 1977). Renfrew (1986) believes that the emergence of new institutions in a given society is partly due to the intensification of production, a process that may be stimulated by long-term warfare. Others see the threat of conflict as stimulating the formation of hierarchies, whereby resolution of disputes was administered by a central authority (Wittfogel 1957; Johnson and Earle 1987; Netting 1990). Nissen (1988) takes this model further, proposing that, in instances where conflict was unresolved, violence would result. Warfare inevitably led to the subordination of one group by another, creating social stratification.

As Netting (1990, 57) illustrates, the risk of violence must have been substantial:

> Any effort to concentrate population and build defences would demand the investment of farmers time and . . . physical relocation, military service and tribute payments would all decrease agricultural efficiency. . . . Thus the economic costs of voluntary incorporation into a chiefdom would be considerable. Perhaps only the threat of warfare and destruction would justify the economic advantages foregone . . . [yet] the benefits of voluntarily joining a new political order that was successful in war and impressive in ritual, regalia, and accumulated wealth must have been obvious.

EXCHANGE

Warfare is not the only form of external relationship in which societies engage. Nonviolent interactions have also been cited as contributing to the rise of political complexity, although Kipp and Schortman (1989) posit that strength of arms may well play a role in these transactions as well. They believe that trade and militarism have long been associated, a force of arms often being necessary to protect trade from theft and disruption of exchange activities.

These same authors stress the importance of terminology, trying to differentiate trade and exchange. Trade, they say, has been used for such a broad range of exchange behavior that its role in the development of political hierarchies remains inconclusive (Kipp and Schortman 1989). Although Renfrew (1975) believes trade and exchange to be synonymous, Kipp and Schortman prefer the definition provided by Adams (1974), where trade involves risk, profit, and entrepreneurial behavior, tending to involve "middlemen." Exchange, they say, is more commonly face to face and direct rather than through traders or a specialized merchant class. Exchange of luxury goods is often undertaken for personal or political reasons, such as wedding gifts, funeral offerings, and other life crisis gifts between kin, and also through reciprocal gift giving between leaders (Kipp and Schortman 1989). Strictly defined, trade involves transactions that are impersonal and based upon profit maximization, and the value of items traded is determined by the laws of supply and demand (Kipp and Schortman 1989).

It is also important to distinguish between internal and external exchange, or redistribution and reciprocity. The former will be discussed in more detail below, and so here the latter will be examined. Reciprocity involves exchange activities between different cultural nodes. The type of exchange activity may play a role in the development of complexity, and the type of material being traded is significant. The nature of trade or exchange has implications in understanding the nature of the societies involved in such transactions. It may also be possible to infer, to a degree, the state of political and cultural development of a society based on the items exchanged. It is significant whether the materials being traded were subsistence products, technological items, or luxury goods. Some may argue that societies involved in the exchange of subsistence products and technological items may not exhibit sociopolitical development as complex as those engaged in the exchange of luxury goods. This, however, may simply be a reflection of environmental constraint; yet the absence of surplus would suggest an inability to support a social hierarchy.

Gilman (1981) believes that, if we are to posit trade/exchange as a motivating factor in the emergence of social stratification, the goods exchanged must be essential to the participants. He believes that trade/exchange must involve, directly or indirectly, the basic subsistence sector of the economy. In examining political development in Bronze Age Europe, Gilman (1981) rules out widespread exchange of agricultural products based upon transportation logistics and the lack of archaeological evidence. The exchange of subsistence products is usually restricted to internal exchange networks, as was the case in prehistoric Hawaii (Kirch 1984) and the southeastern United States (Muller and Stephens 1990). Gilman (1981) similarly dismisses the exchange of metal tools, cited as essential in land clearance

(Childe 1951; 1954), arguing that it is doubtful that these would have substantially increased production. He argues that it is only in late Bronze Age contexts that substantial numbers of utilitarian metal artifacts are found. It is his view that metals were valued more for social and ideological reasons. Anderson (1994) believes that the prestige goods exchange networks existed in many areas long before the development of chiefdoms, including Western Europe, some parts of Central and South America, and the Eastern Woodlands of North America. As control over such networks evolved so did the authority structures prevalent in many chiefdoms.

EXCHANGE AS A MEASURE OF COMPLEXITY

The type of exchange activity pursued by a prehistoric culture is arguably a measure of political complexity and adaptation. Exchange of goods, other than subsistence products, infers a degree of specialization within a society. Full-time specialization is usually possible only where an agricultural surplus is produced. The procurement and manufacture of export items come at the expense of subsistence activities. This implies the existence of a central authority that has the power to subvert subsistence products for the support of specialists. The ability to acquire exchange items in an external network also requires the control of surplus. Hutterer (1977) believes there is evidence for this kind of activity in the Philippine Islands where pots were produced by part-time specialists in certain villages. The vessels are found distributed across several ethnic and linguistic subdivisions, suggesting the existence of an interethnic and intraethnic nonsubsistence exchange system, something Hutterer (1977) believes is indicative of chiefdom-level society.

Evidence of exchange in sumptuary items (Levy 1979; Arnold 1995), luxury goods (Ardika 1987), and symbolic items (Malinowski 1922) is often found archaeologically, especially among chiefdom societies. This type of exchange will be found both within the internal and external networks, as the chief carries out redistribution and reciprocity. Prestige goods may devolve upon members of the chief's family, priests, and/or warriors, as well as being used to cement alliances between chiefs.

Kipp and Schortman (1989) argue that most of the exchanges between prehistoric chiefs were direct and did not involve a third party. The purpose of such transactions was to cement personal or political bonds and usually involved luxury items. The acquisition of foreign items also served to enhance the owner's prestige; as Earle (1987) illustrates, it was not the goods themselves that were important but the knowledge and power they embodied. Some have suggested that the bonds engendered through such exchange may have resembled an exclusive ethnic identity (Friedel 1979; 1986; Schortman and Urban 1987; Kipp and Schortman 1989; Schortman

1989). Earle (1991, 7) takes this argument further, suggesting that elite exchange engendered an international style "used to set the ruling elites as a people apart." This encouraged the creation of new wealth items and exchange. In owning foreign objects, leaders visibly set themselves apart from the rest of their society, legitimizing their sacred and special role (Hastorf 1990).

Elites may maintain their superordinate position by monopolizing intersocietal exchange of prestige markers and luxury goods (Earle 1987). Intercultural similarities in grave furniture are not uncommon among elite burials. These similarities span wide regions and politically autonomous societies where the material culture of the nonelite majority varies noticeably by locale. Styles of architecture and burial treatment diffuse along with portable items and, like them, create and index status differences. Some imported items are employed as political currency; a paramount may distribute exotic items in order to assure the loyalty of subchiefs. According to Kipp and Schortman (1989), this translates into a chief's ability to mobilize labor, encourage surplus production, and call up defensive forces.

EFFECTS OF EXCHANGE ON POLITICAL DEVELOPMENT

There is little doubt that both redistribution and external trade/reciprocity had an effect on the sociopolitical developments of prehistoric societies. These relationships may have had both positive and negative effects on the cultures involved. In some instances, a more efficient operation may have resulted, whereas in others they may have been responsible for the complete collapse of political structures. Marxist analysis might suggest, for example, that external trade in luxury items by the leaders of early chiefdoms may have generated conflict between the chief's family and the common people due to issues of unequal distribution (Kipp and Schortman 1989). Such a conflict of interests may eventually have thrown a chiefdom into disarray leading to social transformation (Schultz and Lavenda 1995). At the same time, however, it was usually in the chief's best interest to exploit opportunities presented from outside his power sphere. Steponaitis (1991, 194) believes that "local success in chiefly politics may depend . . . on access to external knowledge, commodities, and alliances." Monopolies of external trade can also serve to reinforce a chief's internal control (Ekholm 1972; Rathje 1972; Schortman and Urban 1996). Similarly, the importance of trade and external ties is stressed by Earle (1991) who lists these among the strategies essential for gaining and extending power. He also believes that the success or failure of various political strategies may depend upon the existence of external markets and proximity to avenues of trade and exchange, as well as to needed, non-food resources.

Upham (1982 in Hastorf 1990) does not believe that interregional or long-distance exchange is responsible for the onset of ranking. This type of exchange probably first occurred in societies that were already ranked, and the external transactions only served to extend the power of leaders (Earle 1987; Brumfiel and Earle 1987). Due to the increased distances and the higher costs involved, groups engaging in this type of exchange must be able to produce a consistent surplus (Drennan 1984; Brumfiel and Earle 1987 in Hastorf 1990).

There is strong evidence for the occurrence of social change as a result of exchange interactions in the Philippines. Hutterer (1977) believes that the growth of maritime exchange was related to the formation of large nucleated coastal settlements, drastic changes in the economic system such as the development of a primitive market economy, and changes in the social structure of coastal communities. During the period under consideration in the Philippines (10th–12th centuries C.E.), a system of social ranking developed within coastal groups. Spanish sources indicate that this was primarily based upon accumulated wealth and not related to descent. It appeared to observers that political leaders were from the upper economic classes. Individuals and their families would bind themselves to a leader through reciprocal social and economic obligations. The leaders of such alliance groups in turn entered into alliances with more powerful leaders and formed political federations of a higher order. Larger settlements contained two or more levels of political leadership and controlled some of the hinterland. The principle means of demonstrating wealth and rank were ostentatious display of expensive foreign trade goods and the espousal of foreign religious ideologies (Hutterer 1977; Junker 1993). A similar sociopolitical trajectory is charted by Brun (1995) for central Europe during the period 600–450 B.C.E., in which elites used exchange goods to reinforce their control.

The effects of foreign trade were far reaching and caused social upheaval not only among coastal groups but also among those living inland. Because many of the products in demand for export were not in the control of the coastal centers, they were forced to exchange with inland hunters and swidden agriculturalists. This had repercussions on the exploitative patterns and economic systems of these inland populations, causing alterations in their subsistence patterns (Hutterer 1977; Junker 1993).

The repercussions of chiefdom-level societies engaging in transactions with state-level societies are no less disruptive. Chiefs must assure their status positions by ensuring they are the only individuals capable of supplying the demands of state-based traders, as well as ensuring that access is restricted to any introduced commodities. The state-based traders would in all likelihood be interested in locally produced goods, thus creating new sources of wealth.

Johnson and Earle (1987) contend that external exchange could not be conducted by individual commoners because it usually requires politically negotiated agreements or elaborate technology, such as long distance canoes, or both. According to Kipp and Schortman (1989), status and wealth become linked all the more strongly and new levels of coercion also come into play. They also link the rise of militarism to interaction with state-based traders, in that chiefs must protect themselves from pirate traders. Militarism, however, is a double-edged sword, in that, while leaders in more complex chiefdoms may use armed force to extract tribute and labor from subordinates, they must use most of what is gained to maintain the force. In the chief's favor, the demands placed on the populace assures that individuals are unable to amass wealth to buy the luxuries that define power (Kipp and Schortman 1989).

Interactions and their consequent results have been considered by Renfrew (1986) in the presentation of a model he terms "peer-polity interaction." This includes the full range of interaction (imitation and emulation, competition, warfare, and the exchange of material goods and information) that can take place between autonomous sociopolitical units, developed chiefdoms, or early states, situated beside or near one another within a single geographic region.

Renfrew (1986) seeks a median between those explanations that posit exogenous reasons for change and those that promote endogenous factors. He feels both these approaches have consistently ignored the role of neighboring polities of similar size and status. Renfrew's model sees sociopolitical change occurring at a regional level through the interaction of polities. The emphasis is on the flow of information, not just material.

The model ties in many of the facets discussed above, all hinged upon the intensification of production and peer polity interaction. Increased production permits not only increased population density, but also the accumulation of production beyond subsistence, allowing craft specialization (Renfrew 1986). A major component of Renfrew's model is competitive emulation in which neighboring polities are engaged in displays of wealth, a process that further stimulates production.

Symbolic entrainment is another, perhaps more effective, form of change in which the developed symbolic system of one society is incorporated by another less developed society with which it does not conflict (Renfrew 1986). Accompanying such interactions are innovations that are not of a symbolic nature, which may have a profound effect on the sociopolitical structure of the adoptive society.

Although Renfrew (1986) emphasizes information exchange, he states that there is little doubt that an increased flow in the exchange of goods can also further structural transformations as new institutions may develop to cope with reception, production, and distribution of goods.

IDEOLOGY

The manner in which the subsistence economy may be redirected to finance the chiefly apparatus and the way in which control is maintained has been reviewed in the discussion of redistribution. I have examined the role of the military in protecting and expanding societal interests. The control of force may also be used coercively by a chief to ensure compliance, although this is a tactic more common at the state level (Wright 1994). More powerful than force of arms in the consolidation of power is ideology. Some of the surplus may be used by the ruling elite to support a warrior class and for ceremonies, which establish their legitimacy (Earle 1991).

Ideology is one way in which elites seek to legitimize the status quo, using familiar cosmological referents (Pauketat 1994). In Service's (1962) view the consolidation of religion is one of the most prominent aspects of the chiefdom-level society. There is a proliferation of ceremonies and rituals, often dedicated to ancestor worship, which underscore the importance of primogeniture and the rank-order (Renfrew 1986). Ancestor worship in the chiefdom may be coordinated by a priest who holds a permanent hereditary office, similar to that of the chief. Service (1962) noted that it is not uncommon for the office of chief and priest to be combined, creating, in effect, a theocracy.

The internal conflicts and exploitative nature of the chiefly society demand the institution of a complex ideology to ensure stability. The ideology of many chiefdoms involved new systems of symbolism and cognition (Earle 1987), a mystification of the control of resources, and hereditary inequality (Blanton et al. 1996). Control of land was assured through ceremonies that created a sacred landscape in which the ancestors of the chiefs were seen as gods and the living chiefs were their earthly representatives (Kirch 1984). The principles of descent, common in many chiefdoms, lend themselves to exploitation by the elite. Service (1962) found that deified ancestors were often ranked in death as they were in life.

Land, productivity, and religion were closely integrated in Polynesia, and the chief was expected to "liaise" with the gods to ensure a high yield (Kirch 1991). The role of the paramount chief in prehistoric Hawaii is an excellent example of such a situation. The paramount was unlikely to be sanguinally affiliated with the populace in all of the subordinate chiefdoms and so assumed a role that would ensure his position. The paramount did this by making the populace ritually dependent upon him as the only individual able to appease the deities (Peebles and Kus 1977).

Many Polynesian societies offer evidence of the existence of shamans and sorcerers, but in most cases these positions did not diminish the power of the chiefs. The importance of the role of conduit to the gods is evident in the Marquesas Islands, where most of the power of the hereditary chiefs was usurped by a priestly class. These individuals made most of the important decisions regarding warfare and ritual, as it related to production (Kirch 1991). In the Marquesas, the allegiance of the populace was successfully moved from the chief to the priests.

STRATIFIED SOCIETIES

Kristiansen (1991) calls for a reexamination of organizational properties in chiefdoms, arguing that there is a fundamental divide between tribal societies, of which he feels chiefdoms are a variant, and state societies. He prefers to view stratified societies as archaic states that comprise the basic features of state organization, such as strong social and economic divisions, and an emphasis on territory rather than kinship. The presence of developed bureaucracies is, however, lacking in stratified societies, an omission which distinguishes it from the proper state (Kristiansen 1991). Stratified societies may be either decentralized or centralized. The former have decentralized subsistence production and a population living in villages scattered across the land. The rulers are separated from the populace by a retinue of warriors. Without the bonds of kinship, the chiefs demand the payment of tribute and tax, which Kristiansen (1991) says allows them to control, undermine, and exploit the farming communities. Kristiansen (1991) believes that the flow of produce ran through trading communities that were controlled by the central authority. These settlements may evolve into towns but large communities are not a trait of this type of polity. Many of the trade items would be produced by specialists and slaves.

Kristiansen's (1991) centralized archaic state has a centralized economy with the potential for sustaining a state apparatus and the ritualized genealogical structure of the ruling class. These polities may develop in regions of high productivity, where surplus can be generated and controlled. Surplus production is converted into large-scale ritual activities, building of ceremonial centers, organization of craft production, and centralized trade. Chiefs demand either tribute or corvée labor from their followers and must furnish the same to a paramount.

According to Kristiansen (1991), archaic states may be distinguished from chiefdoms based upon the organization of labor used to construct monumental structures. The occasional mobilization of a work force through social obligations, rewarded by feasting, is commonplace in chiefdoms, whereas formalized control of communities through land ownership is a hallmark of the archaic state. Among chiefdoms, economic and political processes are organized along kinship lines, and social groups have not been transformed into classes. The centralized archaic state formalized the basic components of a developed bureaucracy to administrate production, trade, and religious activities.

Fried (1967) also introduced the stratified society as an intermediate between ranked groups and the state. Among stratified societies there is differential economic access to basic subsistence resources, which may lead to the accumulation of wealth by a minority. Such a situation, according to Fried, would result in the formation of dominant-subordinate relationships. Stratified society lacks the complex social, economic, and political institutions seen in states, as well as the stability and duration of states. These political formations could either develop into a primary state or devolve into simpler socioeconomic forms. It should be noted that the cyclic nature of chiefdoms is also well documented and is indeed posited to be a fundamental aspect of societies organized as chiefdoms (Anderson 1994). Fluctuations in the number and composition of the administrative and decision-making levels in chiefdoms appear to have been frequent occurrences. Societies are thought to have alternated or cycled between one, two, and sometimes three decision-making levels. Such fluctuations must be understood on a regional scale rather than being seen as occurring independently within societies, or social units within societies, because the collapse or increased complexity of one group may affect another. "Cycling is thus the recurrent process of the emergence, expansion, and fragmentation of complex chiefdoms amid a regional backdrop of simple chiefdoms" (Anderson 1994, 9).

Fried believed that only self-generating states passed through the stratified stage and that it was usually not encountered in societies that were influenced by preexisting states. The stratified society is best described as a rank society in which access to the basic resources, upon which life depends, is restricted by those holding power (Fried 1967). Further, this societal form will render the exploitation of human labor possible. Such a situation creates social stresses that are unable to be controlled by traditional kinship mechanisms. The result is the destruction of the kinship system and the supersession of a non-kin based regulation system (Fried 1967). The stratified society is not known ethnographically and, as Fried states, has probably not existed for well over two thousand years, but he feels confident in reconstructing this societal type based on historical evidence (Fried 1967).

The stratified society with weakening kinship ties and increasing population is faced with a dilemma. It may either develop formal, specialized mechanisms of coercion to maintain control or revert to an egalitarian form (Fried 1967). The acme in Fried's (1967, 229) model of cultural evolution is the state, which is the "complex of institutions by means of which the power of the society is organized on a basis superior to kinship." He posits two types, the pristine and secondary. The former is an entity that evolved of its own accord, whereas the secondary state was one that came into existence due to the influence of a preexisting state (Fried 1967).

Although Service does not broach the subject of the archaic state, he does offer some points of departure useful in distinguishing these from chiefdoms, a fundamental difference being the nature of the polity. Among chiefdoms, social order is based upon kinship, whereas, in the archaic state, it is based on a civic society. The primitive state may retain corporate kin structures, but their political significance is superseded by the office and institutions associated with leadership. Kinship still plays an important role in the primitive state, where succession is concerned, although the rules concerning this are more definitive (Gibson and Geselowitz 1988). The archaic state may further be distinguished by the presence of a permanent armed force, controlled by an authorized individual. Service (1975) underscores this distinction, writing that it is the monopoly of force by the head of state, as opposed to the advantage of force held by a chief, that most clearly separates the two political forms.

States are socially differentiated from chiefdoms by the existence of political classes. Among chiefdoms, differences in rank and social strata are based upon rules, whereas, in the state, social position will often be determined by political or economic factors (Service 1975). It is important to remember, however, that Service, in positing redistribution as the primary causative factor of political development, believed that chiefdoms were essentially economic in function and origin (Carneiro 1981). States may be economically distinguished from chiefdoms in the bureaucratization of production, where agricultural and craft production are brought further under control by elites through managers (Gibson 1988).

Johnson and Earle (1987) follow Fried (1967) and Service (1962) in using terms of social organization based on economic factors. Once regional control is established, the evolutionary development of chiefdoms toward greater centralization depends on investment opportunities and the costs of controlling, or defending, whatever investments are made. Some investments, such as irrigation, offer an extremely large potential for control and growth. These characteristically underlie the evolution of states.

The rise of the "primitive" state is well documented in Europe. The development from the Bronze Age societies into more complex Iron Age political entities is well understood. It has been argued that formal political roles developed from informal leadership positions and power was individualized (Brun 1995). Polities merged and social inequality became institutionalized (Dietler 1995). Brun (1995) believes that many of these changes were underwritten by agricultural intensification, made possible by technological innovation. Agricultural surpluses during the Iron Age permitted the development of nonagricultural populations based in large settlements. There is a notable increase in the number of fortified sites, which rather than serving to protect their inhabitants are thought to have been constructed more to impress them (Brun 1995; Büchsenschütz 1995). According to Haselgrove (1995, 81) "many scholars see [fortified settlements] as an expression of deeper social change, involving increased political centralisation and stratification." There is also consensus on the role of increasing long-distance exchange in the rise of the state in Europe (Brun 1995; Büchsenschütz 1995; Haselgrove 1995). Transactions were made more fluid with the introduction of coinage, often cited as an important component of statehood.

Yoffee (2005) has argued that semiautonomous social groups developed in the earliest states around the world. These groups comprised patrons and clients organized hierarchically in which power struggles erupted. The resulting recombination of these groups under new leaders resulted in the rise of states. Yoffee states that new ideologies were created to legitimize the new leadership and were accompanied by the use of symbols, sustained and controlled by the elites. A convention was established for the perpetuation, maintenance, and display of the new ideology and the representative symbols of the ideology.

Yoffee argues that the catalyst for the formation of a state apparatus in most societies has been the evolution of the city, that the city was the environment in which the idea of a more structured social order was conceived, and that an important aspect of this development was the interaction between the urban area and the rural territory surrounding it. The rural area provided the city the means of survival through labor, food, and military service, yet also represented a counterpoint of power. Yoffee's hypothesis is that the rural area represented a potential threat to the stability of the society and was in some cases a powerbase for those who may have wanted to resist the desires of the urban elite. Thus the elite often granted country estates to those living in the city as a means of mitigating the threat (Yoffee 2005). At the same time, rural elites played a role in urban politics as well. Yoffee believes that "the stability of the state often lay in the balance between the status and legitimacy provided by [political-religious] ceremonies to rural leaders and the tangible support in goods and labour that rural elites and their dependants had to provide to urban leaders."

THEORIES ON COMPLEX SYSTEMS

All of the variables discussed above including trade, population, environment, access to resources, and conflict may be considered "inputs" into a system. These variables act in conjunction with preexisting socioeconomic and cultural inputs, forming a complex web of interrelationships each affecting the other and in a constant state of flux. These socioeconomic and cultural inputs are, then, adaptable and are affected by the "external" system inputs. However, these inputs will affect the outcome in a changing cultural and political landscape. Preexisting socioeconomics include the political system, the role of prestige, power and economy, conflict resolution strategies, religion, sexual politics, and of course human agency— individual personalities. Such a system may be considered complex and adaptive, forming a "network of interacting parts that exhibit a dynamic, aggregate behaviour" (Yoffee 2005).

Prior to the widespread acceptance of chaos theory, apparently random behavior may have been explained as a result of external interference or systemic complexity. In the former, complex behavior could be explained as the result of uncontrolled external factors. Random behavior attributed to systemic complexity is also understandable. Most systems comprise uncountable atoms and molecules that cannot be controlled, which, it may be argued, results in random behavior. The problem with these explanations is that chaotic behavior is encountered in many simple systems that are free of external influences or "noise." Chaos theory allows the order and universality of these systems to be described and classified (Hilborn 1994). It is, in fact, a search for order in the universe. Much of the order apparent to us in the natural world is attributed to the action of natural selection in evolutionary processes. In other words, the order we see has been determined by chance and circumstance. Nonlinear dynamics promotes the belief that the order found in nature may instead result from the spontaneous order of self-organized systems. These systems include only opportunistic organisms. This differentiates the order found in these systems from that present in natural elements, such as crystals. The behavior of the system is "controlled" by the interaction of its parts. System equilibrium can never be reached, and there is no optimal state of system performance. It is the nature of the system to fluctuate and oscillate beyond the control of any one input or combination of inputs. Minor input changes can result in the alteration of the entire system and vice versa (Yoffee 2005).

Although in a seminal state, the search for evidence of self-organization and natural order have far-reaching consequences for evolutionary theory, be it biological, economic, or social. Kauffman (1995) aims to formulate a body of theory capable of addressing complex questions regarding the nature of functional wholes. The most promising avenue is a model that envisages functional wholes as strings of symbols that interact and act upon one another—so-called autocatalyctic polymer systems. The symbols in a string may represent any number of things. Depending on the system modeled, they may be amino acids or cultural roles, such as shaman, chief, or warrior (Kauffman 1993, 1995). According to Kauffman's theory, the strings act upon one another, governed by rules known as grammars. The "grammar specifies indirectly the function connections among the symbol strings. It defines which sets of strings acting on other sets of strings, which produce sets of output strings." (Kauffman 1993, 370). Kauffman (1993, 387) believes that broad "grammar regimes" exist that will allow the development of predictive evolutionary models. These could be applied to any system to understand and explain functional integration, interaction, transformation, and coevolution. Acknowledging the lack of real laws in the social sciences, Kauffman (1995, 283–84) proposes that abstract models may be useful, provided they belong to the same "universality class" and demonstrate the same "robust behaviour" as that which is found in reality. The details of the model are inconsequential as long as the real world and the model inhabit the same universality class.

The implications of underlying order in social development are clearly vast. Their value to our understanding of the development of social complexity lies in the fact that there may be a finite number of permutations that human social organizations may assume. This theory may also provide a number of useful concepts that will assist our understanding of sociopolitical development.

The departure from lineal thought is perhaps the most useful aspect of self-organization science and nonlinear dynamics. There are, however, other concepts in these theories that are useful in the attempt to understand the development of human social organization. The concept of bifurcation—any sudden change in the behavior of a system as some parameter is varied (Hilborn 1994)—is of particular interest. When a system is near a bifurcation point, it is relatively unstable and small or chance disturbances can be decisive in determining the branch taken (Scott 1991). Systems are thought to progress in a predictable manner up until the bifurcation point, after which the direction taken is unpredictable. Scott (1991, 8) believes that history comprises "successive phases of perhaps relatively predictable evolution 'along' a particular branch, separated by moments of instability during which the future of the system is laid down by some rather indeterminate chance events which push it onto one or another branch."

Systemic development between bifurcation points is not necessarily lineal. Along the path of development there exist "deterministic attractors," which are thought to generate rhythmic behavior. These may be either "point attractors" or "limit cycle attractors," which cause a system to be attracted during its evolution to the same cycle. This attraction may cause the system to "go round and round and round like a machine" (Scott 1991, 10).

It is not intended that heterarchy be slotted into the procession of societal forms proposed under most evolutionary models. Rather it is hoped that it will pervade the theory of social organization and help us better understand its mechanisms. As Brumfiel (1995, 128) says, it is "not any single type of social structure, rather, it is a principle of social organisation, like kinship, that is reworked and assumes different roles depending upon its structural context. . . . We should use heterarchy to look at [the tribes-chiefdoms-states] constructs differently."

Viewing social structures from a heterarchical perspective, one sees a complex system of interconnections that are time and space dependent. The complexity of human relationships renders a pandemic interpretation of social organization difficult. The difficulty is intensified in the case of societies identified archaeologically. It is important to consider the multidimensional aspect of human interaction. There is an array of levels on which every person operates, and the interactions on each are of varying intensity and intricacy. These relationships are not, of course, static but undergo constant metamorphoses. The true value of the heterarchical model lies in its ability to embrace these truths and recognize the flexible and transient nature of human interaction. To this end, both the vertical and horizontal planes of human interaction are viewed as dynamic. Archaeological data represent points in time along a continuum and often give an impression of stasis. The reality, however, is that the social organization may vary from simple to complex or any permutation in between.

It is important to note that the heterarchical model does not negate the existence of ranked hierarchical societies, but encompasses them. All societies may be viewed as heterarchical in the scope of time. Limited evidence for long-term hierarchic or egalitarian structures is necessary for the implementation of the heterarchical model. The heterarchical perspective simply acknowledges the complex web of human and environmental interaction.

CONCLUSION

The preceding pages have outlined the theoretical development of sociopolitical forms that likely existed during the late first millennium B.C.E. and into the first millennium C.E. in Southeast Asia. The various theories for the development of these entities are applicable in the current discussion of the rise of complex polities in Southeast Asia. The rise of increasingly complex political entities in the region was, likely, the result of the interaction of changing system inputs. The genesis and collapse of discreet systems may be understood through an examination of all of the parameters of the system. This, of course, even in the best of circumstances, would prove extremely difficult. It is even more difficult when we are forced to rely upon archaeological evidence alone, as is the case with the early polities of the remote past in Southeast Asia. A fuller understanding of the cycle of development, collapse, and reformulation of complex systems in the past can only be advanced through the accumulation of further evidence of these societies. Although taxing it is an endeavor worthy of pursuit and will result in a better understanding of the development of human political systems and their consequent, inevitable collapse.

8

Sociopolitical Change
in Early Southeast Asia

The dramatic social and political changes that occurred in insular and mainland Southeast Asia during the late first millennium B.C.E. and first millennium C.E. have been discussed from the earliest periods of scholarship on Southeast Asia. The apparent transformation of indigenous cultures and the adoption and absorption of many of the traits of Indian culture has been termed "Aryanization," "Hinduization," and "Sanskritization." The most common term applied to the process, however, has been "Indianization." Scholars have remarked upon the apparent adoption of India's cultural vocabulary and wondered about the catalyst and process of "Indianization" (Wheatley 1961; Coedés 1966; 1968; Wolters 1982).

INDIA: THE FORMATION OF THE MAURYAN EMPIRE

For the most part the period of interaction between South and Southeast Asia spanned the end of the Mauryan rule in India and the rise of Kushanas and the Gupta. It is perhaps apropos, then, to present a brief overview of Indian history as it pertains to the period of interest in Southeast Asia. To do so it is necessary to set the stage in the years prior to the first millennium C.E. At the time the most powerful ruler in the subcontinent was Chandragupta Maurya (r. circa 321–292 B.C.E.), who founded the Mauryan Empire. This empire came to control all of India north of the Narmada River in central modern India and was at its most powerful under Asoka (r. circa 272–232 B.C.E.), who had continued an ambitious campaign of conquest.

Mauryan rulers invested a great deal of energy in uniting their diverse empire under an ethos of universal order and aggressive military expansion

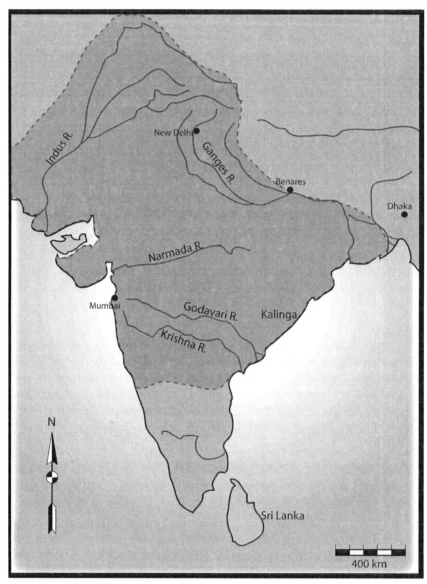

Map 8.1. Map of Indian subcontinent showing the probable boundaries of the Mauryan Empire.

(Farmer et al. 1986). The ruler was the paramount in the government, attended to by a council. The ruler was said to be loved by the gods, and it appears that a great deal of pomp and ceremony surrounded the throne. The empire was divided into provinces each ruled by a governor who was often a relative of the king.

Asoka, however, renounced war after witnessing the destruction and misery he had created and converted to Buddhism. This ruler is largely responsible for the spread of Buddhism throughout South Asia and beyond. Buddhism did not remain the state religion for long, however.

The Mauryans were toppled by the short-lived dynasty of Shunga (183–173 B.C.E.), who instituted a persecution of Buddhists and reinstated Brahmanism as the state religion. By 173 B.C.E. the Shunga line was feeling the pressure of incursions by foreign peoples, including the Parthians, Sakas, Bactrian Greeks, and Kushanas, who dominated India for centuries. The Kushanas invaded India from eastern China. These peoples were eventually absorbed by the subcontinent and became patrons of Buddhism. It was under the Kushana rule, which lasted from the 1st century B.C.E. to the 1st century C.E., that the recently destroyed Bamiyan Buddha effigies in Afghanistan were created.

As powerful and long lasting as the Kushana rule was it did not cover the whole of the subcontinent, being restricted to northwest India and Pakistan. Control of the subcontinent was accomplished under the Gupta rule beginning circa 328 C.E. Events in South Asia, such as the accession and eventual religious conversion of the emperor Asoka in the 3rd century B.C.E., have direct bearing on Southeast Asia. Asoka was largely responsible for the spread of Buddhism throughout South Asia. Contemporaneously, the people of South Asia had begun to adopt the Hindu caste system and Sanskrit language of northwest India.

The Gupta period was one of great enlightenment. Literature, art, architecture, and science flourished under the rule of the Gupta kings. The Hindu religion underwent a renaissance, and other religions prospered due to the Gupta policy of religious tolerance. The Gupta period saw the spread of Indian ideas to the far reaches of the known world. Buddhism was introduced to China and other parts of Southeast Asia during this period.

The Gupta empire lasted until about 467 C.E., when invasions by the nomadic Huns from western Asia weakened the empire. The Hun invaders were eventually expelled from India by a confederation of kings and a pan-Indian empire reestablished by Harsha of Kanauj (r. 606–648 C.E.). Upon Harsha's death the empire collapsed, and the subcontinent came under the sway of the Muslim Turks who established the Sultanate of Dili. The Sultanate lasted until the beginning of the 13th century.

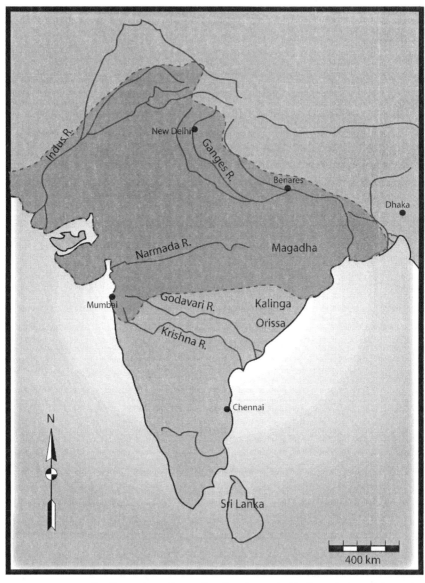

Map 8.2. Map of Indian subcontinent showing the probable boundaries of the Gupta Empire.

VESTIGES OF INDIGENOUS CULTURE IN SOUTHEAST ASIA

There are tantalizing hints regarding the royal regalia in ancient Southeast Asia. As Brown (1996) illustrates, the king of Chitu and the king of Funan both sat before the image of a flaming golden disc. Such a symbol is not present in Indian royal regalia, and it may reflect a deep-rooted Southeast Asia tradition.

The Dong Son culture existed in the Ma and Ca River basins of northern Vietnam. Although most of our knowledge of Dong Son comes from interment sites, there is one settlement site attributed to the culture, Co Loa (Higham 2002). Co Loa is a moated site with two round external moats and an inner, rectangular rampart. The Dong Son culture produced a variety of unique artifacts, mostly in bronze, some of which entered a regional trade network. These include the famous bronze drums, as well as bronze bells decorated with a geometric pattern. The bells have been found in Vietnam, peninsular Malaysia, and Cambodia, with two more being discovered in 2003 at Pursat, Cambodia.

Dong Son drums are more widely distributed, and all share similar decorative motifs. The most prominent aspect of the drums is the flying bird and a "star" on the tympanum. Loofs-Wissowa (1991) hypothesizes that the drums were created in northern Vietnam where the greatest concentration of them is found and that they are symbols of authority conferred upon other regional chiefdoms. If proven correct, this idea has far-reaching implications on our understanding of the development of intraregional trade networks and requires a reassessment of our understanding of the sophistication of Southeast Asian chiefdoms prior to Indian contact. As Jacq-Hergoualc'h (2002, 76) writes, it indicates that "there existed in SE Asia a network of political entities whose chiefs attempted to obtain recognition of their authority through the possession of emblems of power." According to Jacq-Hergoualc'h (2002, 78), the instance of the Dong Son drums demonstrates the existence of a political network from very early on in which chiefs obtained recognition through the possession of emblems of power.

Miksic (1999d, 76) concurs with the idea that the drums were symbols of authority. He feels that early Malaysian chiefs were using their ability to obtain rare and valuable objects such as the drums to demonstrate their power.

One may speculate that the star symbol in the center of Dong Son drums was a precursor to the royal symbol reported by the Chinese. Perhaps the symbolism of these drums, which were spread throughout Southeast Asia, was perpetuated.

One of the earliest sites evidencing contact with India is Ban Don Ta Phet, Thailand, near the Three Pagodas Pass on the upper Malay Peninsula. This Iron Age burial site, dated to the 4th century B.C.E., shows connections between India and Vietnam at a very early date. The site has surrendered bronze artifacts with a high concentration of tin, a technique similar to that found in south India (Glover 1998). Bronze bowls from the site are decorated with scenes reminiscent of Indian art (Glover et al. 1984; Glover 1990). Other artifacts include beads of likely Indian origin and a carved carnelian lion, thought to represent the Buddha. Of particular interest is the presence of an artifact usually found in Vietnam, a bicephalous nephrite earring as well as a bronze situla or bucket. The former artifact is characteristic of the Sa Huynh culture and the latter reminiscent of Dong Son.

Other sites with evidence for early contact include Khao Sam Kaeo, near Chumpon in peninsular Thailand. Here etched agate and carnelian beads have been found. This technology is firmly established in an early period in India, but it is unlikely to have been practiced by indigenous artisans during the period the site is thought to have been occupied (circa early 1st century C.E). Also found were stone seals inscribed with Sanskrit writing dated to the 2nd century B.C.E. (Srisuchat 1986).

In Krabi Province, peninsular Thailand, the site of Khuan Lukpad has yielded similar seals dated to the late 1st and early 2nd century C.E. (Glover 1990). Some of these seals are decorated with figures from Greco-Roman mythology. The trade at this early date clearly stretched as far as the Mediterranean Sea. There is a significant amount of evidence of commercial links between India and Rome, including amphorae and Arretine-ware and the Roman gold coins found throughout the subcontinent (Bellina and Glover 2004).

There is some evidence suggesting that Khuan Lukpad was a manufacturing center of Indian-inspired stone beads. Unfinished beads and partly processed glass indicate that the site was using imported raw materials to produce jewelry for the local market (Bronson 1990).

Brown (1996, 184) presents other possible prehistoric vestiges in protohistoric Southeast Asia. The popularity of *sema* stones in northeast Thailand may have derived from the worship of menhir stones.

The *cakras* popular in Dvaravati are also not wholly Indian conceptions according to Brown (1996, 185). He feels that these are amalgams of Indian and indigenous features. This amalgam is symptomatic of the whole process of Indianization in Brown's opinion.

Wales (1936) theorized that Indian artistic influence swept over Southeast Asia in successive waves. He felt that Dvaravati, Myanmar, and the Malay Peninsula bore the brunt of this artistic Indianization. Cambodia, Indonesia, and Vietnam were less affected by Indian culture (Wales 1974).

Mabbet (1997, 343) notes that the word "Indianization" has transformed from a label for a factual process to the label for a theory that is now open to criticism. He notes that our conceptions of India as the only actor in an engagement between many different cultures across South and Southeast Asia have changed. This change is due, in large part, to the advances made in archaeological science in Southeast Asia. Archaeology has shed some light on the prehistoric past of Southeast Asia and shown that it was not completely populated by barbarians with no political sophistication. Scholars interested in the interaction between the Indian and Southeast Asian cultures now understand that there were likely changes already afoot in Southeast Asia. The chiefdoms or paramountcies may have taken advantage of the new set of political tools presented to them in the form of complex Indian social and cultural beliefs. Evidence of this is particularly strong at sites in north-central and northeast Thailand where the bulk of the research has been undertaken (Higham 1977; 1989a; 1998a; 1998b; 2002; Veerapan 1979; Higham et al. 1982; Higham and Kijngam 1982; Pautreau, Matringhem et al. 1997a; 1997b; Higham and Thosarat 1998; O'Reilly 1998; 1999; 2000; 2003; Pautreau and Mornais 1998). There is strong indication that political complexity was developing as early as the Bronze Age (circa 1500–500 B.C.E.), and hierarchical political organizations appear to have been strongly entrenched by the beginning of the Iron Age (circa 500 B.C.E.).

The evidence from the sites excavated in Thailand appears to suggest that large groups of people were being marshaled to construct settlements surrounded by moats and ramparts. The number of people inhabiting these Iron Age sites appears to have been greater than in the preceding era. The burials from these sites seem to indicate an increase in social stratification from that seen in the Bronze Age sites (O'Reilly 1999; 2000; 2003).

Mabbet (1997) feels that the cause of the social changes evident in the sites of Thailand may be explained by a number of factors. Predominantly he feels that the introduction of improved agricultural technology must have played a role, particularly the introduction of the plough. This innovation along with other tools would have allowed widespread clearing of forest and increased the capability of communities to create surplus stores of rice, setting into effect a chain of sociopolitical consequences. The surplus would have freed many from the demands of food production generating new "classes" of people, including craftsmen, warriors, administrators, and priests.

Exploring alternative motive factors, Mabbet (1997) looks to the work of Carneiro (1970) and his theory of environmental circumscription. This theory involves societies located in geographical settings that are spatially bounded. If all of the desirable land is occupied, the land in turn becomes a point of friction between settlements leading to warfare. More powerful communities subjugate the weak, and these communities are, in turn, incorporated into the lower rungs of a social hierarchy. Mabbet (1997, 345) feels that this scenario is applicable to Southeast Asia where the available land for growing rice was circumscribed due, mainly, to the limited available agricultural technology.

Welch (1985) feels that the rise of political complexity in northeast Thailand may have been the result of environmental unpredictability. Bountiful supplies of water tempered by long dry periods may have resulted in a rising population that in times of stress needed to expand territorially. He feels that the introduction of iron technology would not have had that great an impact on the development of complex societies in Thailand due to the nature of agriculture practiced. Wet rice farming, he feels, would have been able to support large densities of people even without the introduction of iron ploughs. The main challenge to the ancient farmer was the unreliability of the water supply to sustain his crops. In an effort to improve efficiency, Welch (1985) believes that farmers needed to develop complex bunding systems to retain water. The labor demand for this encouraged farmers to have larger families, which in turn placed stress on the existing sociopolitical organization.

An alternative explanation for the rise of more complex political entities in Southeast Asia is that population began to rise, creating a demand for territory. In this view, a settlement, for indeterminate reasons, begins to grow, reaching a critical population threshold. The theory sees the community faced with insurmountable difficulties and facing two options. Either the community fragments and founds new settlements or a hierarchical system is introduced (Johnson 1982). The institution of the latter results in further demands being placed on the society in question. The hierarchic system needs reinforcement through a system of tribute and regalia, materials that must be supplied by lower-ranking members of the society.

It is likely that there were a number of factors that acted as catalysts to the development of social stratification and political complexity in Southeast Asia prior to the introduction of foreign models. At the present it is impossible to isolate any particular event or series of events based on the evidence available to us. What is clear is that there were nascent moves toward political sophistication in areas that were clearly not in direct contact with India.

Contact with India is evident in many of the sites in Southeast Asia dated to the Iron Age. We see foreign influence trickling into these indigenous societies in the form of imported objects, such as glass beads and beads of semiprecious stone, such as carnelian and agate. It is unlikely that these indigenous inland groups had any sustained contact with Indian traders if they had any contact at all. The imported materials were probably incorporated into a preexisting network of exchange of exotic and valuable goods rather than acting as an impetus for political change. The majority of evidence we have for direct contact between Indians and Southeast Asians dates to circa 50 B.C.E. to the second century C.E., by which time there is strong evidence for sociopolitical development in Mainland Southeast Asia (Mabbet 1997).

Mabbet (1997, 347) proposes that there are three distinct phases apparent in pre- and protohistoric Southeast Asia, the first represented by the development of protourban centers in Southeast Asia in the middle of the first millennium B.C.E. and the second represented by the widespread appearance of Indian artifacts. The third phase, Mabbet proposes, is the phase that saw the full incorporation of South Asia ideas of government and religion.

The model of riverine exchange and the development of exchange systems described by Bronson (1977) (see chapter on Malaysia for detail) has few detractors. This is a hypothesis that proposes that indigenous settlements based at the mouth of a river basin were able to attract foreign trade. These settlements had in their favor substantial surrounding areas with the potential for supporting a large population. The river basin isolated the settlements from surrounding polities. Trade goods flowed downstream from the hinterland areas through a network of collection points from their source. Over time, as the power of the river mouth settlement grew through the accumulation of wealth, its populations would develop the agricultural base necessary to sustain the growing polity.

Mabbet (1997) feels that Bronson's model could be used to explain the development of complex societies in the hinterlands. Because there was an existing network of trade downstream, prior to the arrival of foreign traders, a system was in place that would allow the development of increasing political complexity. As Mabbet (1997, 347) writes:

> It is easy to imagine that some groups, living at the places where the middle men came or where the local products were available, found themselves happily possessed of the means to control both access to these goods and the collection of local commodities desired by the Indians (especially for products such as aromatic timber and gold). Thus they could turn to their advantage a new distribution of wealth and influence. They gathered followers around them; they promoted increases in the extent and efficiency of farming for the sustenance of their communities; and they collected weapons for power and costly ornaments for display.

Jacq-Herougalc'h (1997, 124) characterizes the early polities of Malaysia as having a hierarchical structure, capped by Indianized city states. These coastal polities, he believes, were situated in good rice-growing margins along the coasts of Malaysia. These centers, the first to engage Indian traders, were transformed by their leaders, adopting a "social, political, military and religious system based on the Indian model." As well as the Indianized ports, Jacq-Herougalc'h (1997) believes, traders also dealt with non-Indianized ports, probably organized as chiefdoms. Both of these political nodes were supplied by collecting centers. These were settlements located near the sources of local products. These probably became important centers for the redistribution of foreign products to inland areas. The raw forest materials that were being traded were initially gathered at "feeder points" and were located closest to the resources, often at the confluence of rivers or in areas of mineral wealth (Jacq-Hergoualc'h 1997).

EARLY THEORIES OF "INDIANIZATION"

Some early scholars looked at the remains of the protohistoric and historic period in Southeast Asia and envisaged that "Hindu culture was transplanted to this distant corner of Asia . . . [that it] might be a colonial kingdom . . . fed by constant streams of civilization flowing from the motherland, and at last met with inevitable decline when this perennial source itself decayed and ceased to flow" (Majumdar 1944, 45).

Majumdar (1944, 21) envisioned a colonization of Southeast Asia by Indian migrants. Colonies, in his view, sprung up at different times and in different places populated by Indians from the homeland or other regional Indian colonies. This is an idea that, according to Das (1975), is supported by folklore that states that the ruler of Kalinga in India sent twenty thousand families to live in Java. Myanmar was likewise colonized during the Pyu times. The Chinese texts were interpreted as depicting the Funan natives as naked and tattooed semisavages (Majumdar 1944, 26).

There is some evidence in the Indian records that lend support to the theory of colonization. In 603 C.E. the king of Gujarat dispatched five thousand settlers to Java and further supplemented this with two thousand more (Raffles 1817, 87). The theory of dominant colonization has been framed as the *Kshatriya* theory, after the warrior caste of Hindu religion.

An alternative hypothesis to the military colonization of Southeast Asia is the Brahman theory which proposes that Indian culture was brought to the region by Hindu priests and scholars. There are references in the Chinese historic texts to Brahmans at the royal courts of the Southeast Asian kingdoms. The likelihood of Brahmans traveling to Southeast Asia has been debated due to the *smrti* prohibition against foreign travel. According to this prohibition Brahman become impure in crossing the sea or leaving India. Wheatley (1983) contends that this prohibition was not heeded during the early centuries C.E. Despite the fact that Brahman were said to become impure through crossing the sea, there seems to be little doubt that their influence was felt in the court rituals of early Southeast Asia.

These learned men introduced a host of magical rituals to consecrate a ruler, connecting him with mythological genealogies and surrounding him with the appropriate iconography (Wheatley 1961). Wolters (1979) has proposed that Hinduism was adopted by Southeast Asian chiefs who practiced *bhakti*, which can be translated as "being attached to god." This involved personal asceticism to purify oneself. The Brahman surrounding early chiefs likely validated their royal position through a Brahmanic rite known as *vratyastoma*. This ritual officially inducted the ruler into the *Kshatriya* caste (Wolters 1979, 295).

It is equally arguable that Indian traditions were introduced to Southeast Asia by the means of the *vaisya* caste of traders and craftsmen. Detractors of this theory argue that these people would not have been educated in the highly complex rituals recorded by the Chinese historians at the courts of Southeast Asia.

Coedès (1964b; 1968) interpreted the process of Indianization as one in which the indigenous people of the region simply copied the Indian model of religion, government, and law. Coedès (1964a, 183) felt that aspects of Indian culture, including art, literature, religion, and government, were kept by the elite of Southeast Asia, whereas "the way the people lived, their beliefs, the social and economic conditions" were indigenous (Coedès 1964b). This concept was widely supported during the early 20th century (e.g., Pelliot 1903; Aymonier 1903; Mukerji 1912; Bose 1927; Majumdar 1927; 1963; Coedès 1968).

RECENT INTERPRETATIONS OF "INDIANIZATION"

There is no doubt that the culture of India had a profound effect on the cultures of Southeast Asia and that Indian ideals, art, and religion left an indelible mark on the region. However, the idea of the process of Indianization has begun to change. Scholars now place more emphasis on the role of native cultures in the rise of political complexity in Southeast Asia (Wheatley 1983; Higham 1989a; Brown 1992; 1996; Jacq-Hergoualc'h 1997; 2002; Vickery 1998; Jacques and Freeman 1999).

Governmental Evidence

Vickery (1998) believes that there is no evidence in Southeast Asia for the arrival of Indian aristocrats nor for the establishment of states on the Indian model. The acceptance of Indian culture does not appear to have been instantaneous, as we know that in the 3rd and 4th centuries, in Cambodia, local rulers retained their indigenous titles. At this time the political organization and religious beliefs appear to have been predominantly indigenous (Adams 1980, 47). Vickery (1998) is of the opinion that the ruling *fan* of Cambodia forced the less powerful local rulers to alter traditional customs with the aim of securing power within their family. The *fan* did so by assuming Indian titles and customs, which imposed patrilineal succession on the Khmer. According to Hall (1985), however, the adoption of Indian culture did not occur in a significant manner until the mid-5th century C.E.

This "Indianization" may have been due to a change in the dynastic succession in Funan, the new rulers possibly coming from peninsular Malaysia (Hall 1985). From the 5th century onward Sanskrit came to be the official language of the ruling elite, and the Indian dating system, gods, and titles came into widespread use (Hall 1985, 69).

Vickery (1998, 178) feels that a monarchy evolves in one of two ways—either it develops internally within a given society or it is imposed from without. Vickery feels that the first option does not exclude influence on a society introduced through contact with other more complex polities.

Sastri (1949, 125–26) believes that the spread of Indian culture may be attributed mostly to the role of merchants rather than proselytizing Brahmans or Buddhists. After the initial introductions of Indian culture, he feels it may have been strengthened through the introduction of religious figures. We gain some insight, however, into the degree of contact between India and Funan through the meeting of Fan Ch'an, ruler of Funan, and an Indian merchant. This interlude is of interest as it suggests that the monarch had only occasional opportunities to meet Indians. This implies that the Indian population must have been concentrated in the Malaysian peninsula rather than in Funan's ports (Hall 1985, 70).

Trade and "Indianization"

Manguin (1996) has undertaken research on early shipping in Southeast Asia. Archaeological ship remains dating before the 14th century C.E. belong to a technological tradition known as the lash-lug and stitched plank tradition. The vessels were constructed by raising planks that are stitched together on either side of a keel via holes in the planks or lugs. The earliest example of a vessel constructed in this way comes from Malaysia and is dated to the 3rd to 5th century C.E., and the remains of similar vessels have been discovered at Oc Éo, Vietnam, which date between the 1st and 6th century C.E. (Manguin 1996, 185).

The Chinese reported vessels, which had superstructures and reached as much as fifty meters in length, in Southeast Asian harbors in the early first millennium C.E. The Chinese report that they were held together using palm fiber lashing, and that no iron was used in their construction. The ships sported multiple masts (Manguin 1996, 189).

Manguin's research has confirmed that there was a well-developed indigenous tradition of boat building in Southeast Asia that was, at least, contemporary to that of India or China. It appears likely that there was significant exchange in technical expertise between India and Southeast Asia, although our knowledge of the oceangoing vessels of the former is poor.

It is apparent that there was a florescence of trade in the early centuries C.E., as similar artifacts begin to appear at various locations around Southeast Asia, including jewelry molds from Chansen, Oc Éo, U-Thong, and Beikthano, "Pyu" coins are found throughout the region, and seals bearing strong similarities have been recovered from Sri Lanka, Arakan, and the Thai peninsula (Gutman 2001; Miksic 2003; Ratnayake 2003).

More recent research (Bellina and Glover 2004) has allowed the delineation of phases of Indian contact with Southeast Asia. The first phase of contact began around the mid-first millennium B.C.E. and lasted through to the second century C.E. This initial phase of contact is evidenced by the presence of foreign artifacts, including glass and stone beads, Indian-style ceramics, and bronzes, in prehistoric Southeast Asian archaeological sites. Semiprecious stones begin to replace serpentine, limestone, marble, and shell beads in sites dating to the late first millennium B.C.E./early first millennium C.E. It is unclear whether these beads were imported or locally made, but the former, at this early date, seems more likely as these exotic stones make a sudden appearance during the Iron Age. There is now evidence that these ornaments began to be manufactured on the western coast of the Malaysian peninsula and at Oc Éo in present-day southern Vietnam (Bellina 2003). It is likely that Indian craftspeople were involved in the manufacture of beads in Southeast Asia (Bellina 2001).

Another class of artifact that appears during the first phase of contact with Indian traders is glass, a material that appeared in northern India circa 1000 B.C.E. The glass most commonly found in early Iron Age sites in Southeast Asia originates in the Tamil Nadu area of coastal south India. This area is famed for the production of brick-red glass beads that appear in archaeological sites across mainland and insular Southeast Asia (Francis 1996). Translucent glass beads begin to appear as well, but it is thought that some of these may have been manufactured in Southeast Asia (Bellina and Glover 2004). Indeed some evidence of possible glass manufacture has been found at a site dated to circa the fourth century C.E. in Thailand (O'Reilly 1999).

A second phase of Indian contact may be discerned based on an increase in the number of artifacts and a decrease in the diversity of artifacts found that originated in India. Also indigenous ceramics are seen to be modeled on Indian styles such as the kendi (Bellina and Glover 2004). The kendi is a bulbous vessel with a thin neck and a spout. These vessels, often used in Hindu rituals, are found at Southeast Asian sites dating from the early centuries up to the seventh century C.E. (Bellina and Glover 2004).

Artistic Evidence

Regarding the art and architecture of Cambodia, de Casparis (1979, 282) feels that there is no architecture or art in India that "show[s] the model, the archetype of Khmer décor."

Bénisti (1970), with particular reference to Cambodia, proposes that Indian artistic influence found its way into the Southeast Asian repertoire through portable objects such as small statues, plaques, jewelry, votive stupas, etc. The theory may explain why some *very* early Indian motifs are present in Khmer art. These motifs may have been represented on moveable objects from the earliest of times and carried through onto larger structural and sculptural objects. Bénisti (1970) does not support the idea that Indian artists trained Khmer craftsmen either in India or in Southeast Asia. Nor does she believe that the skills were transferred through manuals or texts. She also rejects the idea that the now lost, wooden art of ancient Cambodia was derived from Indian tradition. Brown (1996), while supporting most of Bénisti's theory, feels that the idea of a shared wooden art tradition could explain many developments in Southeast Asian art. According to Brown (1996, 191), the idea allows us to imagine "parallel artistic developments, that began from shared artistic models, in India and Southeast Asia." Further, according to Brown it may explain why the search for Indian sources for much of the Southeast Asian repertoire is fruitless. This is an idea proposed by Kulke (1990, 28), who felt that it was the "social nearness between the societies of both sides of the Bay of Bengal rather than the social distance between imperial Indian states and Southeast Asian chiefdoms which made the Indian model so attractive to Southeast Asian rulers."

This is a contentious and poorly understood process, and Brown (1996) feels that it cannot be applied to the Southeast Asian example. The fact that Indian culture is not a single entity but a conglomerate of traditions complicates our understanding of cultural transference. The continuation of individual cultural traditions in India, even though they have been dramatically transformed by "Sanskritization," illustrates the difficulty of understanding the process (Brown 1996, 187). The fact that Sanskritization was so closely linked to the caste system is another reason to reject an acceptance of its application in Southeast Asia. There is no evidence in Southeast Asia for the widespread adoption of the Hindu caste system. Brown (1996) prefers to interpret the adoption of Indian cultural styles as a tool used by the elite. This set of parameters allowed the elite to share a "cultural vocabulary" and thereby elevate themselves within their own societies.

Brown (1996, 194) proposes that art was a means to power in early Southeast Asia. He feels that during times of political instability more art would have been produced as a means of legitimizing a ruler's claim to power.

The idea that the production of art in a noncentralized political environment would have restricted the type of art produced is rejected by Brown (1996). He feels the loose political organization of the *mandala*-type was in no way an impediment to artistic achievement. Brown (1996) feels that the idea that Dvaravati kingdoms failed to construct monumental structures akin to those in Cambodia due to a less centralized state is too simplistic. He prefers to present the argument that the religious affiliation of Dvaravati may play a role. Early Buddhist beliefs, as opposed to Hindu doctrine, did not encourage the construction of large edifices glorifying the Buddha. It may have been the adoption of Hinduism as opposed to Buddhism by the elite of ancient Cambodia that was the impetus for a different political trajectory. As Brown (1996) says, the building of large temples may have been what caused Cambodia and not Dvaravati to develop a state organization. According to Brown (1996, 195), temples were statements of power, illustrating the connection between the elite and the gods, a process that encouraged centralization. Understood in Hindu terms, kingship was divine, but in Buddhist understanding kingship was related to *karma*. These beliefs affected the development of state-sponsored construction, as the first priority under a Hindu leader was the erection of a state temple to the god. Under a Buddhist monarch the erection of a palace for the king was the priority (Heine-Geldern 1963; Brown 1996). Brown (1996, 196–97) suggests that Cambodian art evolved to serve the needs of the ruler, developing to more and more complex forms to perpetuate and underscore the divine nature of kingship. In Dvaravati, due to the Hinayana beliefs prevalent there, artistic development was not driven by the same demands and could fulfill its religious and political role with little need for change.

Khmer temples of the Angkorian period may be seen to follow the general tenets laid out in the Indian Hindu holy texts. They do differ in minor details, however. Siva worship in Cambodia involved the erection of eight linga around a central linga, whereas in India only eight linga are used (Haendel 2004).

Linguistic Evidence

Based on the absence of loan words from some Indian languages in inscriptions written in Indonesian languages, van Leur (1967) has argued that there was no colonization of the archipelago.

Vickery feels it impossible that Indic writing was brought to Southeast Asia and taught there only by Indians (Vickery 1998, 54). He believes that, as well as Indian sailors and merchants visiting Southeast Asia, Southeast Asians also ventured to India. Upon their return they brought with them models and ideas. Brown (Brown n.d., 39, quoted in Vickery 1998) supports this idea and feels that there were few Indian artists or even Indian-trained artists working in Southeast Asia.

The source within the Indian subcontinent seems to have been the Southeast, particularly the coast of Kalinga, now Orissa, and what was the Pallava empire covering most of south India. The name endings borne by Khmer kings, *-varman*, are rare in India but were used by the Pallava (Vickery 1998, 56).

To date, the earliest evidence of Indian script in Southeast Asia is found in Vietnam. The Vo Canh inscription, although controversial, is dated to the 3rd century C.E. Das (1975, 12) argues that the Vo Canh inscription is evidence of a link between the royal family of Kalinga, south India, and Southeast Asia. Rather than representing a colonial transplanting of Indian culture in Southeast Asia, Southworth (2001, 203) believes that the inscription represents the adaptation of "Indian cultural forms by an indigenous elite." He goes on to write: "It is probable that the Vo Canh inscription, although presented within the context of a sophisticated use of Sanskrit grammar, classical *kavya* metres, and Indian philosophical concepts, was nevertheless primarily motivated by indigenous social concerns" (Southworth 2001, 204).

This opinion is echoed by Jacq-Hergoualc'h (2002, 94), who writes that the "chiefs of certain tribes [in the Malaysian peninsula] felt the need to authenticate their local ancestral authority by drawing on more sophisticated concepts." He feels that the sociopolitical-religious concepts that originated in northwest India began to spread to south India and through trade to Southeast Asia within the space of one or two generations. This is similar to the idea expressed by Kulke (1990), in which he differentiates the large north Indian empires from those of the southeast. The latter were much smaller and probably less sophisticated. They were, in fact, probably somewhat similar to the early urban settlements of Southeast Asia. Kulke (1990) feels that the two societies were closely related developmental stages and that the process of Indianization should be seen as a convergence of similar societies, not as domination by one of the other.

CURRENT VIEWS ON "INDIANIZATION"

Some view the process of Indianization more as a process of Brahmanization or Sanskritization (Mabbett 1977a). This is a process that occurred in India as the subcontinent was culturally dominated by the Aryan civilization. According to Brown (1996), Sanskritization is a process that was used by groups to better position themselves within Indian society, especially with reference to the caste system.

Brown (1996, 193) feels that the process, whereby Indian culture was adopted in Southeast Asia, was executed by the indigenous elite. They used this exotic and supernaturally charged repertoire to secure their positions in their own society, legitimizing their social roles as leaders. Further, the foreign cultural vocabulary allowed them to maintain their intraregional relationships (Brown 1996, 193). A similar view is expressed by Wheatley (1961, 186), who feels that it was Southeast Asian rulers who realized the value of Indian concepts in legitimizing their political positions and "possibly, of stratifying their subjects."

Brown (1996) believes that the sociopolitical organization of 7th and 8th century C.E. Thailand and Cambodia is best portrayed as being structured as a *mandala*. This organizational model seems to have been altered somewhat, at least in Cambodia, with the advent of the 9th century (Brown 1996, 193).

Brown (1996, 198) rejects the idea that Indian culture was brought to Southeast Asia by a particular segment of Indian society, be it the Brahman or the Kysatria, and instead suggests that it was transmitted by *all* the varied groups of India. This is a view also expressed by de Casparis (1983, 19, cited in Jacq-Hergoualc'h 2002), who wrote that "Indianization is . . . a complicated network of relations, both between various parts of each of the two great regions and between the two regions themselves."

Brown (1996, 199) concludes that his interpretation of the process of Indianization was predominantly a religious process if presented from the point of view of a modern, western understanding. Religion, he feels, was inextricably bound up with conceptions of power. As he writes, "the spiritual and mundane worlds were a continuum, with the gods the means to this-worldly power and goals." (Brown 1996, 199).

There is strong evidence for the presence of Indian traders who lived, at least for part of the year, in Southeast Asia. We know from inscriptional evidence that Indian merchant guilds wielded considerable power in Malaysia, being able to build, maintain, and protect water reservoirs (Wheatley 1961; Jacq-Hergoualc'h 2002). It is unlikely, however, that the protection provided by these merchants for their investment represented Indian troops as has been suggested by some (Sastri 1932); rather troops were likely locally employed (Jacq-Hergoualc'h 2002).

Others support the idea that Indian culture, religion, laws, etc. introduced a transformative political element to Southeast Asia. The appeal of this ethic, according to Pollock (2000, 604), was its nebulous nature. He paints a picture of a Sanskrit cultural empire in which populations were never enumerated, and there was no standardization of the legal system. This was an "empire" in which no core-periphery conception took hold and in which space was conceived of as flexible and mirroring cosmological conceptions held at the time. Pollock's (2000) assessment is embraced by Day (2002), who feels that little of Indian culture permeated society's lower echelons and that the cultural elements introduced from India were "predominantly self-referential for the elite and foreign to the country at large, one that never became localized." Day (2002, 99) summarizes the concept by stating that, in Southeast Asia, "cosmological state formation could be beautiful, coercive, and illusory all at the same time."

In studying Indian history, scholars are confronted with problems of evidence. Most of what we know of ancient India is derived from religious texts or scriptures that inform us of teachings but shed little light on the nuances of everyday life or alternative cultural beliefs.

Wolters (1999) feels that a gap exists between prehistory and protohistory represented by Funan. This is the case because some scholars posit Funan as a "fully-fledged state." He goes on to assert that Funan's depiction as a state is based primarily on Chinese records, biased by what the Chinese, at the time, perceived a state to be. The true nature of Funan is difficult to assess, as modern scholars evaluate the polity biased toward the level of economic development and the ancient Chinese interpreted the political organization of this foreign power from their own perspective. Wolters believes there was likely little difference in the "political system" of prehistoric and protohistoric Southeast Asia as pertains to Funan.

Wolters (1999) develops a thesis that Southeast Asian society is and always has been organized bilaterally, with no particular importance attached to lineage. The existence of cognatic kinship is a cornerstone in his attempts to depict the rise of Southeast Asian protostates headed by individuals who were exemplary by right of their ability to win followers. According to Wolters, protohistoric polities were organized as *mandalas*. The *mandala* is an ancient Indian conception of how a government should be modeled. The concept was written about during the 4th century B.C.E. by Kautilya in a treatise on government called the *Arthasastra*.

The geographic area covered by a mandala is flexible, and the polity can expand and contract. A *mandala* is centered around a powerful individual whose court was encircled by provinces, usually governed by princes or trusted associates. The provinces were organized identically to the center. Surrounding the provinces were weaker polities that were vassals of the center. Tambiah (1977) cites a Javanese description of the political power of *mandala* as being similar to a torch whose light becomes weaker the farther from the flame one goes.

Wolters (1999) uses the concept of heterarchy to reinforce his argument that the prehistoric cultures of Southeast Asia were dominated by "men of prowess." He feels that this system had a continual influence on the organization of polities from the prehistoric to the historic period. Wolters is attracted to White's (1995) definition of heterarchic organization of the Bronze Age in Southeast Asia and feels that this can be extrapolated to cover later periods.

Mabbet (1997) is critical of the way in which scholars have approached the study of ancient Indian culture. He feels that there is a dogmatic adherence to the study of historical sources and a tendency to divorce these sources from time and place, thereby simplifying Indian culture, usually along religious lines. He feels that Indian historical research would benefit from the marriage of textual analysis and archaeology.

Because archaeology examines the remains of past behavior as represented by the archaeological evidence of past activity, we may temper the view given by historical texts. This approach seeks to link the literary evidence with actual evidence of behavior. Religious doctrines are of interest only if there is concrete evidence for their implementation through the remains of a past culture.

Mabbet (1997) feels that the study of historical religious documents and texts has dominated the study of ancient India to date. The result has been the creation of an image of India as an "ordered system of ideas, doctrines, rules and rituals, or of a fairly small number of such systems corresponding to major cultural constellations or stages of development." This has had an effect on the understanding of the archaeological remains uncovered in Southeast Asia because, as Mabbet (1997, 349) says, describing something as "Indian" bestows the meaning of an "abstract conceptual system of morality and philosophical beliefs." Anything outside of this conceptual system is automatically labeled "local." The result is that we are given the impression of Southeast Asia as a place that held on to a great many of its local traditions, while we conceive of "India" as a place dominated by Hindu and Buddhist doctrine with little deviation.

The same deviations from the monolithic religions do appear in India, which is clear to anyone who does not treat "India" as a literary construct (Mabbet 1997). "The danger is that of seeing the Indian contribution to Southeast Asian society as more alien, and therefore more superficial, than it actually is, forgetting or failing to recognize that Hinduism and Buddhism in India have been, in their historical development, just as much embodied in a medley of often contradictory local traditions as they have been in Southeast Asia" (Mabbet 1997, 349).

Even if we accept that indigenous Southeast Asian polities were already developing and we further accept that these were not completely dominated by a superior culture, we must still account for the asymmetry seen in the influence of one upon the other (Mabbet 1997). There is no discounting the profound influence Indian literature, language, government, and religion had on Southeast Asia, yet there is scant evidence for reverse influence.

Mabbet (1997) seeks the underlying reason for the adoption of Indian culture in Southeast Asia. Why did the importation of foreign religious figures and the trappings of Indian culture take hold? Why were the people of Southeast Asia seemingly impressed by their leaders who adopted these roles and trappings? As Mabbet says, a plausible theory that adequately answers these questions has not yet been advanced.

Indianization has been explained as a process involving a core and periphery, a process that was repeated many times as the sociopolitical culture of northeast India expanded (Mabbet 1997). This idea is shared by Sastri (1949, 122), who feels that the "Indianization" of Southeast Asia was an extension of the process by which the Deccan and south India were Aryanized and Hinduized by northern influences.

Societies on the periphery of this cultural core were put under great cultural and psychological stress as smaller communities aggregated. These smaller communities, facing great demographic, social, and economic pressure from larger communities, needed a common cultural language comprised of symbolic ritual components from known cultural repertoires. This "new" cultural language assists the people of developing states to "find ways of expression that can carry people through a crisis of social identity" (Mabbet 1997, 350). Mabbet (1997) stresses that the symbolism of the core was adopted, not forced upon the new communities. These communities incorporated the core beliefs, making room for them around their own, long-held beliefs. The emerging states needed cultural symbols that did not violate the ancestral cultural symbols of the smaller communities being absorbed.

THE ROLE OF RELIGION IN POLITICS

Burmese tradition dictates that kingship has three components—the human, the superhuman, and the divine. The kingly duties of administering the kingdom required human qualities, but to conquer other territories and become "universal monarch" required superhuman attributes. For leading his people on the righteous path of the dharma he was thought divine (Aung Thwin 1984). During the Pagan period, about which we are relatively well informed, the responsibility of leading the populace to salvation fell upon the elite (Aung Thwin 1984).

The view of the king as a divine being was also supported by Indian religious tenets. The belief in *avatars* (reincarnations in various forms) supported the idea that the king was actually a god or a *bodhisattva* in human form, sent to help the devout. Inscriptions from the Pagan era illustrate that royals perpetuated this belief, claiming several past lives. The transformation from god/*bodhisattva* was formalized in the coronation ceremony during the Pagan era (Aung Thwin 1984, 48).

Equally important in Burmese religion are the existence of *nats*, supernatural beings. *Nats* are animist spirits that take many forms. They may protect specific areas of forest, a province of the kingdom, people's homes, or oversee the well-being of the royal household. Nats of the latter kind are known as the thirty-seven *nats* and require the respect of the king (Aung Thwin 1984, 52). All of these *nats* died unnaturally, and many represent usurpations of the throne. These spirits needed to be appeased and were accorded the highest honors. Aung Thwin (1984, 52) sees the creation of the royal *nat* pantheon as "an attempt to counterbalance the use of unmitigated power." By according them a place in the pantheon, the royalty released them from the wait associated with karmic rebirth. The importance of *nats* in modern Myanmar is a testament to the influence of indigenous religious beliefs throughout the region's history.

The Burmese kings of Pagan times often portrayed themselves as superhuman beings, the *dhammaraja* and *Cakravatti* (Aung Thwin 1984, 56). Aung Thwin (1984) believes that the concept of *dhammaraja* was instituted in difficult times. If, for example, the Buddhist *sangha* or monkhood became too powerful they would be reminded that the king was the *dhammaraja*, the incarnation of a bodhisattva. The concept was also used to justify the existing hierarchy as divinely sanctioned. In times of war the concept was used to justify military action as a necessary evil. As Aung Thwin (1984, 57) says, "wars of unification became efforts to seek the holy relics, proselytize Buddhism, and acquire the pure scriptures." The process of conquering neighboring states made the king, in effect, the *Cakravatti* (world conqueror/universal monarch). It is of paramount importance to understand that the king was not seen as a god in totality, but bearing supernatural authority as an incarnation. The king was always human, for even the Buddha was but a man during his time on earth.

THE CASTE SYSTEM

Mabbet (1977b, 429) asserts that, no matter how powerful a king in ancient India, the ruler did not possess true religious authority, whereas in Southeast Asia rulers did possess this authority. Further, he believes, the rulers of ancient Southeast Asia controlled social organization.

Examining the evidence for a later period in Khmer history, Mabbet (1977b) believes that the kings of Angkor created, controlled, and manipulated a caste system. He does not, however, view this as a case of social engineering. Many scholars feel that ancient Khmer society was divided along the lines of *varnas* or castes (Chatterjee 1928; Lingat 1949; Kishore 1965). It is clear from these studies that some form of caste system was in existence, but its nature is difficult to define. There is agreement on the fact that the caste system of Southeast Asia was quite different from that of India, being more flexible (Chatterjee 1928). The ability of a monarch to create new *varnas* is unprecedented in India, yet appears to have been possible in ancient Cambodia (Lingat 1949). The fact that *varnas* appear to have been a political tool was revealed by the Indian scholar Chakravarti (Chakravarti 1970).

The nature of the Angkorian *varnas* is unclear. We cannot ascertain, with any certainty, whether society was divided along occupational lines or by social/hereditary lines (Mabbet 1977b, 432). Based upon the inscriptional evidence available to us we cannot even discern whether the entire population was divided into castes or if it was just the elite.

The Angkorian inscriptions, written as they were to glorify the king, must be carefully evaluated. Did the king really control the *varnas* or was this mere poetic license? In the Khmer translations of the Sanskrit poems we are afforded a better understanding of the *varnas* in Angkorian times. It seems that the king had the power to create a caste and give to this caste grants of land.

Based on the available evidence it seems that Angkorian castes may have been divided along professional lines, which implies that they were not hereditary (Mabbet 1977b, 435). It is noted, however, that these castes do not seem to incorporate the lowliest or most common professions and appear to be associated with royal service (Mabbet 1977b, 435). It is likely that this was structured as a reward for an elite group of Angkorian society (Mabbet 1977b, 434–35). It is likely that the Angkorian *varnas* described in the inscriptions were divisions of the royal household and elite class of ancient Cambodia, rather than a broad spectrum system that included all ranks.

The texts we have regarding Siva worship in Cambodia indicate that Indians came from all over the South Asian continent, although the region of Mathura seems to have had more influence than others. The epigraphy follows styles used in both southern and northern India. The localization of the Siva cult is also apparent in these texts, as certain appellations of Siva are completely unknown in India yet are found in Cambodia (Haendel 2004, 45).

CONCLUSION

Early theorists argued that the complex and highly developed nature of Indian culture, politics, and religion awed the early peoples of Southeast Asia and that, through a process of colonization and domination, the ideals of the dominant culture were forced upon the indigenous populations (Majumdar 1944). Gradually, as data are collected through inscriptions, texts, and archaeology we are able to paint a more accurate picture of the process of cultural evolution and amalgamation involving the subcontinent and Southeast Asia. It is apparent that the peoples of Southeast Asia were not passive players in the process. Early Southeast Asians were competent mariners who ventured far, encountering different cultures and returning with new ideas. It is also becoming clear that the process of political development was well underway in Southeast Asia prior to encounters with Indian culture. There is little doubt that Indians came to live and work in Southeast Asia from at least the early centuries of the first millennium, but it does not appear that this was a formal colonization nor did it involve the military domination of new territories. We have seen that the process of cultural interaction took place in two phases, the first in which artifacts from India were adopted into the indigenous culture as prestige items and the second phase which saw the use of Indian items and manufacture of artifacts to an Indian design in societies that increasingly were using Indian religious, linguistic, governmental, and artistic themes that originated from all over India. The amalgamation of Indian and indigenous cultures occurred through the natural interaction between these peoples, driven by trade and the desire by indigenous political players to establish their claims to power more securely. Doubtless, Hindus and Buddhists were eager to proselytize their religions, further fueling the synchronism between the cultures of Indian kingdoms and Southeast Asia's early polities.

Our understanding of the processes that led to the incorporation of aspects of Indian culture into that of the varied cultures of Southeast Asia has progressed thanks to the contributions of archaeological research. It is now clear that theories of Indian colonization cannot be supported, although it is also clear that small colonies of foreign merchants were allowed to reside in certain ports.

The incorporation of Indian cultural motifs into the fabric of the Southeast Asian polities was likely spurred, initially, by a desire to fortify fledgling power structures. Chiefs may have sought to further legitimize their control and perhaps saw in the new suite of beliefs the opportunity to circumvent long-held traditional beliefs about succession. The Indian model, it appears, may have offered early leaders in Southeast Asia a way to heredetize power. Indian ideals may also have enhanced the prestige of chiefs through the acquisition of trade goods, connections with external powers, and the possibility of military support from afar.

Whatever the reasons for the adoption of Indian belief systems in the varied cultures of Southeast Asia, it is clear they had a powerful and lasting impact on all aspects of society from language, art, and religion to politics. Even today the impact of Indian culture is inescapable. Brahman priests still officiate in the palace ceremonies of some Southeast Asian countries. The script of many countries is based upon Sanskrit, and many words are derived from Sanskrit and Pali. It seems unlikely that a process which had such profound impact was short lived. It appears that Indian culture was steadily absorbed throughout Southeast Asia from before the 1st century C.E., when significant developments on the political scene were already underway throughout Southeast Asia.

It is possible to argue that the process of "globalization" began in the early centuries of the first millennium C.E. At this juncture civilizations from North Asia, Southeast Asia, the Indian subcontinent, and the Mediterranean Basin became involved in a vast trade and exchange network. Goods flowed from east to west and vice versa overland and via sea routes. The rise of Indo-Roman trade relations stimulated trade in Southeast Asia and in

China, as demand for exotic forest products rose in the west and the demand for gold and products from Europe grew in the east. This trade came to affect societies at differing levels of sociopolitical development, and the interaction in international exchange brought these groups into contact with more politically complex societies. In many instances involvement in the trade network spurred political, religious, technological, and social evolution and adaptation. It is suspected that bronze technology was brought to Southeast Asia from China, while the technology for making iron may have come from India. Throughout the early centuries C.E., Indian artifacts appear in Southeast Asia, including vessel shapes and possibly glass and carnelian beads. Artifacts with an origin in the Mediterranean have also been found from this period, including coins bearing the image of Roman emperors.

It appears that there were two phases of contact between India and Southeast Asia, one from the fourth century B.C.E. to the second century C.E. and another from then to the fourth century C.E. (Bellina and Glover 2004). The first period of contact is hypothesized to have been steady but of limited impact, at least archaeologically. The following phase sees an intensification of the contact and consequently an increase in the archaeological evidence. As we have seen in the preceding chapters, the ideals of Indian government and religion were embraced by the leaders of the nascent polities in Southeast Asia from around the middle of the first millennium C.E. This should not be taken to indicate that the development of state-level societies was a direct result of contact with India. Complex polities, at least to the level of complex chiefdoms, probably already existed in Southeast Asia prior to the arrival of Indian or Chinese traders. The trappings of Indian culture may have served to enhance the political, social, and religious standing of the indigenous rulers of Southeast Asia. Exotic goods seem to have played an important role in the process of enhancing the prestige of indigenous leaders. This is a process that can be seen to accelerate during the Iron Age in Southeast Asia as artifacts that likely came from India begin to appear in cemeteries. These prehistoric cemeteries often exhibit increased evidence for hierarchical social organization (O'Reilly 2003). Hierarchization of settlements is seen as increasing from the Iron Age into the proto-historic period in Thailand (Onsuwan Eyre 2006).

The polities that arose in the early centuries of the first millennium C.E. may be best characterized, based on present evidence, as exclusionary or individualizing. The exclusionary power strategy discussed by Blanton et al. (1996), similar to Renfrew's (1974) individualizing chiefdoms, sees the development of a political system in which an individual monopolizes sources of power. What caused the emergence of these polities in the different parts of Southeast Asia is difficult to pinpoint but may be clarified by future archaeological research. It is clear that that external stimuli, aspects of culture that have developmental priority and events perceived to be beyond the control of the human population, played a prominent role. Southeast Asia has been, as we have seen, the crossroads for many different technologies over the millennia, and the same can probably be said for cultural and political ideologies. The subsequent development of these fledgling polities may have been dependent upon their environment. It may be that the decline of Funan could be attributed to its failure to secure more agricultural land or that the polities of the Malaysian peninsula failed to become more powerful due to the constricting nature of the peninsula in terms of agricultural production. The production of large surpluses above the subsistence level is crucial to the development of complex societies because they allow hierarchical centralization. Population growth is also often cited as a factor in the development of political complexity. Regrettably it is difficult to assess this factor in Southeast Asia during the period under review, but there are indications that there were significant movements of cultural groups into Myanmar and Thailand at this juncture and possibly pressure in northern Cambodia, which could have spurred political change.

Another oft-cited catalyst for the development of political complexity is conflict. Evidence from Thailand and Cambodia seems to indicate that there was a trend toward militarization during the Iron Age. There is certainly an indication that sites occupied by the Tircul were well defended, and historic documents refer to fortified settlements in Funan and Malaysia. It is possible that competition over trade led to an increase in political tensions and that this, in turn, led to an intensification of social hierarchies in the early political organizations of Southeast Asia. Force of arms and trade are often coincidental, the former needed to ensure the continuation of the latter and the profits from trade used to support an armed force. Although it is likely that long-distance exchange networks existed from the Bronze Age in Southeast Asia, as the stakes grew so did attempts to gain control over these networks. Consequently, the authority structures prevalent in many of the early chiefdoms evolved. It is not difficult to envisage certain individuals or societies seeking to secure a monopoly over exchange, a move that would serve to reinforce a chief's internal political control. The success of various political entities probably depended upon the existence of external markets, proximity to avenues of trade and exchange, and access to needed, non-food resources. Evidence from the Philippines indicates that the effects of foreign trade were far reaching and caused social upheaval not only among coastal groups but also among those living inland. Many of the products exported were not accessible by the coastal centers, and they were forced to exchange with inland populations. As a result, the sociopolitical patterns of these peoples seems to have been altered (Hutterer 1977; Junker 1993).

As we have seen, the exploitative nature and internal conflict prevalent in chiefly societies probably demanded the institution of a complex ideology that would ensure stability. The ideology of many chiefdoms involved new systems of symbolism and cognition (Earle 1987), a mystification of the control of resources and hereditary inequality (Blanton et al. 1996). Control of land was assured through ceremonies that created a sacred landscape in which the ancestors of the chiefs were seen as gods and the living chiefs were their earthly representatives (Kirch 1984). The principles of descent, common in many chiefdoms, lend themselves to exploitation by the elite. Service (1962) found that deified ancestors were often ranked in death as they were in life. All of these strategies appear in the Southeast Asian context and were probably entrenched with the adoption of aspects of Indian religious beliefs.

The early polities of Southeast Asia are probably best thought of as being complex chiefdoms rather than state-level societies. The difference between these political forms may be found in the nature of the social order, which in chiefdoms is based upon kinship whereas in a state the political significance of kinship is superseded by the office and institutions associated with leadership. The archaic state may further be distinguished by the presence of a permanent armed force, controlled by an authorized individual.

States may be further socially differentiated from chiefdoms by the existence of political classes. In chiefdom societies, differences in rank and social strata are based upon social rules. Conversely, social position in a state-level society is often determined by political or economic factors. We begin to see these changes in Chenla, but the evidence that is available for the other polities of the region suggest chiefdom-level societies. It is difficult to evaluate the mode of production in the polities we have examined in the preceding chapters, but there is no evidence to suggest that agricultural and craft production were bureaucratized.

It is possible that the complex political systems that appear to have been functioning in Southeast Asia prior to the rise of "state-level" systems formed the collective basis of the state system. Yoffee (2005) has suggested that the earliest states resulted from the formation of semiautonomous, hierarchical social groups. He believes that states could have formed as a result of the recombination of these groups under a centralized leadership. We see that the cultures of Southeast Asia certainly embraced new ideologies in the form of Indian religious beliefs, laws, and literature, and these early "states were legitimized, through central symbols, expensively supported and maintained by inner elites who constituted the cultural and administrative core of the state" (Yoffee 2005).

References

Adams, R. E. W. 1980. Swamps, Canals and the Location of Ancient Maya Cities. *Antiquity* 54: 206–14.

Adams, R. McC. 1966. *The Evolution of Urban Society*. Chicago: Aldine Publishing.

———. 1974. Anthropological Perspectives on Ancient Trade. *Current Anthropology* 15: 239–58.

Allen, J. 1991. Trade and Site Distribution in Early Historic-Period Kedah: Geoarchaeological, Historical and Locational Evidence. In vol. 1 of *Indo-Pacific Prehistory 1990*, ed. P. Bellwood. Canberra: Indo-Pacific Prehistory Association.

Anderson, A. 1982. A Review of Economic Patterns During the Archaic Phase in Southern New Zealand. *New Zealand Journal of Archaeology* 4: 45–75.

Anderson, D. 1994. *The Savannah River Chiefdoms: Political Change in the Late Prehistoric Southeast*. Tuscaloosa: Univ. of Alabama.

Anon. 2001. A Rare Find. *Enchanting Myanmar*. 1.

Ardika, I. W. 1987. Bronze Artifacts and the Rise of Complex Society in Bali. Master's thesis, Australian National Univ.

Arnold, B. 1995. The Material Culture of Social Structure: Rank and Status in Early Iron Age Europe. In *Celtic Chiefdom, Celtic State*, eds. B. Arnold and D. B. Gibson, 43–52. Cambridge: Cambridge Univ. Press.

Aung, M. H. 1970. *Burmese History Before 1279: A Defense of the Chronicles*. Oxford: The Asoka Society.

Aung Thaw, U. 1968. *Report on the Excavations at Beikthano*. Rangoon: Ministry of Union Culture, Government of the Union of Burma.

———. 1978. *Historical Sites in Burma*. Rangoon: Ministry of Union Culture, Government of the Union of Burma.

Aung Thwin, M. 1984. Political Ideology: Conceptions of Kingship. Paper for the symposium on Southeast Asia in the 9th to 14th centuries, Australian National Univ., Canberra.

Aurousseau, L. 1914. Le Royaume de Champa. *BEFEO* 14(9): 8–43.

Aymonier, É. 1903. Le Founan. *Journal Asiatique* (Dixieme série) 1: 109–50.

Bagchi, P. C. 1930. On Some Tantrik Texts Studied in Ancient Kambuja. *The Indian Historical Quarterly* VI(1): 97–107.

Baker, P., and W. Sanders. 1972. Demographic Studies in Anthropology. *Annual Review of Anthropology* 1: 151–78.

Bargatzky, T. 1984. Culture, Environment, and the Ills of Adaptionalism. *Current Anthropology* 25: 399–415.

Bayard, D. 1980. An Early Indigenous Bronze Technology in Northeastern Thailand; Its Implications for the Prehistory of East Asia. In *The Diffusion of Material Culture*, ed. H. Loofs-Wissowa, 191–214. Honolulu: SSRI.

———. 1984. Agriculture, Metallurgy and State Formation in Mainland Southeast Asia. *Current Anthropology* 25(1): 103–5.

Beal, S. 1884. *Si-yu-ki: Buddhist Records of the Western World. Translated from the Chinese of Hiuen Tsiang*. London: Trubner and Co.

Beckwith, C. I. 1987. The Tibetan Empire in Central Asia. Princeton, N.J.: Princeton Univ. Press.

Bulletin de l'École Française d'Extrême-Orient. 1933. Angkor Borei. *Bulletin de l'École Française d'Extrême-Orient*: 491.

Bellina, B. 2001. Les réseaux d'échanges entre le sous-continent indien et l'Asie du Sud-Est à travers le matériel archéologique des perles en cornaline et des sceaux de marchands en pierre dure (VIe siècle ap. J.C.). Paris, Sorbonne-Novelle-Paris III.

———. 2003. Beads, Social Change and Interaction between India and South-east Asia. *Antiquity* 77: 286–97.

Bellina, B., and I. Glover. 2004. The Archaeology of Early Contact with India and the Mediterranean World, from the Fourth Century BC to the Fourth Century AD. In *Southeast Asia from Prehistory to History*, ed. I. Glover and P. Bellwood, 68–88. London: RoutledgeCurzon.

Bellina, B., and P. Silapanth. 2006. Khao Sam Kaeo and the Upper Thai Peninsula: Understanding the Mechanisms of Early Trans-Asiatic Trade and Cultural Exchange. In *Uncovering Southeast Asia's Past: Selected Papers from the Tenth Biennial Conference of the European Association of Southeast Asian Archaeologists, London, 14th–17th September 2004*, ed. E. A. Bacus, I. C. Glover, and V. C. Pigott, 379–92. Singapore: National Univ. Press.

Bellwood, P. 1985. *Prehistory of the Indo-Malaysian Archipelago*. New York: Academic Press.

———. 1992. Early Burmese Urbanisation: Inspired Independence or External Stimulus? Review of *The Ancient Pyu of Burma. Volume 1: Early Pyu Cities in a Man-Made Landscape. The Review of Archaeology* 13(2): 1–7.

———. 1993. Cultural and Biological Differentiation in Peninsular Malaysia: The Last 10,000 Years. *Asian Perspectives* 32, no. 2 (Fall 1993), 37–59.

———. 1995. Austronesian Prehistory in Southeast Asia: Homeland, Expansion and Transformation. In *The Austronesians*, ed. P. Bellwood, J. J. Fox, and D. Tryon. Canberra: Dept. of Anthropology, Australian National Univ.

———. 1997. *Prehistory of the Indo-Malaysian Archipelago*. Honolulu: Univ. of Hawaii Press.

Bénisti, V. M. 1970. Rapports Entre le Premier Art Khmèr et l'Art Indien. *BEFEO Mémoire Archéologique* V.

Bergaigne, A. 1888. L'Ancien Royaume de Champa. *Journale Asiatique* 11: 5–105.

Bhattacharya, K. 1961. Précisions sur la Paléographie de l'Inscription Dite de Vocanh. *Artibus Asiae* 24: 219–24.

Bishop, P., D. Penny, et al. 2003. A 3.5 ka Record of Paleoenvironments and Human Occupation at Angkor Borei, Mekong Delta, Southern Cambodia. *Geoarchaeology* 18(3): 359–93.

Bishop, P., D. C. Sanderson, et al. 2004. OSL and Radiocarbon Dating of a Pre-Angkorian Canal in the Mekong Delta, Southern Cambodia. *Journal of Archaeological Science* 31: 319–36.

Blagden, C. O. 1911. Tircul Faces. *Journal of the Royal Asiatic Society.* 365–87.

Blanton, R., G. Feinman, et al. 1996. A Dual-Processual Theory for the Evolution of Mesoamerican Civilization. *Current Anthropology* 37(1): 1–14.

Boeles, J. 1964. The King of Sri Dvaravati and His Regalia. *Journal of the Siam Society* LII: 1.

Boisselier, J. 1956. Arts du Champa et du Cambodge Préangkorien: La Date de Mi-so'n E-1. *Artibus Asiae* 19(3/4): 197–212.

———. 1965. Nouvelles Données sur l'Histoire Ancienne de la Thailande. Conference, Alliance Française, Centre culture.

———. 1968. Dvaravati Arts, (Part 1). *Silapakon* 2(6).

———. 1969. Recent Investigations at Muang Nakhon Pathom. *Archaeology* 2(4).

———. 1971. U-Thong et son Importance pour l'Histoire de Thailande. *Silapakon* 9(1): 27–30.

———. 2001. The Art of Champa. In *Cham Art*, ed. E. Guillon, 28–63. Bangkok, River Books.

Bose, N. D. 1927. *The Indian Colony of Siam*. Lahore: Punjab Sanskrit Book Depot.

Boserup, E. 1965. *The Conditions of Agricultural Growth: The Economics of Agrarian Change Under Population Pressure*. Chicago: Aldine Press.

Briggs, L. 1951. *The Ancient Khmer Empire*. Philadelphia: The American Philosopical Society. Vol. 41:1.

Bronson, B. 1977. Exchange at the Upstream and Downstream Ends: Notes toward a Functional Model of the Coastal State in Southeast Asia. In *Economic Exchange and Social Interaction in Southeast Asia: Perspectives from Prehistory, History and Ethnography*, ed. K. L. Hutterer, 39–52. Ann Arbor: Center for South and Southeast Asia Studies, Univ. of Michigan.

———. 1979. The Late Prehistory and Early History of Central Thailand with Special Reference to Chansen. In *Early Southeast Asia*, ed. R. B. Smith and W. Watson, 315–37. New York: Oxford Univ. Press.

———. 1990. Glass and Beads at Khuan Lukpad, Southern Thailand. In *Southeast Asian Archaeology 1986, Proceedings of the First Conference of the Association of Southeast Asian Archaeologists in Western Europe*, ed. I. Glover and E. Glover, 213–30. London: British Archaeological Reports International Series.

———. 1996. Chinese and Middle Eastern Trade in Southern Thailand during the 9th Century A.D. *Ancient Trades and Cultural Contacts in Southeast Asia*, ed. A. Srisuchat, 181–200. Bangkok: The Office of the National Culture Commission.

Bronson, B., and G. F. Dales. 1972. Excavations at Chansen, Thailand. *Asian Perspectives* 15: 26–46.

Bronson, B., and J. Wisseman. 1976. Palembang as Srivjaya; The Lateness of Early Cities in Southern Southeast Asia. *Asian Perspectives* XIX: 220–39.

Brown, R. L. 1992. Indian Art Transformed: The Earliest Sculptural Styles of Southeast Asia. In *Panels of the VIIth World Sanskrit Conference, Vol. X, Indian Art and Archaeology.* ed. J. Bronkhorst. Leiden: Brill.

———. 1996. *The Dvaravati Wheels of the Law and the Indianization of South East Asia.* Leiden: Brill.

———. n.d. Indian Art Transformed: The Earliest Sculptural Styles of Southeast Asia. Unpublished manuscript.

Brumfiel, E. 1976. Regional Growth in the Eastern Valley of Mexico: A Test of the "Population Pressure" Hypothesis. In *The Early Mesoamerican Village*, ed. K. V. Flannery, 234–48. New York: Academic Press.

———. 1995. Heterarchy and the Analysis of Complex Societies: Comments. In *Heterarchy and the Analysis of Complex Societies*, ed. R. Ehrenreich, C. Crumley, and J. Levy, 125–31. Washington, D.C.: American Anthropological Association.

Brumfiel, E., and T. Earle. 1987. Specialization, Exchange, and Complex Society. In *Specialization, Exchange, and Complex Society*, ed. E. Brumfiel and T. Earle. Cambridge: Cambridge Univ. Press.

Brun, P. 1995. From Chiefdom to State Organization in Celtic Europe. *Celtic Chiefdom, Celtic State*, ed. B. Arnold and D. B. Gibson, 13–25. Cambridge: Cambridge Univ. Press.

Büchsenschütz, O. 1995. The Significance of Major Settlements in European Iron Age Society. *Celtic Chiefdom, Celtic State*, ed. B. Arnold and D. B. Gibson, 53–63. Cambridge: Cambridge Univ. Press.

Buhler, G, trans. 1886. *Manu-smriti: The Laws of Manu.* Oxford: Oxford.

Bui Phat Diem, Vuong Thu Hon, et al. 1997. Research Achievements of the Archaeology Before "Oc Éo Culture" in the Lower Bam Co River Basin, Southern Part of Vietnam. *Journal of Southeast Asian Archaeology* 17(6): 72–82.

Bulbeck, D. 2004. Indigenous Traditions and Exogenous Influences in the Early History of Peninsular Malaysia. In *Southeast Asia from Prehistory to History*, ed. I. Glover and P. Bellwood, 314–36. London: RoutledgeCurzon.

Carneiro, R. 1967. On the Relationship between Size of Population and Complexity of Social Organization. *Southwestern Journal of Anthropology* 23: 234–43.

———. 1970. A Theory of the Origin of the State. *Science* 169: 733–38.

———. 1981. The Chiefdom: Precursor of the State. In *The Transition to Statehood in the New World*, ed. G. D. Jones and R. R. Kautz, 37–79. Cambridge: Cambridge Univ. Press.

Cassels, R. 1974. Explanations of Change in New Zealand Prehistory. New Zealand Archaeological Association, Blenheim, New Zealand, unpublished mimeograph.

Chakravarti, A. K. 1970. The Caste System in Ancient Cambodia. *Journal of Ancient Indian History* 71: 14–59.

Chataratiyakarn, P. 1984. The Middle Chi Research Programme. In *Prehistoric Investigations in Northeast Thailand*, eds. C. F. W. Higham and A. Kijngam. British Archaeological Reports (International Series) 231: 565–643.

Chatterjee, B. R. 1928. *Indian Cultural Influences in Cambodia.* Calcutta: Calcutta Univ. Press.

Chavannes, E. 1894. *Mémoire Composé à l'Époque de la Grande Dynastie T'ang sur les Religieux Éminents qui Allèrent Chercher la Loi dans les Pays d'Occident par I'Tsing.* Paris: Ernest Leroux.

Childe, G. 1951. *Social Evolution*. New York: Schuman.

——. 1954. *What Happened in History*. Baltimore: Penguin.

Chutintaranond, S. 1990. "Mandala," "Segmentary State" and Politics of Centralization in Medieval Ayudhya. *Journal of the Siam Society* 78(1): 89–100.

Civico, A. 1991. Pumtek: Some Beads from Burma, their Ethnographic Occurrence and Methods of Manufacture: Report Submitted in Partial Fulfillment of the Requirements for the Degree of B.S.C. Hons, The Institute of Archaeology, Dept. of Prehistory, Univ. of London. London: Institute of Archaeology.

Claessen, H. J. M., and P. Skalnik. 1981. The Early State: Theories and Hypotheses. In *The Early State*, ed. H. J. M. Claessen and P. Skalnik, 3–29. The Hague: Mouton Publishers.

Coedès, G. 1918. Le Royaume de Çrivijaya. *Bulletin de l'École Française d'Extrême-Orient* XVIII(6): 1–36.

——. 1924a. L'expansion du Cambodge vers le Sud-Ouest au VIIe siècle (Nouvelles inscriptions de Chantaboun). *Bulletin de l'École Française d'Extrême-Orient* 24: 352–58.

——. 1924b. *Recueil des Inscriptions du Siam*. Bangkok: Bangkok Times Press.

——. 1931. Deux Inscriptions Sanskrites du Fou-Nan. *Bulletin de l'École Française d'Extrême-Orient* 31: 1–12.

——. 1937–1966. *Les Inscriptions du Cambodge*. Hanoi and Paris: L'École Française d'Extrême Orient.

——. 1939. La Plus Ancienne Inscription en Langue Cham. Special issue, *New Indian Antiquary* 1: 46–49.

——. 1940. The Date of the Sanskrit Inscription of Vo-canh (South Annam). *The Indian Historical Quarterly* XVI: 484–88.

——. 1942. *Inscriptions du Cambodge*. Hanoi: L'Ecole Francaise d'Extreme-Orient.

——. 1943–1946. Études Cambodgiennes - XXXVI: Prècisions sur la fin du Funan XXXVII: Le site de Janapada d'après une inscription de Prasat Khna. *Bulletin de l'École Française d'Extrême-Orient* XLIII: 1–8.

——. 1958. Nouvelles Données Épigraphiques sur l'Histoire de l'Indochine Centrale. *Journal Asiatique* 246: 129–31.

——. 1964a. *Les États Hindouisés d'Indochine et d'Indonésie*. Paris: E. de Boccard.

——. 1964b. Some Problems in the Ancient History of the Hinduized States of South-East Asia. *Journal of Southeast Asian History* 5-2: 1–14.

——. 1966. *The Making of Southeast Asia*. London: Routledge & Kegan Paul.

——. 1968. *The Indianized States of Southeast Asia*. Honolulu: East-West Center Press.

Coedès, G., and P. Dupont. 1943–1946. Les Stèles de Sdok Kak Thom, Phom Sandak et Prah Vihar. *Bulletin de l'École Française d'Extrême-Orient* 43: 56–134.

Collins, J. 1999. Language. *The Encyclopedia of Malaysia: Early History*, ed. N. H. Shuhaimi and N. A. Rahman, 102–104. Kuala Lumpur: Archipelago Press.

Coser, L. 1956. *The Functions of Social Conflict*. London: Routledge & Kegan Paul.

Cowgill, G. 1975. On Causes and Consequences of Ancient and Modern Population Changes. *American Anthropologist* 77: 505–25.

Creamer, W., and J. Haas. 1985. Tribe Versus Chiefdom in Lower Central America. *American Antiquity* 50(4): 738–54.

Czuma, S. 1980. Mon-Dvaravati Buddha. *The Bulletin of the Cleveland Museum of Art* September: 235.

D'Altroy, T., and T. Earle. 1985. Staple Finance, Wealth Finance and Storage in the Inca Political Economy. *Current Anthropology* 26(2): 187–206.

Dang Van Thang, and Vu Quoc Hien. 1997. Excavation at Giong Ca Vo site, Can Gio District, Ho Chi Minh City. *Journal of Southeast Asian Archaeology* 17(6): 30–44.

Dao Linh Con. 1995. The Graves in Oc Éo Culture (in Vietnamese). Report, Dept. of Archaeology. Ho Chi Minh City.

——. 1998. The Oc Éo Burial Group Recently Excavated at Go Thap (Dong Thap Province, Vietnam). In vol. 1 of *Southeast Asian Archaeology 1994: Proceeding of the 5th International Conference of the European Association of Southeast Asian Archaeologists*, ed. P.-Y. Manguin, 111–17. Hull: Centre for Southeast Asian Studies, Univ. of Hull.

Dars, J. 1979. Les Jonques Chinoises de Haute Mer Sous les Song et les Yuan. *Archipel* 18: 41–56.

Das, S. A. C. 1975. Kalinga, the Ancient Maritime Power. *Orissa Historical Research Journal* 16(4): 6–16.

Day, T. 2002. *Fluid Iron: State Formation in Southeast Asia*. Honolulu: Univ. of Hawai'i Press.

de Casparis, J. G. 1979. Palaeolography. In *Early South East Asia*, ed. R. Smith and W. Watson, 380–94. Oxford: Oxford University Press.

Dega, M., and Latinis, D. K. 1996. Recent Archaeological Investigation of Angkor Borei: The Material Culture of a Funan-Period Site. In *Proceedings of the 5th Annual East-West Center Centerwide Conference*, 71–81. Honolulu: East-West Center.

Dharma, P. 2001. The History of Champa. In *Cham Art*, ed. E. Guillon, 14–27. Bangkok: River Books.

Dhida, S. 1985. Si Thep was Sricanasa (in Thai). *Muang Boran Journal* 11(1): 64.

——. 1999. *(Sri) Dvaravati: The Initial Phase of Siam's History*. Bangkok: Muang Boran Publishing.

Di Crocco, V. 1991. Ceramic Wares of the Haripunjaya Area. *Journal of the Siam Society* 79(1): 84–98.

Dietler, M. 1995. Early Celtic Socio-Political Ideological Representation and Social Competition in Dynamic Comparative Perspective. In *Celtic Chiefdom, Celtic State*, ed. B. Arnold and D. B. Gibson, 64–71. Cambridge: Cambridge Univ. Press.

Diffloth, G. 1984. *The Dvaravati Old Mon Language and Nyah Kur*. Bangkok: Chulalongkorn Univ. Printing House.

Diskul, M. C. S. 1956. Mueng Fa Daed, an Ancient Town in Northeast Thailand. *Artibus Asiae* 19: 362–67.

Donovan, D. G., H. Fukui, and T. Itoh. 1998. Perspective on the Pyu Landscape. *Southeast Asian Studies* 36(1):19–126.

Dowling, N. H. 1999. A New Date for the Phnom Da Images and its Implications for Early Cambodia. *Asian Perspectives* 38(1): 51–61.

Drennan, R. 1984. Long Distance Transport Costs in Prehispanic Mesoamerica. *American Anthropologist* 88 (1): 105–14.

Drennan, R. 1991. Pre-Hispanic Chiefdom Trajectories in Mesoamerica, Central America and Northern South America. In *Chiefdoms: Power, Economy, Ideology*, ed. T. Earle, 263–87. Cambridge: Cambridge Univ. Press.

Dunn, F. L. 1975. *Rain-forest Collectors and Traders. A Study of Resource Utilization in Modern and Ancient Malaya*. Kuala Lumpur: Malaysian Branch of the Royal Asiatic Society.

Dupont, P. 1943–1946. La Dislocation du Tchen-la et la Formation du Cambodge Angkorien. *Bulletin de l'École Française d'Extrême-Orient* 43: 17–55.

———. 1959. *L'archaeologie Mone et Dvaravati*. Paris: Ecole Francaise d'Extreme Orient.

Duroiselle, C. 1926–1927. *Excavations at Hmawza*. Archaeological survey of India, 171–81.

Earle, T. 1973. *Control Hierarchies in the Traditional Irrigation Economy of Halelea District, Kaua'i Hawaii*. Ann Arbor, Michigan: Univ. Microfilms.

———. 1975. *Redistribution: A Reappraisal*. PhD thesis, Los Angeles, Univ. of California.

———. 1977. A Reappraisal of Redistribution: Complex Hawaiian Chiefdoms. In *Exchange Systems in Prehistory*, ed. T. Earle and J. Ericson, 213–29. New York: Academic Press.

———. 1978. Economic and Social Organization of a Complex Chiefdom: The Halelea District, Kaua'i Hawaii. *Anthropological Papers*. Museum of Anthropology, Univ. of Michigan. 63.

———. 1987. Chiefdoms in Archaeological and Ethnohistorical Perspective. *Annual Reviews in Anthropology* 16: 279–308.

———. 1991. The Evolution of Chiefdoms. In *Chiefdoms, Power, Economy and Ideology*, ed. T. Earle, 1–16. Cambridge, Cambridge Univ. Press.

Earle, T., and T. D'Altroy. 1982. Storage Facilities and State Finance in the Upper Mantaro Valley, Peru. In *Contexts for Prehistoric Exchange*, ed. J. Ericson and T. K. Earle, 265–90. New York: Academic Press.

Ekholm, K. 1972. *Power and Prestige: The Rise and Fall of the Kongo Kingdom*. Uppsala: Scriv Service.

Farmer, E., G. Hambly, et al., eds. 1986. *Comparative History of Civilizations in Asia*. Boulder, Colo.: Westview Press.

Feinman, G. 1991. Demography, Surplus and Inequality: Early Political Formations in Highland Mesoamerica. In *Chiefdoms: Power, Economy, and Ideology*, ed. T. Earle, 229–62. Cambridge: Cambridge Univ. Press.

Filliozat, J. 1968. Les Symbols d'une Stele Khmère du 7ème Siècle. *Arts Asiatiques* 17: 111–18.

Fine Arts Department, The. 1968. *The Survey and Excavation of Muang Fa Daed Song Yang, Ban Sema, Tambon Nong Pan, Amphoe Kamalasai, Changwat Kalasin 1967–1968*. Bangkok: Fine Arts Dept.

Finney, B. 1966. Resource Distribution and Resource Structure in Tahiti. *Ecology* 5: 80–86.

Finot, L. 1902. Notes d'Épigraphie I: Deux nouvelles inscriptions de Ghadravarman Ier, roi de Champa. *BEFEO* 2: 185–91.

Firth, R. 1936. *We, the Tikopia*. New York: Macmillan.

Fox, J. J., and J. Ledgerwood. 1999. Dry-season Flood-recession Rice in the Mekong Delta: Two Thousand Years of Sustainable Agriculture? *Asian Perspectives* 38(1): 37–50.

Fox, R. B. 1970. The Tabon Caves: Archaeological Explorations and Excavations on Palawan Island, Philippines. National Museum of Manila, monograph 1.

———. 1979. The Philippines in the First Millennium B.C. In *Early South-East Asia: Essays in Archaeology, History and Historical Geography*, ed. R. Smith and W. Watson, 232–41. Oxford: Oxford Univ. Press.

Francis, P. 1991. Glass Beads in Malaya: A Reassessment. *Journal of the Malayan Branch of the Royal Asiatic Society* 64: 97–118.

———. 1996. Bead, the Bead Trade and State Development in Southeast Asia. In *Ancient Trades and Cultural Contacts in Southeast Asia*, ed. A. Srisuchat, 139–52. Bangkok: The Office of the National Culture Commission.

Fried, M. 1960. On the Evolution of Social Stratification and the State. In *Culture and History: Essays in Honor of Paul Radin*, ed. S. Diamond. New York: Columbia Univ. Press. Reprinted in Fried, Morton, ed. Vol. 1 of *Readings in Anthropology*. New York: Thomas Y. Crowell Company.

———. 1967. *The Evolution of Political Society: An Essay in Political Anthropology*. New York: Random House.

Friedel, D. 1979. Culture Areas and Interaction Spheres: Contrasting Approaches to the Emergence of Civilization in the Maya Lowlands. *American Antiquity* 44(1): 36–54.

———. 1986. Maya Warfare: An Example of Peer Polity Interaction. In *Interaction and Socio-Political Change*, ed. C. Renfrew and J. Cherry, 93–116. Cambridge: Cambridge Univ. Press.

Gaspardone, É. 1953. La Plus Ancienne Inscription d'Indochine. *Journal Asiatiqué* CCXLI: 477–85.

Gibson, B. 1982. Unreferenced citation in Gibson, D. B. and Geselowitz, M. N. 1988. The Evolution of Complex Societies in Late Prehistoric Europe: Toward a Paradigm. In *Tribe and Polity in Late Prehistoric Europe*, ed. D. B. Gibson and M. N. Geselowitz, 3–37. New York: Plenum.

———. 1988. Agro-pastoralism and Regional Social Organisation in Early Ireland. In *Tribe and Polity in Late Prehistoric Europe*, ed. D. B. Gibson and M. N. Geselowitz, 243–67. New York: Plenum.

Gibson, B., and M. Geselowitz. 1988. The Evolution of Complex Societies in Late Prehistoric Europe: Toward a Paradigm. In *Tribe and Polity in Late Prehistoric Europe*, ed. D. B. Gibson and M. N. Geselowitz, 3–37. New York: Plenum.

Gilman, A. 1981. The Development of Social Stratification in Bronze Age Europe. *Current Anthropology* 22(1): 1–23.

———. 1991. Trajectories Toward Social Complexity in the Later Prehistory of the Mediterranean. In *Chiefdoms, Power, Economy and Ideology*, ed. T. Earle, 146–69. Cambridge: Cambridge Univ. Press.

Giteau, M. 1957. *Histoire du Cambodge*. Paris: Didier.

Glover, I. C. 1989. *Early Trade between India and Southeast Asia: A Link in the Development of a World Trading System. Occasional Paper No. 16*. Hull: The Univ. of Hull Centre for South-East Asian Studies.

———. 1990. Ban Don Ta Phet: The 1984–1985 Excavation. In *Southeast Asian Archaeology 1986*, ed. I. Glover and E. Glover. Proceedings of the first conference of the Association of Southeast Asian Archaeologists in Western Europe. Oxford: British Archaeological Reports, International Series 561: 139–83.

———. 1991. The Bronze-Iron Age in Western Thailand. Paper presented at conference on The High Bronze Age of Southeast Asia and South China, Hua Hin, Thailand.

———. 1998. The Role of India in the Late Prehistory of Southeast Asia. *Journal of Southeast Asian Archaeology* 18: 21–49.

Glover, I. C., P. Charoenwongsa, et al. 1984. The Cemetery of Ban Don Ta Phet, Thailand, Results from the 1980–1981 Season. In *South Asian Archaeology*, ed. B. Allchin, F. R. Allchin, and M. Sidell, 319–30. Cambridge: Cambridge Univ. Press.

Goldman, I. 1970. *Ancient Polynesian Society*. Chicago: Univ. of Chicago Press.

Grave, P. 1995. Beyond the Mandala: Buddhist Landscapes and Upland-Lowland Interaction in North-west Thailand AD 1200–1650. *World Archaeology* 27(2): 243–65.

Green, R. 1967. Fortifications in Other Parts of Tropical Polynesia. *New Zealand Archaeological Association News Letter* 10: 96–113.

Groslier, B. P. 1962. *The Art of Indochina, including Thailand, Vietnam, Laos and Cambodia*. New York: Crown Publishers.

———. 1980. Prospection des Sites Khmers du Siam. *Coûts et Profits en Archéologie*. Paris: Centre de Recerches Archéologiques, 33–57.

Guillon, E. 1999. *The Mons: A Civilization of Southeast Asia*. Bangkok: Siam Society.

Gutman, P. 1976. *Ancient Arakan: With Special Reference to its Cultural History between the 5th and 11th Centuries*. PhD diss., Department of Archaeology, Canberra, Australian National Univ.

———. 2001. *Burma's Lost Kingdoms: Splendours of Arakan*. Bangkok: Orchid Press.

Haendel, A. 2004. The Temples of King Rajendravarman: Tenth Century Architecture at Angkor. PhD thesis, Dept. of Archaeology and Anthropology, London, School of Oriental and African Studies.

Hagesteijn, R. 1987. The Angkor State: Rise, Fall and In Between. *Studies in Human Society* 2: 154–69.

———. 1989. *Circles of Kings: Political Dynamics in Early Southeast Asia*. Dordrecht, Holland: Foris Publications.

Hall, D. G. E. 1950. *Burma*. London: Hutchinson's Univ. Library.

———. 1955. *A History of Southeast Asia*. London: Macmillan.

Hall, K. R. 1976. An Introductory Essay on Southeast Asian Statecraft in the Classical Period. In *Explorations in Early Southeast Asian History: The Origins of Southeast Asian Statecraft*, ed. K. R. Hall and J. K. Whitmore, 1–24. Ann Arbor: Center for South and Southeast Asian Studies, Univ. of Michigan.

———. 1982. The Indianization of Funan: An Economic History of Southeast Asia's First State. *Journal of Southeast Asian Studies* 13: 81–106.

———. 1985. *Maritime Trade and State Development in Early Southeast Asia*. Honolulu: Univ. of Hawaii Press.

———. 1992. Economic History of Early Southeast Asia. In vol. 1 of *The Cambridge History of Southeast Asia*, ed. N. Tarling, 183–275. Cambridge: Cambridge Univ. Press.

Hansen, M. H. 2000. Introduction: The Concept of City-State and City-State Culture. In *A Comparative Study of Thirty City-State Cultures*, ed. M. H. Hansen, 11–34. Copenhagen: The Royal Danish Academy of Sciences and Letters.

Harner, M. 1970. Population Pressure and the Social Evolution of Agriculturalists. *Southwestern Journal of Anthropology* 26: 67–86.

Harrisson, B. 1968. Malaya: A Series of Neolithic and Metal Age Burial Grottos at Sekaloh, Niah, Sarawak. *Journal of the Royal Asiatic Society—Malaysian Branch* 41(214 pt. 2): 148–75.

Haselgrove, C. 1995. Late Iron Age Society in Britain and North-west Europe: Structural Transformation or Superficial Change? In *Celtic Chiefdoms, Celtic State*, ed. B. Arnold and D. B. Gibson, 81–7. Cambridge: Cambridge Univ. Press.

Hastorf, C. 1990. One Path to the Heights: Negotiating Political Inequality in the Sausa of Peru. In *The Evolution of Political Systems*, ed. S. Upham, 146–76. Cambridge: Cambridge Univ. Press.

Ha Van Tan. 1977. Two-headed Animal Earrings and Relations between Song Son and Sa Huynh (in Vietnamese). *Khao co hoc* 4: 62–67.

——. 1986a. Oc Éo: Endogenous and Exogenous Elements. *Vietnam Social Sciences* 1–2(7–8): 91–101.

——. 1986b. Two-Headed Animal Earrings Recently Discovered Outside Vietnam. *New Discoveries in Archaeology*: 132–34.

Heine-Geldern, R. 1963. *Conceptions of State and Kingship in Southeast Asia*. Ithaca, N.Y.: Cornell Univ.

Higham, C. 1977. The Late Prehistory of the Southern Khorat Plateau, North East Thailand with Particular Reference to Roi Et Province. In *Modern Quaternary Research in Southeast Asia*, ed. W. A. Casparie, I. Glover, G.-J. Bartstra Rotterdam, and A. A. Balkema. 3: 103–41.

——. 1984. The Social Structure of the Ban Na Di Prehistoric Population. In *Southeast Asian Archaeology at the XV Pacific Science Congress*, ed. D. T. Bayard, vol. 16, 72–85. Dunedin: Univ. of Otago Studies in Prehistoric Anthropology.

——. 1989a. *The Archaeology of Mainland Southeast Asia; From 10,000 B.C. to the Fall of Angkor*. Cambridge: Cambridge Univ. Press.

——. 1989b. The Later Prehistory of Mainland Southeast Asia. *Journal of World Archaeology* 3: 235–82.

——. 1996. *The Bronze Age of Southeast Asia*. Cambridge: Cambridge Univ. Press.

——. 1998a. Noen U-Loke and the Implications for the Origins of Early States. Unpublished paper presented at the 16th Congress of the Indo-Pacific Prehistory Association. Melaka, Malaysia.

——. 1998b. The Transition from Prehistory to the Historic Period in the Upper Mun Valley. *The Transition to History in Southeast Asia, Part I: Cambodia and Thailand* 2(3): 235–60.

——. 2002. *Early Cultures of Mainland Southeast Asia*. Bangkok: River Books.

Higham, C., A. Kijngam, et al. 1982. Site Location and Site Hierarchy in Prehistoric Thailand. *Proceedings of the Prehistoric Society* 48: 1–27.

Higham, C., and A. Kijngam. 1982. Irregular Earthworks in Northeast Thailand: New Insight. *Antiquity* LVI: 102–10.

Higham, C., and R. Thosarat. 1994. *Khok Phanom Di: Prehistoric Adaptation to the World's Richest Habitat*. Fort Worth, TX: Harcourt Brace College Publishers.

——. 1998. *Prehistoric Thailand: From Early Settlement to Sukhothai*. Bangkok: River Books.

Hilborn, R. 1994. *Chaos and Nonlinear Dynamics*. Oxford: Oxford Univ. Press.

Hla, N. P. 1991. The Major Role of the Mons in Southeast Asia. *Journal of the Siam Society* 79(1): 13–21.

Hla, U. K. 1979. Ancient Cities in Burma. *Journal of the Society of Architectural Historians* 38(2): 95–102.

Ho, C. 1991a. Ceramics Found at Excavations at Ko Kho Khao and Laem Pho, Southern Thailand. *Journal of Trade Ceramic Studies* 11: 53–80.

———. 1991b. Chinese Presence in Southern Thailand before 1500 A.D. from Archaeological Evidence. In *China and the Maritime Silk Road*, ed. J. Guy, 290–307. Quangzhou, China: Quangzhou International Seminar on China and the Maritime Routes of the Silk Roads Organization Committee.

———. 1994. Problems in the Study of Zhejiang Green Glazed Wares with Special References to Ko Kho Khao and Laem Pho-Payang, Southern Thailand. *New Light on Chinese Yue and Longquan Wares. Archaeological Ceramics Found in Eastern and Southern Asia A.D. 800–1400*, ed. C. Ho, 187–212. Hong Kong: Centre of Asian Studies, Univ. of Hong Kong.

Ho, C., P. Charoenwongsa, et al. 1990. Newly Identified Chinese Ceramic Wares from Ninth Century Trading Ports in Southern Thailand. *SPAFA Digest; Journal of SEAMO Project in Archaeology and Fine Arts* 11(3): 12–17.

Ho Xuan Tinh. 1993. The Proto-historic Cam Ha Burial Jars in Hoi An, Quang Nam-Da Nang. *Ancient town of Hoi An*. Hanoi: The Gioi Publishers, 82–85.

Hoshino, T. 1993. Puram; Earliest Chinese Sources on Sri Thep and Lopburi. Paper presented at the Symposium sur les sources de l'histoire du pays khmer, Paris.

———. 1999. The Kingdom of Red Earth (Chitu Guo) in Cambodia and Vietnam from the Sixth to the Eighth Centuries. *Journal of the Siam Society (1996)* 84(2): 55–74.

Hudson, R. 2004. *The Origins of Bagan: The Archaeological Landscape of Upper Burma to AD 1300*. Sydney: Univ. of Sydney.

Hutterer, K. 1977. Prehistoric Trade and the Evolution of Philippine Societies: A Reconsideration. In *Economic Exchange and Social Interaction in Southeast Asia: Prehistory, History and Ethnography*, ed. K. L. Hutterer, 177–96. Ann Arbor: Center for South and Southeast Asian Studies, Univ. of Michigan.

———. 1991. The High Bronze Age in Southeast Asia: Introductory Remarks. Unpublished paper read at the Conference of the High Bronze Age, Hua Hin, Thailand.

Indrawooth, P. 1984. Results from the Excavation within the Ancient Town of Nakhon Phathom, Tambon Phra Praton, Amphoe Muang, Changwat Nakhon Phathom (in Thai). Special issue, *Journal of Silapakon University*: 148–68.

———. 1991. Archaeological Excavation at the Ancient City of Fah Daed Soang Yang. *Muang Boran Journal* 17(3).

———. 1994. Dvaravati Culture in the Chi Valley: A Study on Muang Fa Daed Song Yang. *Muang Boran Journal* 20(1).

———. 2004. The Archaeology of the Early Buddhist Kingdoms of Thailand. In *Southeast Asia from Prehistory to History*, ed. I. Glover and P. Bellwood, 120–48. London, RoutledgeCurzon.

Indrawooth, P., S. Krabuansang, et al. 1991. Muang Fa Daed Song Yang: New Archaeological Discoveries. In *Récentes Recherches en Archéologie en Thailande: Deuxieme Symposium Franco-Thai*, 98–111. Bangkok: Silpakon Univ.

Ishizawa, Y. 1995. Chinese Chronicles of 1st–5th century AD: Funan, Southern Cambodia. In *South East Asia and China: Art, Interaction and Commerce; Colloquies on Art and Archaeology in Asia No.17*, ed. R. Scott and J. Guy, 11–31. London: Univ. of London.

Jacob, J. M. 1979. Pre-Angkor Cambodia: Evidence from the Inscriptions in Khmer concerning the Common People and their Environment. In *Early South East Asia: Essays in Archaeology, History and Historical Geography*, ed. R. B. Smith and W. Watson, 406–26. New York: Oxford Univ. Press.

Jacobsen, T. 2003. Autonomous Queenship in Cambodia, 1st–9th centuries CE. *Journal of the Royal Asiatic Society* 13(3): 357–75.

Jacq-Hergoualc'h, M. 1997. Archaeological Research in the Malay Peninsula. *Journal of the Siam Society* 85(1 and 2): 121–32.

———. 2002. *The Malay Peninsula: Crossroads of the Maritime Silk Road (100 BC–1300 AD)*. Leiden: Brill.

Jacques, C. 1969. Notes sur la Stèle de Vo-Canh. *Bulletin de l'École Française d'Extrême-Orient* 55: 117–24.

———. 1972a. La Carrière de Jayavarman II. *Bulletin de l'École Française d'Extrême-Orient* 59: 205–20.

———. 1972b. Sur l'Emplacement du Royaume d'Aninditapura. *Bulletin de l'École Française d'Extrême-Orient* 59: 193–205.

———. 1979. "Funan," "Zhenla": The Reality Concealed by these Chinese Views of Indochina. In *Early South East Asia: Essays in Archaeology, History and Historical Geography*, ed. R. B. Smith and W. Watson, 371–77. New York: Oxford Univ. Press.

———. 1985. The Kamraten Jagat in Ancient Cambodia. In *Indus Valley to Mekong Delta: Explorations in Epigraphy*, ed. K. Norbu, 269–86. Madras: New Era Publications.

———. 1986. Le Pays Khmer Avant Angkor. *Journal des Savants* Jan.–Sept.: 85.

———. 1988. Le Pays Khmer Avant Angkor. *Dossiers Histoire et Archeologie* 125: 28–33.

———. 1989. Les Khmers en Thailande: Ce que nous disent les inscriptions. *SPAFA Digest* 10(1): 19.

———. 1990. New Data on the VII–VIIIth Centuries in the Khmer Land. *BAR International Series* 561: 251–60.

Jacques, C., and M. Freeman. 1999. *Ancient Angkor*. Bangkok: River Books Guides.

Jenny, M. 2001. *A Short Introduction to the Mon Language, The Mon Culture and Literature Survival Project*. 2002.

Jermsawadi, P., and C. Charuphananon. 1989. Votive Tablets from Excavation at Wat Nakhon Kosa. *Silpakon Journal* 32(6): 40–55.

Johnson, A., and T. Earle. 1987. *The Evolution of Human Societies*. Stanford, Calif.: Stanford Univ. Press.

Johnson, G. 1982. Organizational Structure and Scalar Stress. In *Theory and Explanation in Archaeology*, ed. C. Renfrew, M. Rowlands, and B. Segraves, 389–421. New York: Academic Press.

Junker, L. L. 1993. Craft Goods Specialization and Prestige Goods Exchange in Philippine Chiefdoms of the Fifteenth and Sixteenth Centuries. *Asian Perspectives* 32(1): 1–35.

———. 2004. Political Economy in the Historic Period Chiefdoms and States of Southeast Asia. In *Archaeological Perspectives on Political Economies*, ed. G. Feinman and L. M. Nicholas. Salt Lake City: Univ. of Utah Press.

Kappel, W. 1974. Irrigation Development and Population Pressure. In *Irrigation's Impact on Society*, ed. T. Downing and G. McGuire, 159–69. Tucson: Univ. of Arizona Press.

Kasetsiri, C. 1976. *The Rise of Ayudhya: A History of Siam in the Fourteenth and Fifteenth Centuries*. Kuala Lumpur/London: Oxford Univ. Press.

Kauffman, S. 1993. *The Origins of Order: Self-Organisation and Selection in Evolution*. Oxford: Oxford Univ. Press.

——. 1995. *At Home in the Universe: The Search for the Laws of Self-Organization and Complexity*. New York: Oxford Univ. Press.

Kennedy, J. 1977. *A Course Toward Diversity: Economic Interaction and Cultural Differentiation in Prehistoric Mainland Southeast Asia*. Honolulu: Univ. of Hawaii Press.

Khai, V. S. 1998. Plans architecturaux des ancients monuments du Delta du Mékong du 1er au 10 e siècles A.D. In vol. 1 of *Southeast Asian Archaeology 1994: Proceeding of the 5th International Conference of the European Association of Southeast Asian Archaeologists*, ed. P.-Y. Manguin, 207–14. Hull: Centre for Southeast Asian Studies, Univ. of Hull.

——. 2003. The Kingdom of Funan and the Culture of Oc Éo. In *Art and Archaeology of Fu Nan: Pre-Khmer Kingdom of the Lower Mekong Valley*, ed. J. Khoo, 36–85. Bangkok: Orchid Press.

Kipp, R., and E. Schortman. 1989. The Political Impact of Trade in Chiefdoms. *American Anthropologist* 91(2): 370–85.

Kirch, P. 1984. *The Evolution of the Polynesian Chiefdoms*. Cambridge: Cambridge Univ. Press.

——. 1991. Chiefship and Competitive Involution: The Marquesas Islands of East Polynesia. In *Chiefdoms, Power, Economy and Ideology*, ed. T. Earle, 119–46. Cambridge: Cambridge Univ. Press.

Kirchoff, P. 1959. The Principles of Clanship in Human Society. In *Readings in Anthropology II Cultural Anthropology*, ed. M. Fried, 259–70. New York: Thomas Y. Crowell Co.

Kishore, K. 1965. Varnas in Early Kambuja Inscriptions. *Journal of the American Oriental Society* LXXXV: 566–69.

Kohl, P. 1987. The Use and Abuse of World Systems Theory: The Case of the Prehistoric West Asian State. In vol. 11 of *Advances in Archaeological Method and Theory*, ed. M. B. Schiffer, 1–35. Orlando: Academic Press.

Kosse, K. 1994. The Evolution of Large, Complex Groups: A Hypothesis. *Journal of Anthropological Archaeology* 13: 35–50.

Krairiksh, P. 1977. *Art Styles in Thailand: A selection from National Provincial Museums; An Essay in Conceptualization*. Bangkok: Dept. of Fine Arts.

Kristiansen, K. 1991. Chiefdoms, States and Systems of Social Evolution. In *Chiefdoms, Power, Economy and Ideology*, ed. T. Earle, 16–44. Cambridge: Cambridge Univ. Press.

Kulke, H. 1986. The Early and the Imperial Kingdom in Southeast Asian History. In *Southeast Asia in the 9th–14th Centuries*, ed. D. G. Marr and A. C. Milner, 1–23. Singapore: Australian National Univ. and the Institute of Southeast Asian Studies.

——. 1990. Indian Colonies: Indianization or Cultural Convergence? In *Onderzoek in Zuidoost-Azie*, ed. S. H. Nordholt. Leiden: Rijksuniversiteit te Leiden.

——. 1993. "Kadatuan-Srivijaya"—Empire or *kraton* of Srivijaya? A Reassesment of the Epigraphical Evidence. *Bulletin de l'École Française d'Extrême-Orient* LXXX(1): 159–80.

Kus, S. M. n.d. Unreferenced citation. In Peebles, C. S., and S. M. Kus. 1977. Some Archaeological Correlates of Ranked Societies. *American Antiquity* 42: 421–48.

le May, R. 1964. *The Culture of South-East Asia: The Heritage of India*. London: George Allen and Unwin Ltd.

Le Thi Lein. 2002. Gold Plates and Their Archaeological Context in Oc Éo Culture. Paper presented at the 17th Indo-Pacific Prehistory Association conference, Taipei, Republic of China.

Le Xuan Diem, Dao Linh Con, et al. 1995. *The Oc Éo Culture: New Discoveries* (in Vietnamese). Hanoi: Social Sciences Publishing House.

Levy, J. 1979. Evidence of Social Stratification in Bronze Age Denmark. *Journal of Field Archaeology* 6: 49–56.

Lingat, R. 1949. L'influence Juridique de l'Inde au Champa et au Cambodge d'apres l'Epigraphie. *Journal Asiatique*: 23.

Lombard, D. 1987. Le Campa Vu du Sud. *Bulletin de l'École Française d'Extrême-Orient* 76: 311–17.

Loofs, H. H. E. 1979. Problems of Continuity between the Pre-Buddhist and Buddhist Periods in Central Thailand, with Special Reference to U-Thong. In *Early South East Asia: Essays in Archaeology, History and Historical Geography*, ed. R. B. Smith and W. Watson, 342–51. New York: Oxford Univ. Press.

Loofs-Wissowa, H. 1991. Dongson Drums: Instruments of Shamanism or Regalia? A New Interpretation of their Decoration May Provide the Answer. *Arts Asiatiques* XLVI: 39–49.

Luce, G. H. 1925. The Tan (AD 97–132) and the Ngai-lao. *Journal of Burma Research Society* XIV(2).

———. 1937. The Ancient Pyu. *Journal of Burma Research Society* 27: 239–53.

———. 1965. Dvaravati and Old Burma. *Journal of the Siam Society* 53(1): 9–25.

———. 1976. Sources of Early Burma History. In *Southeast Asian History and Historiography: Essays Presented to D. G. E. Hall*, ed. C. D. Cowan and O. W. Wolters, 31–42. Ithaca/London: Cornell Univ. Press.

———. 1985. *Phases in Pre-Pagan Burma*. Oxford: Oxford Univ. Press.

Lyons, E. 1965. The Traders of Ku Bua. *Archives of the China Art Society*: 52–56.

———. 1979. Dvaravati, A Consideration of Its Formative Period. In *Early South East Asia*, ed. R. Smith and W. Watson. Oxford: Oxford Univ. Press: 352–59.

Ma Tuan-Lin. 1876. *Ethnographie des Peuples Étrangers à la Chine*. Geneva: Georg.

Mabbett, I. W. 1977a. The "Indianization" of Southeast Asia: Reflections on the Pre-Historic Sources. *Journal of Southeast Asian Studies* 8(1): 1–14.

———. 1977b. Varnas in Angkor and the Indian Caste System. *Journal Of Asian Studies* xxxvi(3): 429–42.

———. 1997. The "Indianization" of Southeast Asia: A Reappraisal. In *Living a Life in Accord with Dhamma: Papers in Honor of Professor Jean Boisselier on his Eightieth Birthday*, ed. N. Eilenberg, S. M. C. Diskul, and R. Brown, 342–55. Bangkok: Silpakorn Univ.

Mahlo, D. 1998. Fruhe Munzen aus Birma: Thesen (Early Coins from Burma: Some Theories). *Indo-Asiatische Zeitschrift* 2: 88–94.

Majid, Z. 1982. The West Mouth, Niah, in the Prehistory of Southeast Asia. *Sarawak Museum Journal* 31.

Majumdar, R. C. 1927. *Ancient Indian Colonies in the Far East: Vol. 1 Champa*. Lahore: Punjab Sanskrit Book Depot (Greater India Society Publication 1).

———. 1944. *Kambuja-desa or An Ancient Hindu Colony in Cambodia*. Madras: Univ. of Madras.

———. 1963. *Hindu Colonies in the Far East.* Calcutta: Firma KLM Private Limited.

Malinowski, B. 1922. *Argonauts of the Western Pacific: An Account of Native Enterprise and Adventure in the Archipelagoes of Melanesian New Guinea.* London: G. Routledge & Sons.

Malleret, L. 1959. *L'Archeologie du Delta du Mekong.* Vol. 1. Paris: Publications de l'École Française d'Extrême Orient.

Malleret, L. 1960. *L'Archéologie du Delta du Mekong.* Vol. 2. Paris: Publications de l'École Française d'Extrême Orient.

———. 1960–1962. *L'Archéologie du Delta du Mekong.* Vol. 3. Paris: Publications de l'École Française d'Extrême Orient.

———. 1962. L'Archéologie du Delta du Mekong: La Culture du Fou-nan. *École Française d'Extrême Orient* XLIII(3).

Manguin, P.-Y. 1983. Comments on the Concept of Trans-Peninsular Routes. In *SPAFA Final Report, Consultative Workshop on Archaeological and Environmental Studies on Srivijaya (T-W3), Bangkok and South Thailand, March 29–April 11, 1983.* Bangkok: SPAFA, 297–98.

———. 1987. Etudes Sumatranaises I Palembang et Sriwijaya: Anciennes Hypothèses, Recherches Nouvelles (Palembang Ouest). *Bulletin de l'École Française d'Extrême-Orient* LXXVI: 337–402.

———. 1989. The Trading Ships of Insular Southeast Asia: New Evidence from Indonesian Archaeological Sites. In *Proceedings, Pertemuan Ilmiah Arkeologi V, Yogakarta,* 200–219. Jakarta: Ikatan Ahli Arkeologi Indonesia.

———. 1992. Excavations in South Sumatra 1988–1990: New Evidence for Srivijayan Sites. In *Southeast Asian Archaeology, 1990,* ed. I. Glover, 63–74. Hull: Centre for South-East Asian Studies, Univ. of Hull.

———. 1996. Southeast Asian Shipping in the Indian Ocean During the First Millenium AD. In *Tradition and Archaeology. Early Maritime Contacts in the Indian Ocean.* Proceedings of the International Seminar Techno-Archaeological Perspectives of Seafaring in the Indian Ocean 4th century BC–15th century AD. New Delhi, Manohar: 181–98.

———. n.d. Unpublished lecture given at the Centre Culturel Francais, December 5, 2002. Phnom Penh, Cambodia.

Maspero, G. 1928. *Le Royaume du Champa.* Paris and Brussels: Librairie nationale d'art et d'histoire.

McNeill, J., and D. Welch. 1991. Regional and Interregional Interaction on the Khorat Plateau. *Bulletin of the Indo-Pacific Prehistory Association* 10: 327–40.

Miksic, J. 1977. Archaeology and Paleogeography in the Straits of Malacca. In vol. 13 of *Economic Exchange and Social Interaction in Southeast Asia,* ed. K. L. Hutterer, 155–76. Ann Arbor: Univ. of Michigan.

———. 1984. A Comparison Between Some Long-distance Trading Institutions of the Malacca Straits Area and of the Western Pacific. In vol. 16 of *Southeast Asian Archaeology at the XV Pacific Sciences Congress,* ed. D. Bayard, 235–53. Dunedin: Univ. of Otago.

———. 1999a. Chinese Traders and Pilgrims. In *The Encyclopedia of Malaysia: Early History,* ed. N. H. Shuhaimi and N. A. Rahman. Kuala Lumpur: Archipelago Press.

———. 1999b. The Cola Attacks. In *The Encyclopedia of Malaysia: Early History,* ed. N. H. Shuhaimi and N. A. Rahman, 120–22. Kuala Lumpur, Archipelago Press.

——. 1999c. The Expansion of Trade. In *The Encylopedia of Malaysia: Early History*, ed. N. H. Shuhaimi and N. A. Rahman, 76–78. Kuala Lumpur: Archipelago Press.

——. 1999d. From Prehistory to Protohistory. In *The Encyclopedia of Malaysia: Early History*, ed. N. H. Shuhaimi and N. A. Rahman, 64–66. Kuala Lumpur: Archipelago Press.

——. 1999e. Indian Traders. In *The Encyclopedia of Malaysia: Early History*, ed. N. H. Shuhaimi and N. A. Rahman, 80–82. Kuala Lumpur: Archipelago Press.

——. 1999f. Protohistoric Settlement Patterns. In *The Encylopedia of Malaysia: Early History*, ed. N. H. Shuhaimi and N. A. Rahman, 66–68. Kuala Lumpur: Archipelago Press.

——. 1999g. Wider Contacts in Protohistoric Times. In *The Encyclopedia of Malaysia: Early History*, ed. N. H. Shuhaimi and N. A. Rahman, 74–75. Kuala Lumpur: Archipelago Press.

——. 1999h. Transformation of Indigenous Religious Beliefs. In *The Encyclopedia of Malaysia: Early History*, ed. N. H. Shuhaimi and N. A. Rahman, 92–93. Kuala Lumpur: Archipelago Press.

——. 1999i. Candi Architecture. In *The Encyclopedia of Malaysia: Early History*, ed. N. H. Shuhaimi and N. A. Rahman, 94–95. Kuala Lumpur: Archipelago Press.

——. 2003. The Beginning of Trade in Early Southeast Asia: The Role of Oc Éo and the Lower Mekong River. In *Art and Archaeology of Fu Nan: Pre-Khmer Kingdom of the Lower Mekong Valley*, ed. J. Khoo, 1–34. Bangkok: Orchid Press.

Millon, R. 1962. Variations in Social Responses to the Practice of Irrigation Agriculture. In *Civilizations in Desert Lands*, ed. R. Woodbury, 56–88. Salt Lake City: Univ. of Utah Press.

Mitchiner, M. 1982. The Date of the Early Funanese, Mon, Pyu and Arakanese Coinages ("Symbolic Coins"). *Journal of the Siam Society* 70: 5–12.

Moore, E. 1986. Moated Settlement in the Mun Basin, Northeast Thailand. In *Southeast Asian Archaeology 1986*, ed. I. Glover and E. Glover, 201–12. Oxford: British Archaeological Reports International Series 561.

Moore, E., and U. A. Myint. 1991. Finger Marked Designs on Ancient Bricks in Myanmar. *Journal of the Siam Society* 79(2): 81–102.

——. 1993. Beads of Myanmar (Burma). *Journal of the Siam Society* 81(1): 55–64.

Mudar, K. 1999. How Many Dvaravati Kingdoms? Locational Analysis of First Millennium A.D. Moated Settlements in Central Thailand. *Journal of Anthropological Archaeology* 18: 1–28.

Mukerji, R. 1912. *Indian Shipping: A History of the Sea-borne Trade and Maritime Activity of the Indians from the Earliest Times*. Bombay and Calcutta: Munshiram Manoharial.

Muller, J. 1987. Salt, Chert, and Shell: Mississippian Exchange and Economy. In *Specialization, Exchange, and Complex Societies*, ed. E. Brumfiel and T. Earle. Cambridge: Cambridge Univ. Press.

Muller, J., and E. Stephens. 1990. Mississipian Sociocultural Adaptation. In *Cahokia and the Hinterlands: Middle Mississippian Cultures of the Midwest*, ed. T. Emersdon and R. Lewis. Urbana: Univ. of Illinois Press.

Murari, K. 1985. *Cultural Heritage of Burma*. New Delhi: Inter-India Publications.

Netting, R. 1990. Population, Permanent Agriculture, and Polities: Unpacking the Evolutionary Portmanteau. In *The Evolution of Political Systems: Socio-Politics in Small Scale Sedentary Societies*, ed. S. Upham, 21–61. Cambridge: Cambridge Univ. Press.

Ng, R. 1979. The Geographical Habitat of Historical Settlement in Mainland South East Asia. In *Early South East Asia*, ed. R. Smith and W. Watson. Oxford: Oxford Univ. Press.

Ngo Si Hong. 1991. Sa Huynh: An Indigenous Cultural Tradition in Southern Viet Nam. Conference on The High Bronze Age of Southeast Asia and South China, Hua Hin, Thailand, unpublished paper.

Ngo Si Hong and T. Q. Thinh. 1991. Jar Burials at Hau Xa, Hoi An District (Quang Nam, Da Nang Province) and a New Understanding of the Sa Huynh Culture. *Khao co Hoc* 1991(3): 64–75.

Ngo Si Hong, Tran Quy Thinh, et al. 1991. Test Dig at the Sa Huynh Site at Hau Xa, Hoi An District (Quang Nam, Da Nang Province). *New Discoveries in Archaeology* 1990: 99–101.

Nguyen Chieu, Lam My Dung, et al. 1991. Ceramics from Excavation at the Ancient Cham Site of Tra Kieu, 1990 (in Vietnamese). *Khao co Hoc* 4: 19–30.

Nimmanhaeminda, K. 1967. The Lawa Guardian Spirits of Chiengmai. *Journal of the Siam Society* 45(2): 197.

Nissen, H. 1988. *The Early History of the Ancient Near East 9000–2000 B.C.* Chicago: Univ. of Chicago Press.

Nitta, E. 1991. Archaeological Study on the Ancient Iron-smelting and Salt-making Industries in the Northeast of Thailand; Preliminary Report on the Excavations of Non Yang and Ban Don Phlong. *Journal of Southeast Asian Archaeology* 11: 1–46.

Oberg, K. 1955. Types of Social Structure among the Lowland Tribes of South and Central America. *American Anthropologist* 57: 472–89.

O'Connor, S. J. 1972. *Hindu Gods of Peninsular Siam*. Ascona: Artibus Asie.

Onsuwan Eyre, C. 2006. Prehistoric and Proto-historic communities in the eastern Upper Chao Praya River Valley: Analysis of site chronology, settlement patterns, and land use. Pittsburgh: Dept. of Anthropology, University of Pennsylvania, 616.

O'Reilly, D. J. W. 1998. The Discovery of Clay-Lined Floors at an Iron Age Site in Thailand: Preliminary Observations from Non Muang Kao, Nakon Ratchasima Province. *Journal of the Siam Society* 85(1): 1–14.

———. 1999. *A Diachronic Analysis of Social Organisation in the Mun River Valley*. Dunedin: Dept. of Anthropology, Univ. of Otago, 324.

———. 2000. From the Bronze Age to the Iron Age in Thailand: Applying the Heterarchical Approach. *Asian Perspectives* 39(1-2): 1–19.

———. 2003. Further Evidence of Heterarchy in Bronze Age Thailand. *Current Anthropology* 44(2): 300–306.

O'Reilly, D. J. W., and S. Peng. 2001. Recent Excavations in Northwest Cambodia. *Antiquity* 75: 265–266.

Orans, M. 1966. Surplus. *Human Organization* 25(1): 24–32.

Paris, P. 1931. Anciens Canaux Reconnus sur Photographies Aériennes dans les Provinces de Takeo & Chau Doc. *BEFEO* XXXI(1–2): 221–25.

Parmentier, H. 1902. Le Sanctuaire de Po-Nagar a Nhatrang. *Bulletin de l'École Française d'Extrême-Orient* II: 17–54.

———. 1909. *Inventaire Descriptif des Monuments Cams de l'Annam, Tome Premier: Description des Monuments*. Paris: Publications de l'École Française d'Éxtreme Orient.

———. 1918. *Inventaire Descriptif des Monuments Cams de l'Annam, Tome II: Étude de l'art cam*. Paris: Éditions Ernest Leroux (Inventaire archéologique de l'Indochine II; Publications de l'École Française d'Éxtreme Orient).

———. 1924. Notes d'Archeologie Indochinoises, I, Relevé des points cams décou-verts en Annam depuis la publication do l'Inventaire. *BEFEO* 23: 267–75.

Pauketat, T. 1994. *The Ascent of Chiefs: Cahokia and Mississippian Politics in North America*. Tuscaloosa: Univ. of Alabama.

Pautreau, J.-P., A. Matringhem, et al. 1997a. Excavations at Ban Wang Hi, Lamphun Province, Thailand. *The Journal of the Siam Society* 85: 161–72.

———. 1997b. Thailande, La Fin des Temps Prehistoriques (in French). *Archeologia* 330.

Pautreau, J.-P., and P. Mornais. 1998. Ban Wang Hi (Thailande) Travaux 1998. Journee Prehistorique et Protohistorique de Bretagne, Université de Rennes 1. Un-published paper.

Peebles, C., and S. Kus. 1977. Some Archaeological Correlates of Ranked Societies. *American Antiquity* 42: 421–48.

Pelliot, P. 1903a. Le Fou-Nan. *Bulletin de l'École Française d'Extrême-Orient* 2: 248–333.

———. 1903b. Textes Chinois sur Panduranga. *Bulletin de l'École Française d'Extrême-Orient* 3: 649–54.

———. 1904. Deux Itinéraires de Chine en Inde: A la fin du VIIIe siècle. *Bulletin de l'École Française d'Extrême-Orient* 4: 131–413.

———. 1925. Quelques Textes Chinois Concernant l'Indochine Hinduisée. *Etudes Asiatiques* 2: 243–63.

Pham Duc Manh. 1996. Proto-history and Pre-history of the Eastern Part of Nam Bo: Past and Modern Perceptions. *Vietnamese Studies 1996/2, Special: Archaeologi-cal Data II New Series* 50(120): 63–119.

Phayre, A. P. 1967. *History of Burma*. London/Santiago de Compostela: Susil Gupta.

Pisnupong, P. 1991. Report on the Excavation of Sra Morakod Monuments (in Thai). Bangkok: Fine Arts Department.

———. 1992. *History and Archaeology of Si Mahood* (in Thai). Bangkok: Fine Arts Dept.

———. 1993. *History and Archaeology of Si Mahood: Two* (in Thai). Bangkok: Fine Arts Dept.

Polanyi, K. 1957. The Economy as an Instituted Process. In *Primitive, Archaic and Modern Economies: Essays of Karl Polanyi*, ed. G. Dalton, 306–34. Boston: Beacon Press.

Pollock, S. 2000. Cosmopolitan and Vernacular in History. *Public Culture* 12 (3): 591–625.

Raffles, S. 1817. *History of Java*. Kuala Lumpur: Oxford Univ. Press.

Rathje, W. 1972. Praise the Gods and Pass the Metates: A Hypothesis of the Devel-opment of Lowland Rainforest Civilizations in Meso-america. In *Contemporary Ar-chaeology*, ed. M. Leone. Carbondale: Southern Illinois Univ. Press.

Ratnayake, H. 2003. The Jetavana Treasure. In Sri Lanka and the Silk Road of the Sea. ed. S. Bandaranayake, L. Dewaraja, R. Silva, and K. G. D. Wimalaratne, 37–52. Colombo, Sri Lanka: Institute of International Relations.

Rattanakun, S. 1992. *Bang Chiang Heritage* (in Thai). Bangkok: Fine Arts Dept., Ar-chaeology Division Publications No. 8.

Redmond, E. 1994. *Tribal and Chiefly Warfare in South America*. Ann Arbor: Univ. of Michigan Museum.

Reid, A. 1983. "Closed" and "Open" Slave Systems in Pre-colonial Southeast Asia. In *Slavery, Bondage, and Dependency in Southeast Asia,* ed. A. Reid, 156–81. New York: St. Martin's.

Renfrew, C. 1974. Beyond a Subsistence Economy: The Evolution of Social Organisation in Prehistoric Europe. In *Reconstructing Complex Societies: An Archaeological Colloquium,* ed. C. B. Moore, 69–95. Ann Arbor, Mich.: Supplemental to the Bulletin of the American Schools of Oriental Research No. 20.

———. 1975. Trade as Action at a Distance: Questions of Integration and Communication. In *Ancient Civilization and Trade,* ed. J. A. Sabloff and C. C. Lamberg-Karlowsky. Albuquerque: Univ. of New Mexico Press for School of American Research.

———. 1986. Introduction: Peer Polity Interaction and Sociopolitical Change. In *Peer Polity Interaction and Sociopolitical Change,* ed. C. Renfrew and J. F. Cherry, 1–18. Cambridge: Cambridge Univ. Press.

Rothman, M. 1994. Evolutionary Typologies and Cultural Complexity. In *Chiefdoms and Early States in the Near East: The Organisational Dynamics of Complexity,* ed. G. Stein and M. S. Rothman, 1–10. Madison, Wisc.: Prehistory Press.

Sahlins, M. 1958. *Social Stratification in Polynesia.* Seattle: Univ. of Washington Press.

———. 1972. *Stone Age Economics.* Chicago: Aldine.

Sanders, W., and B. Price. 1968. *Mesoamerica: The Evolution of a Civilization.* New York: Random House.

Sanders, W., and D. Webster. 1978. Unilinealism, Multilinealism, and the Evolution of Complex Societies. In *Social Archaeology: Beyond Subsistence and Dating,* ed. C. L. Redman, M. J. Berman, E. V. Curtinet, et al., 249–302. New York: Academic Press.

Sanderson, D. C., P. Bishop, et al. 2003. Luminescence Dating of Anthropogenically Reset Canal Sediments from Angkor Borei, Mekong Delta, Cambodia. *Quaternary Sciences Review* 22: 1111–21.

San Win. 2003. Dating the Hpayahtaung Pyu Stone Urn Inscription. *Myanmar Historical Research Journal* 11:15–22.

Sastri, K. A. N. 1932. The Takua-Pa (Siam) Tamil Inscription. *Journal of Oriental Research* 6(4): 299–310.

———. 1936. L'origine de l'Alphabet du Champa. *Bulletin de l'École Française d'Extrême-Orient* 35: 233–41.

———. 1949. *History of Sri Vijaya.* Madras: Univ. of Madras.

Schortman, E. 1989. Interregional Interaction in Prehistory. *American Antiquity* 54: 52–65.

Schortman, E., and P. Urban. 1987. Modeling Interregional Interaction in Prehistory. In *Advances in Archaeological Method and Theory,* ed. M. Schiffer, 37–95. Orlando: Academic Press.

———. 1996. Actions at a Distance, Impacts at Home: Prestige Good Theory and a Pre-Columbian Polity in Southeastern Mesoamerica. *Pre-Columbian World Systems,* ed. P. Peregrine and G. Feinman, 97–114. Madison, Wisc.: Prehistory Press.

Schultz, E., and R. Lavenda. 1995. *Anthropology.* London: Mayfield Publishing.

Schurr, M., and M. Schoeninger. 1995. Associations Between Agricultural Intensification and Social Complexity: An Example from the Prehistoric Ohio Valley. *Journal of Anthropological Archaeology* 14: 315–39.

Schweyer, A.-V. 2000. La Dynastie d'Indrapura (Quang Nam Vietnam). *Southeast Asian Archaeology 1998*, ed. W. Lobo and S. Reimann, 205–18. Hull: Centre for South-East Asian Studies and Ethnologisches Museum, Staatliche Museen zu Berlin, Stifung Preussischer Kulturbesitz, Univ. of Hull.

Scott, G. 1991. *Time, Rhythms, and Chaos in the New Dialogue with Nature.* Ames: Iowa State Univ.

Scott, W. 1983. *Oripun* and *Alipin* in the Sixteenth-Century Philippines. In *Slavery, Bondage and Dependency in Southeast Asia*, ed. A. Reid, 138–55. New York: St. Martin's.

Sedov, L. A. 1978. Angkor: Society and State. *The Study of the State*, ed. H. J. M. Claessen and P. Skalnik, 111–30. The Hague: Mouton.

Sein, C. L. 1979. Weather and Climate. In *South-East Asia: A Systematic Geography*, ed. R. D. Hill, 16–30. Kuala Lumpur: Oxford Univ. Press.

Service, E. 1962. *Primitive Social Organization, an Evolutionary Perspective.* New York: Random House.

——— . 1971. *Primitive Social Organization, an Evolutionary Perspective.* New York: Random House.

——— . 1975. *The Origins of the State and Civilization.* New York: Norton.

Shuhaimi, N. 1984. Art, Archaeology and the Early Kingdoms in the Malay Peninsula and Sumatra c. 400–1400 AD. PhD thesis, London, Univ. of London, School of Oriental and African Studies.

——— . 1991. Recent Research at Kuala Selinsing, Perak. In *Indo-Pacific Prehistory 1990 Proceedings of the 14th Congress of the Indo-Pacific Prehistory Association, Yogyakarta, Indonesia, 26 August to 2 September 1990*, II, ed. P. Bellwood, 141–52.

——— . 1999a. The Bujang Valley. In *The Encyclopedia of Malaysia: Early History*, ed. N. H. Shuhaimi and N. A. Rahman, 68–70. Kuala Lumpur: Archipelago Press.

——— . 1999b. Chi tu: An Inland Kingdom. In *The Encyclopedia of Malaysia: Early History*, ed. N. H. Shuhaimi and N. A. Rahman, 68–70. Kuala Lumpur: Archipelago Press.

——— , ed. 1999c. The Encyclopedia of Malaysia: Early History. In *The Encyclopedia of Malaysia: Early History*, ed. N. H. Shuhaimi and N. A. Rahman. Kuala Lumpur: Archipelago Press.

——— . 1999d. Pulau Tioman: A Port Settlement. In *The Encyclopedia of Malaysia: Early History*, ed. N. H. Shuhaimi and N. A. Rahman, 72–74. Kuala Lumpur: Archipelago Press.

——— . 1999e. Srivijaya. In *The Encyclopedia of Malaysia: Early History*, ed. N. H. Shuhaimi and N. A. Rahman, 118–20. Kuala Lumpur: Archipelago Press.

Sircar, D. C. 1939. Date of the Earliest Sanskrit Inscription of Campa. *The Journal of the Greater India Society* VI: 53–55.

——— , ed. 1942. *Select Inscriptions Bearing on Indian History and Civilization Volume One: From the sixth century B.C. to the sixth century AD.* Calcutta: Univ. of Calcutta.

Smith, R., and W. Watson, eds. 1979. *Early South East Asia.* Oxford: Oxford Univ. Press.

Solheim II, W. G. 1968. Early Bronze in Northeastern Thailand. *Current Anthropology* 9(1): 59–62.

Sørensen, P. 1973. Prehistoric Iron Implements from Thailand. *Asian Perspectives* 16(2): 134–73.

Southworth, W. 2001. *The Origins of Campa in Central Vietnam: A Preliminary Review.* London: School of Oriental and African Studies (SOAS), Univ. of London, 477.

———. 2004. The Coastal States of Champa. In *Southeast Asia from Prehistory to History*, ed. I. Glover and P. Bellwood, 209–33. London: RoutledgeCurzon.

Srisuchat, A. 1986. Antique Jewels from the South (in Thai). In *Encyclopedia of Southern Culture, II.* Bangkok: 552–66.

Stargardt, J. 1983. *Satingpra I: The Environmental and Economic Archaeology of South Thailand.* Oxford: BAR International Series 158.

———. 1985. The Isthmus of the Malay Penninsula in Long-distance Navigation: New Archaeological Findings. In *Trade and Shipping in the Southern Seas: Selected Readings from Archipel 18 (1979).* Bangkok: SPAFA, 11.

———. 1986. Hydraulic Works and Southeast Asian Polities. In *Southeast Asia in the 9th-14th Centuries*, ed. D. G. Marr and A. C. Milner, 23–48. Singapore: Australian National Univ. and the Institute of Southeast Asian Studies.

———. 1990. *The Ancient Pyu of Burma, Volume One: Early Pyu Cities in a Man-made Landscape.* Cambridge: Publications on Ancient Civilization in South East Asia.

Stark, M. 1998. The Transition to History in the Mekong Delta: A View from Cambodia. *The Transition to History in Southeast Asia, Part I: Cambodia and Thailand* 2(3): 175–204.

———. 2003. The Chronology, Technology and Contexts of Earthenware Ceramics in Cambodia. In *Earthenware in Southeast Asia*, ed. J. Miksic. Singapore: Singapore Univ. Press.

———. 2004. Pre-Angkorian and Angkorian Cambodia. In *Southeast Asia: From Prehistory to History*, ed. P. Bellwood and I. Glover, 89–119. London: RoutledgeCurzon.

Stark, M., and S. Bong. 2001. Recent Research on Emergent Complexity in Cambodia's Mekong. *Bulletin of the Indo Pacific Prehistory Association* 5(21): 85–98.

Stark, M., P. B. Griffin, et al. 1999. Results of the 1995/1996 Field Investigations at Angkor Borei, Cambodia. *Asian Perspectives* 38(1): 7–36.

Stein, R. 1947. Le Lin-yi; sa localisation, sa contribution à la formation du Champa et ses liens avec la Chine. *Han-hiue* 2(1–3): 1–335.

Steponaitis, V. 1991. Contrasting Patterns of Mississippian Development. In *Chiefdoms: Power, Economy, and Ideology*, ed. T. Earle, 193–228. Cambridge: Cambridge Univ. Press.

Stern, P. 1942. *L'Art du Champa (Ancien Annam) et son Évolution.* Toulouse: Les frères Douladoure.

Stevenson, R. 1968. *Population and Political Systems in Tropical Africa.* New York: Columbia Univ. Press.

Steward, J. 1949. Cultural Causality and Law: A Trial Formulation of the Development of early Civilizations. *American Anthropologist* 51(1): 1–27.

Stott, P. 1992. Angkor: Shifting the Hydraulic Paradigm. In *The Gift of Water: Water Management, Cosmology and the State in South East Asia*, ed. J. Rigg, 47–58. London: School of Oriental and African Studies.

Sulaksananont, A. 1987. The Study of Muang Phra Rot, Amphoe Phanat Nikhom, Chonburi, from Material Culture and Stratigraphy (in Thai). M.A. thesis, Silapakorn Univ., Bangkok.

Tainter, J. 1978. Mortuary Practices and the Study of Prehistoric Social Systems. *Advances in Archaeological Method and Theory*, ed. M. B. Schiffer, 105–41. New York: Academic Press.

Takakusu, J. 1896. *A Record of Buddhist Religion as Practised in India and the Malay Archipelago (A.D. 671–695) by I-Tsing*. Delhi: Munshiram Monoharlal, 1966.

Tambiah, S. J. 1977. The Galactic Polity: The Structure of Traditional Kingdoms in Southeast Asia. *Annals of the New York Academy of Sciences* 293: 69–97.

Tan, H. 2003. Remarks on the Pottery of Oc-Éo. In *Art and Archaeology of Fu Nan: Pre-Khmer Kingdom of the Lower Mekong Valley*, ed. J. Khoo, 107–18. Bangkok: Orchid Press.

Tankittikorn, W. 1991. *The Settlement Before Muang Sri Thep* (in Thai). Bangkok: Fine Arts Dept.

Taylor, D. 1975. Some Locational Aspects of Middle Range Hierarchical Societies. Doctoral dissertation in anthropology, City Univ. of New York. Ann Arbor: Univ. Microfilms.

Taylor, K. 1992. The Early Kingdoms. In *The Cambridge History of Southeast Asia*, ed. N. Tarling, 137–81. Cambridge: Cambridge Univ. Press.

Than, S. 1982. Alternative Strategies of Irrigation Development in Cambodia. *Agriculture*. Ithaca: Cornell Univ., 169.

Thepchai, K. 1982. Archaeological Surveys, Excavations and Restorations in Searching for More Information About Srivijaya. In *The History and Archaeology of Srivijaya: Papers from the 1982 Surat Thani Seminar*. Bangkok: Fine Arts Dept., 176–92.

———. 1989. *Excavations at Laem Pho*. Bangkok: Fine Arts Dept.

Thurgood, G. 1999. *From Ancient Cham to Modern Dialects, Two Thousand Years of Language Contact and Change*. Honolulu: Univ. of Hawaii.

Tong Enzheng. 1991. Chiefdoms in Southwest China: The Dian Culture as an Example. Unpublished paper read at the Conference on The High Bronze Age of Southeast Asia and South China, Hua Hin, Thailand.

Trigger, B. 1990. *A History of Archaeological Thought*. Cambridge: Cambridge Univ. Press.

Trinh Thi Hoa. 1996. The Vestiges of Oc Éo Culture: Some Reflections. *Vietnamese Studies* 50: 121–34.

Tun Aung Chain. 2003. The Kings of Hpayahtaung Urn Inscription. *Myanmar Historical Research Journal* 11:1–15.

Upham, S. 1982. *Polities and Power: An Economic and Political History of the Western Pueblo*. New York: Academic Press.

Vallibhotama, M. 1987. Where is Thavaravati? *Art and Culture* 9(1): 104–20.

Vallibhotama, S. 1970. Review of Dvaravati by H.G. Quaritch Wales. *Journal of the Siam Society* 58(1): 136.

———. 1976. The Northeast of Thailand During the 7th–11th Century. *Muang Boran Journal* 3(1): 34–55.

———. 1979. The Area of Accumulation Before the 19th c. B.E. in the Northern Northeast. *Muang Boran Journal* 6(1): 29–39.

———. 1982. Nagara Jaya Sri. *Muang Boran* 8(3).

———. 1984. The Relevance of Moated Settlements to the Formation of States in Thailand. In vol. 16 of *Southeast Asian Archaeology at the XV Pacific Science Congress*, ed. D. Bayard, 123–28. Dunedin: Univ. of Otago Studies in Prehistoric Anthropology.

––––––. 1986. Political and Cultural Continuities at Dvaravati Sites. In *Southeast Asia in the 9th–14th Centuries*, ed. D. G. Marr and A. C. Milner, 229–38. Singapore: Australian National Univ. and the Institute of Southeast Asian Studies.

––––––. 1991. Bronze-Iron Age Foundations for the Origin of the State of Chenla. Unpublished paper read at the Conference of the High Bronze Age, Hua Hin, Thailand.

––––––. 1999. Introduction. In *(Sri) Dvaravati: The Initial Phase of Siam's History*, D. Saraya, 7–15. Bangkok: Muang Boran Publishing.

Vanasin and Suupajanya. 1981. *Ancient Cities on the Former Shoreline in the Central Plain of Thailand* (in Thai). Bangkok: Chulalongkorn Univ. Press.

van Leur, J. C. 1967. *Indonesian Trade and Society*. The Hague: Van Hoeve.

van Liere, W. 1980. Traditional Water Management in the Lower Mekong Basin. *World Archaeology* 11(3): 265–80.

––––––. 1988. Fou-Nan. Unpublished paper presented at the Research Conference on La Thailande: Des debuts de son histoire au XVeme siecle. Univ. de Silpakorn, Premier Symposium Franco Thai 18–20 Juillet 1988.

Vayda, A. 1960. Maori Warfare. *Polynesian Society Maori Monograph 2*.

Veerapan, M. 1979. The Excavation of Sab Champa. In *Early South East Asia*, ed. R. B. Smith and W. Watson, 337–41. Oxford: Oxford Univ. Press.

Veeraprajak, K. 1986. Inscriptions from South Thailand. *SPAFA Digest; Journal of SEAMO Project in Archaeology and Fine Arts* 7(1): 7–34.

Veraprasert, M. 1992. Khlong Thom: An Ancient Bead-Manufacturing Location and an Ancient Entrepôt. In *Early Metallurgy, Trade and Urban Centres in Thailand and Southeast Asia*, ed. I. Glover, P. Suchitta, and J. Villiers, 149–61. Bangkok: White Lotus.

Vickery, M. 1986. Some Notes on Early State Formation in Cambodia. In *Southeast Asia in the 9th–14th Centuries*, ed. D. G. Marr and A. C. Milner, 95–116. Singapore: Australian National Univ. and the Institute of Southeast Asian Studies.

––––––. 1992. Evidence for Prehistoric Austronesian-Khmer Contact and Linguistic Borrowing, *Mon-Khmer Studies*, XXI, 185–89.

––––––. 1994. Where and What was Chenla? In *Recherches nouvelles sur le Cambodge*, ed. F. Bizot, 197–212. Paris: EFEO.

––––––. 1996. Studying the State in Ancient Cambodia. International Conference on Khmer Studies, Phnom Penh Univ., Phnom Penh, Cambodia, unpublished paper.

––––––. 1998. *Society, Economics and Politics in Pre-Angkor Cambodia*. Tokyo: The Centre for East Asian Cultural Studies for Unesco, the Toyo Bunko, Hon komagome.

––––––. 2005. Champa Revised. Asia Research Institute, Working Paper Series No. 37, March 2005, www.nus.ari.edu.sg/pub/wps.htm.

––––––. n.d. Funan Reviewed: Deconstructing the Ancients. *Bulletin de l'École Française d'Extrême-Orient*, forthcoming.

Wagely, C. 1973. Cultural Influences on Population: A Comparison of Two Tupi Tribes. In *Peoples and Cultures of Native South America*, ed. D. R. Gross, 145–56. Garden City, N.Y.: Doubleday/ The Natural History Press.

Wales, H. G. Q. 1936. The Exploration of Sri Deva, an Ancient Indian City in Indochina. *Indian Arts and Letters* 10(2): 16–99.

––––––. 1967. *The Indianization of China and of South-east Asia*. London: Quaritch.

––––––. 1969. Dvaravati. *The Earliest Kingdom of Siam (6th–11th Century A.D.)*. London: Quaritch.

———. 1974. *The Making of Greater India*. London: Quaritch.

Wan Chen. n.d. *Nan-chou I-wu Chih apud T'ai-p'ing Yu-lan.*

Wang Gungwu. 1958. The Nanhai Trade: A Study of the Early History of Chinese Trade in the South China Sea. *Journal of the Malayan Branch of the Royal Asiatic Society* 31 (part 2)(185): 1–135.

Wason, P. 1994. *The Archaeology of Rank*. Cambridge: Cambridge Univ. Press.

Watson, J., ed. 1980. *Asian and African Systems of Slavery*. Berkeley: Univ. of California Press.

Webster, D. 1977. Warfare and the Evolution of Maya Civilization. In *The Origins of Maya Civilization*, ed. R. E. Adams, 335–71. Albuquerque: Univ. of New Mexico.

Weeraprajak, K. 1986. *Inscriptions in Thailand*. Bangkok: Fine Arts Dept.

———. 1990. Analysis of the Inscriptions Found at Yarang (in Thai). *The Silapakorn Journal* 33: 35–50.

Welch, D. 1984. Settlement Pattern as an Indicator of Socio-political Complexity in the Phimai Region, Thailand. In *Southeast Asian Archaeology at the XV Pacific Science Congress*, ed. D. Bayard. Dunedin, vol. 16, 129–52. New Zealand: Univ. of Otago.

———. 1985. Adaptation to Environmental Unpredictability: Intensive Agriculture and Regional Exchange at Late Prehistoric Centres in the Phimai Region in Thailand. PhD diss., Manoa: Univ. of Hawaii.

Wen, B. X. Xie, S. Gao, H. Li, H. Shi, X. Song, T. Quian, et al. 2004. Analyses of Genetic Structure of Tibeto-Burman Populations Reveals Sex-Biased Admixture in Southern Tibeto-Burmans. *American Journal of Human Genetics* 74: 856–65.

Wheatley, P. 1961. The Golden Khersonese: Studies in the Historical Geography of the Malay Peninsula to A.D. 1500. Kuala Lumpur: Univ. of Malaya Press.

———. 1974. The Mount of the Immortals: A Note on Tamil Cultural Influence in Fifth-Century Indochina. *Oriens Extremus* Jahrgang 21: 97–109.

———. 1983. Nagara and Commandery: Origins of the Southeast Asian Urban Traditions. Univ. of Chicago, Dept. of Geography Research Paper Nos. 207–208.

White, J. C. 1982. *Ban Chiang: The Discovery of a Lost Bronze Age*. Philadelphia: Univ. of Pennsylvania Press.

———. 1995. Incorporating Heterarchy into Theory on Socio-Political Development: The Case from Southeast Asia. In *Heterarchy and the Analysis of Complex Societies: Comments*, ed. R. Ehrenreich, C. Crumley, and J. Levy, 101–23. Washington D.C.: American Anthropological Association.

White, J. C., and V. Pigott. 1996. From Community Craft to Regional Specialization: Intensification of Copper Production in Pre-State Thailand. In *Craft Specialization and Social Evolution: In Memory of V. Gordon Childe*, ed. B. Wailes, 151–75. Philadelphia: Univ. Museum of Archaeology and Anthropology, Univ. of Pennsylvania.

Wicks, R. S. 1992. *Money, Markets, and Trade in Early Southeast Asia: The Development of Indigenous Monetary Systems to AD 1400*. Ithaca, N.Y.: Southeast Asia Program, Cornell Univ.

Wilaikaeo, J. 1991. *The Archaeology of Muang U-Taphao* (in Thai). Bangkok: Fine Arts Dept.

Wilen, R. 1982–1983. Prehistoric Settlement Patterns in Northeast Thailand: A Critical Review. *Asian Perspectives* 25(1): 63–81.

——. 1987. Excavation and Site Survey in the Huay Sai Khao Basin, Northeastern Thailand. *Bulletin of the Indo-Pacific Prehistory Association* 7: 94–117.

——. 1992. Mortuary Traditions and Cultural Identity in the Khorat Plateau Piedmont, Northeast Thailand. In *Southeast Asian Archaeology, 1990*, ed. I. Glover, 103–110. Hull: Center for South-East Asian Studies, Univ. of Hull.

Wisseman Christie, J. 1995. State Formation in Early Maritime Southeast Asia: A Consideration of the Theories and the Data. *Bijdragen: Tot de Taal—Land en Volkendunde* Deel 151: 235–88.

Wittfogel, K. 1957. *Oriental Despotism. A Study of Total Power.* New Haven, Conn.: Yale Univ. Press.

Wolf, E. 1959. *Sons of the Shaking Earth.* Chicago: Univ. of Chicago Press.

Wolters, O. W. 1973. Jayavarman II's Military Power: The Territorial Foundation of the Angkor Empire. *JRAS* 1(21–30).

——. 1974. North-western Cambodia in the Seventh Century. *Bulletin of the School of Oriental and African Studies* 37: 355–84.

——. 1979. Khmer "Hinduism" in the Seventh Century. In *Early South East Asia: Essays in Archaeology, History and Historical Geography*, ed. R. B. Smith and W. Watson, 427–42. New York: Oxford Univ. Press.

——. 1982. *History, Culture and Region in Southeast Asian Perspectives.* Singapore: Institute of Southeast Asian Studies.

——. 1999. *History, Culture, and Region in Southeast Asian Perspectives.* Ithaca, N.Y.: Southeast Asia Program Publications.

Wright, H. 1984. Prestate Political Formations. In *On the Evolution of Complex Societies: Essays in Honor of Harry Hoijer 1982*, ed. T. Earle, 41–75. Los Angeles: Undena Publishers.

——. 1994. Prestate Political Formations. In *Chiefdoms and Early States in the Near East: The Organizational Dynamics of Complexity*, ed. G. Stein and M. S. Rothman, 67–84. Madison, Wisc.: Prehistory Press.

Wynne-Edwards, V. 1962. *Animal Dispersion in Relation to Social Behaviour.* London: Oliver and Boyd.

Xuanling, F., ed. 578–648. *Jin Shu (Book of the Jin Dynasty).*

Yamamoto, T. 1979. *East Asian Historical Sources for Dvaravati Studies. Proceedings of the Seventh IAHA Conference.* Bangkok: Chulalongkorn Univ. Press.

Yoffee, N. 1993. Too Many Chiefs? (or Safe Texts for the 90s). In *Archaeological Theory: Who Sets the Agenda?*, ed. N. Yoffee and A. Sherratt, 60–78. Cambridge: Cambridge Univ. Press.

——. 2005. *Myths of the Archaic State: Evolution of the Earliest Cities, States and Civilizations.* Cambridge: Cambridge Univ. Press.

Yule, H. 1875. *The Book of Ser Marco Polo, the Venetian, Concerning the Kingdoms and Marvels of the East.* London: John Murray.

Zaini, S. A. M. 2002. Recent Research at the Pyu Settlement of Sriksetra. Burma Studies Conference. Gothenburg, Sweden.

Zuylen van, G. 1991. The Flow of History: Did Khmer Riches Come from Irrigation? *The Nation.* Bangkok.

Index

About the Author

Dougald O'Reilly is a Canadian who was granted an M.A. and PhD in archaeology by the University of Otago, Dunedin, New Zealand. His research involved the exploration of the development of political complexity in Bronze and Iron Age Thailand. He lived in Cambodia from 1999 to 2006. During that time he was employed as a UNESCO lecturer at the Royal University of Fine Arts in Phnom Penh. Whilst there O'Reilly led the excavation of an Iron Age site, Phum Snay, located in the northwest of Cambodia. The site had been extensively looted by locals prior to its archaeological excavation—a trend that expanded to nearly all known prehistoric sites in the region.

In response to the looting, a nongovernmental organization called HeritageWatch was founded by the author in an effort to combat the loss of heritage in Cambodia. HeritageWatch established a nationwide education campaign highlighting the importance of heritage. Through television, radio, and village trainings, the organization encouraged the preservation of Cambodia's heritage. Hotlines allow the reporting of looting or archaeological finds. Rescue excavations and training for young Cambodian archaeologists were implemented by the organization, as well as sustainable development projects at threatened sites as poverty is the root cause of looting. An online petition at www.heritagewatch.org has also been launched with the aim of encouraging the governments of Thailand and Singapore to sign the 1970 UNESCO convention committing these countries to be responsible for heritage preservation and the restriction of the antiquities trade. With a committed staff, several dedicated volunteers, and outside supporters, HeritageWatch has met with great success as one of the few non-governmental organizations working on heritage preservation.

O'Reilly is currently a lecturer in archaeology with the University of Sydney, Australia, and continues his research in Cambodia.